Happy Birthday Tatyana!
Hope this book helps you on your
path to enlightenment
xO Robert

Sit Down and Shut Up

Sit Down and Shut Up

Punk Rock Commentaries on
Buddha, God, Truth, Sex, Death, and
Dogen's *Treasury of the Right Dharma Eye*

Brad Warner

New World Library
Novato, California

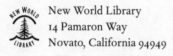 New World Library
14 Pamaron Way
Novato, California 94949

Grateful acknowledgment to Alfred Publishing and Hal Leonard Publishing for use of the lyrics to "Hell Hole" by Spinal Tap on pages 155–56.

Text design and typography by Tona Pearce Myers

Library of Congress Cataloging-in-Publication Data
Warner, Brad.
   Sit down and shut up : punk rock commentaries on Buddha, god, truth, sex, death, and Dogen's Treasury of the right dharma eye / Brad Warner.
      p.   cm.
   ISBN 978-1-57731-559-9 (pbk. : alk. paper)
   1. Meditation—Zen Buddhism. 2. Dogen, 1200–1253. I. Title.
   BQ9288.W377 2007
   294.3'85—dc22   2007002802

First printing, May 2007
ISBN-10: 1-57731-559-6
ISBN-13: 978-1-57731-559-9
Printed in Canada on acid-free, recycled paper

g New World Library is a proud member of the Green Press Initiative.

10   9   8   7   6   5   4

Dedicated to my mother,
Sandra Sue Warner

Contents

Zero Defects at The Dale in Akron, Ohio, sometime in 1982. The guy jumping across the frame is Fraser Suicyde of Starvation Army. This is where we played with MDC, the Meat Puppets, the Crucifucks, DRI, and about a zillion other bands.

Zero Defects at the Cleveland's Screaming show at the Beachland Ballroom, December 5, 2005. My shirt says "Bear Claw" and shows a cute teddy bear ripping up Ronald McDonald's face with a set of metal claws like Wolverine from the X-Men. I bought it in Tokyo. I have no idea what it's supposed to mean.

Chapter 1

Why Dogen Matters

Long before I was a Zen monk, I was a punk rock bass player. Long before I was exposed to the teachings of Dogen Zenji, I studied the teachings of Ian MacKaye, of the DC-based hardcore band Minor Threat, who advocated a remarkably similar philosophy — no drink, no drugs, no smoking, just honest hard work and a commitment to what was true.

When I was seventeen, I saw the hardcore punk band Zero Defects (aka oDFx or Zero Defex) play at a nightclub called The Bank in downtown Akron, Ohio. I thought they were God's gift to music. They were the most over-the-top thing I had ever seen onstage, and to me they remain so to this day. When I found out they were looking for a bass player, I jumped at the chance to join. Zero Defects was Akron's premier punk band — which means we played to crowds of fifty people instead of crowds of five. We were big fish in a very small pond. And we didn't last very long. The band played its last show sometime in the spring of 1983.

In almost no time at all hardcore punk had gone from being a potent force for change to being an excuse for tough dudes to beat the crap out of each other. I loved the guys in the band. But I was ready to do something else. It turned out that we all were ready to do something else. If we could have found a way to do that within the group, I have no doubt that Zero Defects would have been a major force on the music scene in the 1980s rather than a footnote. But such is life.

I moved on to other things. I signed with New York's Midnight Records label and put out five albums of the most antipunk music on earth — psychedelia — with an ever-changing lineup I dubbed Dimentia 13, after a cheesy horror flick made by a young Francis Ford Coppola. I discovered Zen Buddhism. I moved to Japan. Appeared in monster movies. Became a Buddhist monk.* Got married. Moved to Los Angeles. And somewhere in the middle of all that the Internet appeared. Suddenly, kids who had been in diapers when Zero Defects breathed its last wanted to know about the old hardcore scene. The members of the band found each other via a website called ClePunk, dedicated to the Cleveland and Akron punk rock scene. We started talking about playing shows again.

In the meantime I was working on a book. As some of you must surely know, I wrote a book a few years ago called *Hardcore Zen: Punk Rock, Monster Movies, and the Truth about Reality*. I didn't come up with that title, by the way. That's what my publishers decided to call it. But I liked that title, so I went with it.

I wrote the book believing there was no way in hell anyone would ever publish such a thing. I'd been dedicated to Zen for nearly two decades before I'd started working on the book. But my take on Zen seemed to be completely at odds with that of nearly everyone else I encountered who was interested in the philosophy.

The people I met at Zen centers I visited were usually older than me. And smarter, too. And a lot quieter. They were generally almost studiously ignorant of popular culture, the kind of people who don't

---

* You can read all about this in my first book, so I'm skipping the details here.

own TVs or purchase CDs, unless maybe they're recordings of Chinese chants or something. I never met a single Zen practitioner who was into punk rock or who liked Godzilla movies, let alone one who played punk rock and appeared in Godzilla movies.* Zen people tend to be bookish intellectuals in pale-blue pullovers rather than ratty-haired guitarists in ripped-up jeans.

Yet I had found this philosophy to be deeply appealing for the same reasons I had found punk rock appealing. It was a philosophy that asked questions rather than providing pat answers. It didn't have any time for bullshit. It was completely unpretentious. Zen teachers were rude and uncouth, rebellious, real.

I thought that maybe, just maybe, there might be a few people out there who would be interested in Zen if only it weren't presented in such a wimpy, nerdy fashion. So I wrote what I conceived of as a loud book about silence. When I was done, I wasn't sure what to do with it. My most concrete plan was to xerox it myself and see if I could get it distributed by whoever stocks the bookshelves at Tower Records, since they seemed to carry a lot of off-the-wall stuff. But, I thought, I might as well give it a shot with a few publishers before I take it to the local Kinko's.

I got turned down by most of the publishers I sent it to, which was no surprise. But one publisher liked it and wanted to put it out. I was game. So I signed a contract and got down to the work of turning my fanzine-quality writings into a slick, shiny, professional-type book. The result was okay. And there was immediately a demand for another one just like it. But I'd written that book already, and I really didn't want to turn it into some sort of Chicken (Tofu?) Soup for the Zen Soul kind of thing. So I hemmed and hawed for a long time.

Eventually, though, I started writing another book. I wanted it

---

* Actually I've never been in a Godzilla movie — yet. But I've been in a bunch of Ultraman movies, which to the untrained eye often appear to be pretty much the same thing.

to be something completely different from *Hardcore Zen*. It was going to be about a very old book called *Shobogenzo*, or 正法現蔵, if you're into reading it in Japanese (the Japanese language spells out most words in Chinese characters). It means "Treasury of the Right Dharma Eye." Don't ask about the left dharma eye, by the way.* It's by a dead Japanese guy named Dogen, sometimes known as Dogen Zenji, meaning "Zen Master Dogen," or Eihei Dogen, meaning "Dogen, you know, that dude who lives in Eihei temple."

The English translation of Dogen's *Shobogenzo* by my teacher, Gudo Nishijima, and his student, Chodo Cross — which is the source of most of the quotations in this book — had been the cornerstone of the intellectual side of my Zen practice. But Zen isn't really about intellectual stuff like books. It's a philosophy of action, a philosophy you *do* rather than read about. Yet what really sets Dogen apart from all the other Buddhist masters before and since is his ability to express his insights in words. Others may have plumbed the same depths. But none had ever described what they'd discovered quite so well. In order to describe what he'd understood, Dogen almost had to reinvent human language. Even in the original Japanese, his style is full of weird turns of phrase and bizarre grammar. When you first read it, either in translation or in the original, *Shobogenzo* almost sounds like the ramblings of a crazy person. Get into the rhythm a little bit, though, and you discover that Dogen wasn't just a guy who talked crazy. In fact, all his crazy talk has a very clear and consistent logic to it. It may be the sanest material anyone has ever committed to words. I'd gotten a lot out of my reading of Dogen, and I thought I'd try to share some of that. So I bit the bullet and wrote another goddamned book.

To start off with, let me give you a little background on Dogen. He was born in 1200 to an aristocratic family back in the days when all Japan looked like the sets in *The Last Samurai*. His father died

* Sometimes the title is translated as "The True Dharma Eye Treasury." Whatever.

when he was just three years old, and his mother died five years later. Having lost the people children believe to be the most reliable, stable things in the world — parents — at such a young age, he started searching for something that was perfectly reliable. That's what got him into Buddhism.

I can relate to this myself. My parents are both still alive. But several people in my family have contracted a particular disease and died from it while still quite young. I saw some of this happening when I was a child. At the time, I also learned that this disease runs in families. So there was a chance that I would suffer from the same illness and linger for years in a pretty miserable condition until the sickness did me in, as had happened to my grandmother and a couple of my aunts.* So I started looking into religious and philosophical matters at a very early age. In Dogen's case Buddhism was really the only religion he would have encountered. Though Shintoism was around, too, it tends to be confined to rituals and doesn't really address the deeper aspects of human life. In my case, though, the first religion I encountered was Christianity. And, although I was very intrigued by Christian ideas, they didn't really address my concerns.

As a young kid Dogen had a similar problem. Although Buddhism offered a lot of valuable things, he found there was one seemingly simple question that none of the old Buddhist masters he encountered could answer to his satisfaction. Buddhism says that all beings are perfect as they are, with nothing lacking and nothing extra. But it also recommends doing a lot of difficult stuff to try and realize this fact. Different sects of Buddhism recommend different stuff to do — some want you to chant, others want you to meditate, others want you to memorize a lot of stuff out of old books — but they all require you to *do* things, most of which aren't a big barrel o' fun. Why? That's all Dogen wanted to know. If we're already perfect, why do we need all this Buddhist practice to understand that? Why not

---

* And, on January 12, 2007, while I was finishing this book, my mom.

just sit around messing with your PlayStation? It doesn't make any difference anyhow. Right?

In spite of his lingering doubts, Dogen was impressed enough with Buddhism that by the time he was twelve, he became a monk. He studied for a time at a temple called Enryaku, which was part of the Tendai sect, an esoteric line of Buddhism with lots of mudras and mandalas — weird gestures and symbols that are supposed to have mystical meaning and power. He stayed there for three years but eventually found no satisfactory answer to his question. But when he was hanging out at the temple across the street from Enryaku — a place called Miidera (or sometimes Onjyoji for those keeping score at home) — he heard about a teacher in Kyoto named Eisai who lived at a temple called Kenninji.

Kenninji was, at the time, Japan's head temple of the Rinzai sect of Zen Buddhism. Zen was a sect of Buddhism that attempted to strip away a lot of the elaborate ritual that had grown up around the teachings since Buddha's death to find the essential practice. Eisai was supposed to be pretty wise. So Dogen went to his place and put his question to him.* Eisai answered, "I don't know anything about Buddhas of the past, present, or future. But I know that cats exist, and I know that cows exist." Eisai's answer struck Dogen as extraordinarily practical.

Now hold up a second, 'cuz I know what you're thinking — they were both nuts! But let's look at Eisai's answer again. It's not just some Monty Python–type wisecrack. Everything else Dogen had heard was all caught up in theory and intellectualization. Eisai, however, answered on the basis of his own experience. Buddhas of the past, present, and future were matters of theory and speculation. But Eisai himself had seen cats. They probably hung around the temple, as cats often do at Japanese monasteries, and he'd seen cows. Those

---

* Or maybe he didn't. Dogen's own account is a bit vague about whether they actually met face-to-face.

he could confirm. Eisai wasn't interested in theoretical speculation. He was interested in reality.

This was the same thing I discovered when I encountered my first Buddhist teacher, Tim McCarthy. I came to him with loads of deep questions about the meaning of life, heaven, hell, God, and all that stuff. But he had no answers. Well, I shouldn't say no answers. See, I had already come across a few dozen sets of answers to my questions, from Christians, from Hare Krishnas, from New Agers, from scientists, from punk rock philosophers. But none of those answers was any good at all. I couldn't believe in them even when I tried. Tim, on the other hand, made no attempt to fix reality in place and explain it all away with some formula like those guys had. That, in itself, was his answer — that you cannot possibly nail down the answers to questions like that and that it's a waste of energy even to try. But he wasn't a nihilist either. I'd already run into plenty of those, and their attitude of just saying screw it to everything and basically giving up was as unappealing to me as the idea of sitting in church pews listening to a bunch of old stories being repeated over and over and over again. Buddhism was different.

When Dogen found a different, more satisfying, form of Buddhism, he jumped ship and left the Tendai sect to study Zen at Kenninji. Though he spent nine years there trying to find the enlightenment that the adherents of the Rinzai sect said was supposed to come from hours and days and weeks on end of seated meditation practice called zazen, Dogen never found anything that he felt qualified as the kind of enlightenment they promised. By this time Eisai, who was already an old codger when Dogen met him,* had bit the big one. So Dogen decided to take a trip to China to find a style of Buddhism closer to its Indian source.

Meanwhile, back in my real life, I was about to make a trip, too. In December 2005 a guy named Jim Lanza had the idea of getting a bunch

---

* Or didn't meet him.

of the old Cleveland-area hardcore bands together to play a one-off show called Cleveland's Screaming. He worked tirelessly to bring us all together and get it happening. A few people called the reunion show a sham, my friend Johnny Phlegm for one, pointing out that we'd formed those bands as a reaction against fat forty-year-olds dominating the music scene with out-of-date irrelevant nonsense, and here we were, all old and out of shape, playing music that had been cutting-edge twenty years ago but now was the stuff of Pepsi commercials. I tended to agree with Johnny, actually. But I also wanted to rock out with those guys again, so I got me a plane ticket and headed for Ohio.

I also decided I wanted to do more than just play at the show. I wanted to document it. A number of movies about punk rock have been made already. But all of them focus on the national or international scene, the big groups, the movers and shakers. None of those bands mattered much to me. At the time I played with Zero Defects I owned exactly three hardcore punk records, all by bands we'd opened for, all bought from the bands themselves. For me, the hardcore scene was the local scene. I didn't give a shit about Black Flag and the Dead Kennedys. But I loved Starvation Army and the Urban Mutants. As hard as I looked, I never came across a single film about any of the hundreds of local hardcore scenes that existed in the eighties. I figured if nobody else was gonna make a movie like that, it was up to me. So I wrote up a bunch of interview questions, packed up my little digital video camera, and off I went.

Of course, my trip was nothing compared to Dogen's. Remember, folks, making a trip from Kyoto, Japan, to China in 1223 wasn't like it is today, when you can hop on a plane at Kansai International Airport and be in Shanghai in less time than it takes you just to get through traffic on the way to the airport. A trip to China meant a long voyage over the notoriously stormy Sea of Japan in a dodgy wooden ship. In those days lots of people never returned from trips to China. Dogen was willing to risk his life to find the answers to his questions.

But once he got to China, Dogen found the Buddhist teachings he came across there just as unsatisfactory as the ones he'd encountered in Japan. After two years of searching in vain for something different, he was about to give up and go back home when he heard about a teacher named Tendo Nyojo. Actually, his name was pronounced more like Tien-tung Ju-tsing, but in Japan they insist on pronouncing the Chinese characters used to spell out his name their own way; thus he's known in Japanese as Tendo Nyojo. Tien-tung (or Tendo) is the name of the mountain where he had his monastery, while Ju-tsing was his personal name. Master Tendo was supposed to be really different from the other Zen teachers he'd met, so Dogen figured he'd check the guy out. Turns out that Tendo Nyojo was from a school of Zen called the Soto school and taught a way of doing zazen that was fundamentally different from the style practiced in the Rinzai temples where Dogen had studied previously. Though both schools teach the practice of zazen, the Rinzai school emphasizes the idea that zazen is a way to gain enlightenment. Enlightenment is the end, and zazen is the means. Clear and simple. But according to Tendo Nyojo, zazen was its own end, and the mere practice of zazen was enlightenment itself.

Now, that's just a weird idea. If you've never done zazen, you may picture it as a real mystical thing. You sit there with your legs crossed, in some remote old temple. Incense wafts through the still early-morning air. Chants are intoned, bells ring, and you enter into deep *samadhi*, plunging through the depths of the universe and experiencing ever-intensifying insights, the mysteries of creation melting away before your continuously expanding consciousness. Unfortunately, the only time zazen is like that is when you've taken some heavy drugs before sitting down on your cushion. Those sessions almost invariably end up with the practitioner going nutso squirrelly and having to be forcibly ejected from the zendo. No, mostly zazen is nothing like what anyone would hold up as "enlightenment." It's lots of boredom and stiff legs and just trying your best to get through it. Occasionally insights arise, and some of them can be quite amazing. But mostly, your teachers — if they're any good — will tell you to forget about them. If you believe that at the end of all this pain and boredom you'll be rewarded with the peak experience to end all peak experiences, maybe you can get through it. But if someone tells you that the practice itself is enlightenment? Come on! What is *that*?

But Dogen was intrigued anyway. So he checked out Tendo Nyojo and figured the guy was alright. In fact, he ended up canceling his trip back to Japan and staying at Tendo's monastery for two years. At the end of this time Dogen experienced what he called the "dropping away of both body and mind." When Tendo Nyojo gave Dogen his permission to teach Buddhism as part of his lineage, Dogen went back to Japan.

When he got there, folks asked him what he'd brought back from China. "Nothing," he said. Disappointed with this wiseass answer, as well as the fact that they didn't get any souvenirs, they pressed him for more, and he said that he brought back a soft and flexible mind.* Dogen established a temple in Kyoto. But as his no-bullshit style of Zen teaching became more and more popular, the folks at the other temples in town started giving him a hard time. Kyoto was then and still is what you might call a "temple town," the way you'd call Boston a college town. The temples were the foundation of the economy, and no one liked this new, young trouble-maker messing up the status quo. So Dogen moved out to the wilds of Fukui Prefecture far from the big city and set up shop in a new temple he ended up calling Eihei-ji, or the Temple of Eternal Peace.

All this time Dogen wrote his little balls off. He produced a huge amount of literature based on his experiences and understanding of Buddhism. The biggest and fattest of all his books was the ninety-five-chapter monster called *Shobogenzo*.

---

* Ew, gross!

To say that Dogen's book did not exactly catch on like wildfire when it was first written would be a massive understatement. In fact, very few people outside his immediate students and a few later scholarly types who made a point of reading absolutely everything about Buddhism even took a look at it. It wasn't until 1690, more than four hundred years after Dogen wrote it, that *Shobogenzo* was actually printed up and distributed outside that very small group of hardcore Dogen fans. And even that edition quickly went out of print for another 121 years. Think of that. It's as if the book you're reading right now — not that it's anywhere near as good as Dogen's — had to wait till the year 2807, when human beings had mutated into soft-bodied creatures with sixteen tentacles and eyes on stalks living on the moons of Jupiter, before anyone decided it was worth taking a look at. It's hard to fathom the amount of time that had to pass before anybody was ready for what Dogen was laying down all those years ago.*

All of which avoids the question you've probably been asking yourself since you started to plow through this chapter, which is: Why in the hell is this damned Shooby-dooby-whachacallit book by some crazy dead Japanese guy so freakin' important? I'm getting to that.

Every religion has its special books. Even before a true believer reads a word of their chosen religion's special book, a true believer already assumes that everything inside it is God's — or Whoever's — absolute truth. These books cannot be questioned or doubted. Only specially appointed and highly trained experts are even allowed to explain their meaning to the rest of us dunces who couldn't possibly understand what's written in them.

But Buddhism does not have any such holy literature. This is not to say that there aren't a lot of people who consider themselves Buddhists who *do* treat the words of the Buddhist masters in exactly this manner. But Buddha himself is famous for having said, "Do not go upon what has been acquired by repeated hearing; nor upon

---

* And to all of you sixteen-tentacled Jovians reading this in the year 2807— hey!

tradition; nor upon rumor; nor upon what is in a scripture. But when you yourselves know: 'These things are good; these things are not blamable; these things are praised by the wise; undertaken and observed, these things lead to benefit and happiness,' enter on and abide in them." This pretty much removes the whole idea of inerrant scripture from the picture as far as Buddhism is concerned. In fact, if we follow what Buddha's saying here to its logical conclusion, it's clear that even the words of Buddha himself cannot be taken as inerrant, infallible, and beyond all question the way the founders' words of most other religions are treated.

So *Shobogenzo* is not a holy book of any kind. It's just a book, and Dogen was just a guy. What makes *Shobogenzo* important to me is not its status as some infallible work of God. It is the actual contents of the work itself. *Shobogenzo* is simply the single most reliable written interpretation of Buddhism I have ever come across. Dogen's writing is direct and clear and brutally honest in a way I've never seen matched by anyone else. It's a damned good book.

I first heard about the book from Tim. He used to quote it sometimes, and when I moved into his zendo in Kent, there was a tattered copy of the then-standard English translation by Kosen Nishiyama and John Stevens on the shelves. I used to leaf through it from time to time. But it never made a huge impact. It seemed too old and weird and abstract. It was like looking at some piece of surrealist art that everyone says is great but that you just can't quite get. I was much more affected by a book called *Zen Mind, Beginner's Mind*, by Shunryu Suzuki. But Suzuki also quoted Dogen a lot. So I kept *Shobogenzo* on my "things to read one of these days" list for a long time.

It was when I ran into my current teacher, Gudo Nishijima, that I decided I had to read the darned thing for myself. Nishijima is practically obsessed with *Shobogenzo*. To hear him talk, you'd sometimes think it was the only book he'd ever read. He's read it over and over and over for the past sixty years and produced a complete English translation, while also overseeing editions in German, Spanish, and

Korean. Some people are football fanboys; me, I'm a monster movie fanboy, and Nishijima is a *Shobogenzo* fanboy of the highest order. It was his enthusiasm for the book that finally got me to decide I was gonna sit there and make my way through the whole ninety-five chapters, even if it killed me.

What surprised me is that I really enjoyed it. In fact, I read it all the way through again. And then again. In the end I became a Dogen fanboy too. But when I quote Dogen, I'm not doing it the way most religious guys quote their favorite holy books. I'm not saying, "Here is what the voice of ultimate authority says on the subject." I'm saying, "Here are the words of a person who put this difficult subject into words very well." As a writer, no one yet has even come close to matching Dogen's ability to express the inexpressible. Of course, he failed. What he was trying to put into words cannot, by its very nature, be put into words. But in this he failed knowing full well he could not possibly succeed. Yet he tried anyway, and that's what makes Dogen a genius and makes his writing so valuable even eight hundred years after he wrote it. He expressed himself perfectly, even to the point of expressing his own limitations with absolute clarity. Dogen did not tolerate bullshit of any kind, even when it was his own. There are very few, if any, like him.

So what's *Shobogenzo* all about? The best way to find out is to go through all ninety-five chapters yourself. But the best way to understand it is to use the formula Nishijima gives in his introduction. In a nutshell Dogen establishes four basic principles for Buddhist study. The first principle is what he calls "establishing will to the truth." In Sanskrit this is called *Bodhicitta*, with the last bit pronounced "cheetah," as in Tarzan's best friend — though I could never understand why he was named Cheetah when he wasn't a cheetah but a chimp. Anyhow, *Bodhicitta* means you have to regard the truth, the whole truth, and nothing but the truth as your ultimate criterion or goal. You have to be willing to accept what is true, whether or not you like it. It's way tougher than it sounds.

The second principle is what he calls "deep belief in the rule of cause and effect." Most of us don't really believe in cause and effect in a very deep way. Oh, we believe in it. But we always imagine there might be some exceptions. We tend to believe we can get something for nothing, or that the things we do to others will never come back to us. Or we believe in a God who can somehow transcend the law of cause and effect by his magic powers. But Dogen didn't accept that kind of thinking at all. He believed that the whole universe — God included — follows the rule of cause and effect without exception.

Dogen's third principle is that our life is just action at the present moment. The past is nothing more than memory, and the future is nothing but dreams. At best, past and future are no more than reference material for the eternal now. The only real facts are those at the present moment. You cannot go back and correct the mistakes you made in your past, so you better be very careful right now. You can dream about your future, but no matter how well you construct that dream, your future will not be precisely as you envisioned it. The world where we live is existence in the present moment.

The final principle is the practice of zazen itself. Buddhism is not a philosophy you just read about. It is a philosophy you do. So the principles of Buddhism include actual action, which cannot be put into words. In Dogen's view the best way to learn how to truly experience the world just as it is, is through the daily practice of zazen.

The only way to really understand Buddhism is to *do* Buddhism, which means to do zazen for yourself. That's how Dogen came to his understanding of the philosophy. Because Buddhism is not about words, not even Dogen's. It is absolutely impossible to understand Buddhism without the practice of zazen. Try as you might, it ain't a-gonna happen. So read books — even this sloppy piece of work — if you must. But when you're ready to stop farting around and experience real Buddhism, sit down and shut up. That's where the real Buddhism is at.

Chapter 2

"Genjo Koan"

Why on earth did I choose to leave sunny Southern California to plunge straight into an Ohio winter so cold that it felt like the water inside my eyeballs was starting to freeze up the second I stepped outside the Akron airport? Struggling not to slip on the ice as I carried my bass and my luggage out to my rental car, I tried to remember how you're supposed to walk on ice like this. My Ohio instincts were still intact as I automatically headed for the most salt-saturated path. I hadn't experienced cold like this in more than a decade. How did I ever survive my upbringing in this place?

But I braved the notorious Ohio winter for the sake of the big punk rock reunion show. I'd been away from Akron so long that I got completely lost on the same streets I used to drive down every day. I didn't realize until the following morning that I had driven in a huge circle around the city trying to get to an address that was only a block away from the spot where I first decided I was hopelessly lost and had to return to my point of origin.

But I made it to our drummer's house in spite of my confusion and lack of practice driving on snow-covered roads. Turns out

Mickey was on his way back to the house after picking up our singer, Jimi, who doesn't have a car, and arrived at the same time as me. There wasn't a whole lot of time to get ready for the gig, which was only two days away. Since we hadn't even seen each other, let alone rehearsed together, in twenty-some years, we had to get right down to business. The rehearsal went amazingly well, all things considered. The other three members of the band had gotten together a couple of times before I arrived, so it was mainly just a matter of tightening things up. In fact, we sounded a hell of a lot better than we ever did back in the day.

As I walked up the stairs from the basement practice room, I noticed something I hadn't experienced in several years. I get a tremendous buzz from playing music. But it's not the floating, disoriented kind of buzz you get from drugs. The very act of trying to play a song with a group of other people forces you to concentrate very clearly on the here and now. Now, when I say *concentrate*, I do not mean "think very hard about," which is what most people mean when they use that word. A completely different concentration is required. You cannot think at all, or you will screw everything up.

It's funny to me that I rarely notice the changes that have gone on in my mental and physical state when I play music until I take a break. That's when I start to detect the fact that my brain is no longer chattering away, that, in spite of all the racket I've been making, everything seems remarkably quiet and still.

This is much the same effect that zazen has on one. During the practice it's difficult to notice what is actually taking place. It can feel boring, frustrating, even silly. Or, conversely, you can feel elated, high, full of cosmic energy, and all that nonsense. But it's usually not until after you've done the practice that you notice what has just happened. Of course, the very act of noticing what has happened is a small corruption of the practice. As Nishijima Sensei likes to say, "You can never notice your own enlightenment." If you think you've noticed it, that ain't it, brother.

Still, it's only human to try and assess these things. And the only way you can write about what you've learned in your practice is to assess it. Meaning, you're not really writing about the practice itself but about your mental assessment of that practice.

Dogen understood this very clearly. To describe the effects of practice as precisely as possible, he developed an entirely new way to use human language. This involved a fourfold system of logic somewhat related to the four basic principles I mentioned in the previous chapter. Basically you're looking at things from four distinctly different and mutually contradictory points of view all at the same time. It's not easy. These four points of view are idealism, materialism, action, and reality, the last of which synthesizes the previous three. Rather than examining these in terms of abstract theory, let's look at them in terms of something Dogen actually wrote using that formula.

Whenever someone includes a piece by Dogen in an anthology of famous Buddhist writings, "Genjo Koan" (現成公案) is the big favorite. It's the one *Shobogenzo* excerpt to include if you can only include one. Dogen himself was obviously quite fond of it, since he continued to rework and revise this particular chapter almost up to the time of his death. This nice bite-sized chapter kind of sums up most of what's really important in *Shobogenzo*. Plus, it's got some of Dogen's most quotable quotes. So it's a good place to start.

I see that some of you Buddha fans out there have noticed the word *koan* in the title. Ever since Zen was introduced into the West, folks have been gaga over the koans. In case you're a normal person who does not spend all your spare cash on drippy Buddhist books and magazines, I'd better supply some background information. Generally, the word *koan* is used to refer to those weird unanswerable questions often associated with Zen, like "What's the sound of one hand clapping?" or "If a tree falls in a forest and it hits a mime, would he make a noise?" The word *koan* means "public case." So the koans are public records recounting encounters between famous Zen teachers and their students.

There is a school of Zen in which students are given these questions and required to answer them in private meetings with their teachers. Dogen was not part of this school. In fact, he had nothing but bad stuff to say about that particular practice. He devotes an entire chapter of *Shobogenzo* (chapter 75, "Samadhi as Experience of the Self") to a massive rant denouncing the founder of the practice as a fraud. So, obviously, "Genjo Koan" is not one of those types of koans. Which is not to say that Dogen disliked the koans themselves. He often wrote about them, and he even put together a compilation of three hundred of his favorites.

For Dogen, the word *koan* was also a synonym for *dharma*, the profound truth of the universe in the sense that the universe is a mystery. And by that I mean that although the universe is all around us, proclaiming its truth so loudly you'd have to be deaf to miss it, most of us manage to miss it anyhow.

"Genjo Koan" starts off with what sounds like a string of contradictory statements. This is where the fourfold logic system comes into place.

"When all dharmas are the Buddha-Dharma," Dogen says right at the outset, "then there is delusion and realization, there is practice, there is life and there is death, there are buddhas and there are ordinary beings." The word *dharma* can be a kind of catchall word in Buddhism. *Dharma* sometimes means the Buddha's teachings specifically. But here the meaning is much wider. It's almost like saying "stuff." Dharmas could be stuff you're going through — studying for your midterms, getting a divorce, making an egg-salad sandwich. Or it could be the people and things that are going through whatever it is they're going through. The phrase "all dharmas" means the whole universe. When he talks about all dharmas being the Buddha-Dharma, he is just referring to a time when everything is seen from the point of view of Buddhist philosophy. I know that might be a little much to wrap your brain around. But we'll deal with that later.

At any rate, the sentence is pretty straightforward — linguistically, at least. But then Dogen says, "When the myriad dharmas are each not of the self, there is no delusion and no realization, no buddhas and no ordinary beings, no life and no death." Hold it! I thought there were all those things, and now he says there aren't.

And then just to be even more contrary he says, "The Buddha's truth is originally transcendent over abundance and scarcity, and so there is life and death, there is delusion and realization, there are beings and buddhas."

And just when you think he hasn't twisted your cranium enough, he finishes up the paragraph by saying, "And though it is like this, it is only that flowers, while loved, fall; and weeds while hated, flourish."

I happen to like that last line a whole lot. In one sense he's saying something like, "Shit happens. Deal with it." But it goes deeper than that. He's saying that the world will never behave the way we think it should behave, but that isn't so terrible because the self that thinks the world should behave according to its wishes doesn't really exist.

The first line expresses the idealistic or spiritual point of view. When you think about all things in terms of an idealistic interpretation of Buddhist truth, you can make clear distinctions between Buddhas and ordinary, just-plain folks,* between delusion and realization, and between life and death. That's what your brain does. It draws distinctions between things. That's how you sort stuff out.

If you take the materialistic point of view (line two), however, these distinctions vanish. Dogen characterizes the materialistic view as seeing things as "not of the self." It's what we call "objectivity" these days. Science has always strived for pure objectivity, although these days many scientists are starting to see that pure objectivity can never be achieved. Yet there is still the underlying mindset saying that the only way to understand the material world clearly is to be as close to absolutely objective as possible. Anyhow, from a materialistic point of view, Buddhas and ordinary folks, delusion and

* What do you call a Buddhist from Plano, Texas? A Plano Buddhist!

enlightenment, even life and death are exactly the same. They are all just different permutations of material elements, none of which has any greater value than any other.

The third line is purely practical, expressing the viewpoint of action. "The Buddha's truth is transcendent over abundance and scarcity." Meaning that in Buddhism we are taking a view that is entirely different from the first two. In those other views we try to define things, to explain them. To "transcend abundance and scarcity" means to transcend viewing the world and saying there's too much of this and not enough of that. It means giving up your opinions and definitions and seeing things just as they are. In the idealistic view there is an abundance of meaning. In the materialistic view everything is essentially meaningless. In action both views are transcended.

When I am playing the bass line to Zero Defects's ever-popular chant song, "No More Control,"* I am transcending abundance and scarcity. I am in the middle ground between the idealistic phase in which the song is conceived and the materialistic phase in which it becomes a set of sound vibrations for a bunch of thrashing kids in the pit to beat themselves senseless to. I am just playing, just moving my fingers and trying to hit the right notes at the right time. Thought is no longer part of the picture. All forms of action are like this.

Finally, Dogen ties the whole thing together in the fourth line, which is just realism. "Flowers while loved fall, weeds while hated flourish." Whether we like or hate what life hands us, it is what it is, and that's all that it is.

In the next paragraph he gets into this a bit more deeply. "Those who greatly realize delusion are buddhas. Those who are greatly deluded about realization are ordinary beings." In other words, to be a buddha is to understand delusion thoroughly. But just having a lot of cool ideas about realization or enlightenment doesn't mean squat.

---

* Chorus: "No more! No more! Control over you! No more! No more! Control over me! No more! No more! Control over us!!!"

Buddhist practitioners have to be especially careful here because we tend to build up a lot of elaborate fantasies about what realization must be like. When we get to the point in our practice where these fantasies begin to play themselves out in our minds, we can get very confused. Often practitioners start to experience exactly the fantasy of "enlightenment" we've constructed for ourselves. It's absolutely perfect because it conforms precisely to our ego's definition of absolute perfection. If we haven't understood the point that all our thoughts are just thoughts, we can get lost in these delusions about realization for a very long time.

So just what is this Buddha's truth stuff Dogen keeps going on and on about? By way of explanation, he gives us a kooky little passage that goes like this. Ahem. "To learn the Buddha's truth is to learn ourselves. To learn ourselves is to forget ourselves. To forget ourselves is to be experienced by the myriad dharmas. To be experienced by the myriad dharmas is to let our own body-and-mind, and the body-and-mind of the external world, fall away."

Sounds pretty weird and "Zen," don't it? But what he's trying to say here isn't really all that strange. First off, let's take that "to learn yourself is to forget yourself" bit. Dogen does not deny the individual or subjective side of our experience. But to really understand your subjective experience, you need to forget your confused ideas about your "self."

To most of us the existence of "self" is unquestionable, self-evident. What could be more obvious? I think, therefore I am. But to Dogen it was evident that self did not exist at all — as it is to anyone who pursues Buddhist practice deeply enough. Self is just a mental construct, an idea, a way of understanding reality, a slot within our heads into which we place a certain portion of what we experience. But when your practice deepens and it begins to dawn on you that all your thoughts are just thoughts, even that most basic of thoughts, the idea that your thoughts are generated by something called "self," becomes questionable and finally dissolves away.

So what happens if we manage to realize this whole "there is no such thing as self" deal? I mean, do you just disappear? Does your whole personality vanish? Do you end up like some kind of soulless Zen robot or something?

It doesn't really happen that way at all, actually. 'Cuz when the thought of self breaks down, that to which you assigned the name *self* does not similarly disappear. You just discover that "me" was far too limiting a name for what you really are. Here's what Dogen has to say about that: "A person getting realization is like the moon being reflected in water: the moon does not get wet, and the water is not broken. The whole moon and the whole sky are reflected in a dew-drop on a blade of grass. Realization does not break the individual, just as the moon does not pierce the water. The individual does not hinder the state of realization, just as a dew-drop does not hinder the sky and moon."

The thing is, it's not like you get some great realization and then your soul vanishes. The fact is, your soul or "self" or whatever never existed in the first place, except as an ill-formed concept that caused you a lot of unnecessary grief. It doesn't exist right now, so there's nothing that could possibly vanish in some future "enlightenment experience." My first Zen teacher, Tim, is like a stand-up comic; my current teacher, Gudo Nishijima, is like a bulldog. None of the Zen teachers I've known was the least bit like a robot. If anything, their personalities were stronger than other people's because they had fewer illusions about who they were.

But just how do you forget your ideas of "self"? You do, Dogen says, when you are "experienced by the myriad dharmas." In other words, we forget our ideas of self when we stop concentrating exclusively on how we experience the universe and learn how the universe experiences *us*. It's not as impossible as it sounds. In fact, you do it all the time.

When I was in that basement trying to get those old songs together for the first time in two decades, I had to simultaneously play my part while understanding how the bass lines fit into the overall structure of the song and how what I was playing was being perceived and interpreted by the other members of the band.

When I look at you and you look at me, I am experiencing you and being experienced by you at the same time. You don't know what thoughts are in my head when I look at you. And I don't know if you notice that zit on the end of my nose. And yet my experience of you is a real and vital part of your experience, and vice versa. We behave and even think differently in front of others. Maybe if you weren't lookin' at me, I'd pop that zit. If I find out Mickey, our drummer, is playing harder on the downbeat, I might have to hit the bass a little harder on the downbeat, too. And, of course, it goes way deeper than just that. We are always being experienced by everyone and everything we come in contact with. A Buddhist would even say that you're being experienced by this book at some level. The money you paid for it will be experienced by me, for example.* And the book itself, though we conceive of it as being an inanimate object, can be said to have a kind of ability to experience things. Maybe not quite the same as yours, but still, a Buddhist accepts that this kind of stuff is part of the wide, vast universe. Of course, you don't need to take this literally if you don't want to. But I find that this way of viewing things makes me far more respectful of the stuff around me.

At some level we each partake in the overall experiences of the whole universe. A gust of wind comes along, and everyone in the park feels a chill. The sun suddenly goes supernova, and we all burn to a crisp. And even when we think we're not experiencing the experience of the whole universe, we still are. We just don't know it. And our not knowing it is an indispensable part of that overall universal experience. Gosh.

So where do we get this idea of self in the first place? Here's Dogen's take on this question: "When a man is sailing along in a boat

_____

*   Thank you.

and he moves his eyes to the shore, he misapprehends that the shore is moving. If he keeps his eyes fixed on the boat, he knows that it is the boat which is moving forward. Similarly, when we try to understand the myriad dharmas on the basis of confused assumptions about body and mind, we misapprehend that our own mind or our own essence may be permanent." In other words, it's when we conceive of ourselves as having some kind of permanent essence that we get into trouble. It's this permanent essence that we feel we must protect and preserve, that feels slighted when it's mistreated, that seeks revenge, that gets jealous of other people's (nonexistent) permanent essences and does all kinds of idiotic things just to try and prove its worth.

As for the supposed permanence of this nonexistent essence, Dogen gives us a metaphor. He says, "Firewood becomes ash; it can never go back to being firewood. Nevertheless, we should not take the view that ash is its future and firewood is its past." Firewood is firewood; ash is ash. It makes no sense to speak of some kind of essence that changes from firewood into ash.

It's like imagining some kind of permanent essence that starts off as a bunch of wads of cotton, gets shipped off to Taiwan, gets sewn into a T-shirt, gets printed up with the logo of some studly hair-metal band, gets bought for much too much money by a pimply faced teenage boy and worn for three years before ending up as a dishrag, then a cat toy, and finally winds up forgotten at the bottom of a landfill somewhere slowly turning into dirt. From the beginning the T-shirt was just a conglomeration of cotton and ink on the material, or "form," side and the trademark of the hair-metal band along with some merchandiser's greed for making money off of dull-witted teenage boys on the immaterial, or "emptiness," side. You and I are no different. We're no more than a transitional phase of a particular glob of matter and energy within the vast universe. Yet the vast universe is as much a part of us as we are a part of it.

So if it's a mistake to view our past or our future as something that happens to our "self," how can we view either? Dogen says, "Remember, firewood abides in the place of firewood in the Dharma. It has a past and it has a future. Although it has a past and a future, the past and the future are cut off. Ash exists in the place of ash in the Dharma. It has a past and it has a future. The firewood, after becoming ash, does not again become firewood." Our past and our future are cut off from the here and now. We can't revisit the past, and we can't fast-forward to the future. The only real time is now. The only real place is here. And just to make sure we don't miss the full implications of the metaphor, he adds, "Similarly, human beings, after death, do not live again."

So if even life and death can't be thought of as things that happen to our "self," what the heck are they? "Life is an instantaneous situation, and death is also an instantaneous situation. It is the same, for example, with winter and spring. We do not think that winter becomes spring, and we do not say that spring becomes summer."

For what it's worth, let me give you my take on this whole "self" thing. There is something, some segment of the vast and wide universe, that you carve out and call "self" and say belongs to "you." It's an odd idea, you know, that "you" belong to "you." When you were very young, you noticed this aspect of the universe, and your parents and teachers and friends all told you in overt and subtle ways that this something was your unique "self." They might have even referred to this something as your "soul." Everyone has one of these, they told you, and each one is unique, individual, eternally separate from all the others. You accepted this explanation and based your interpretation of all your experiences on this way of looking at things. It's only natural that you did so because nearly all the great religious, scientific, and philosophical works across the world are based on this understanding. There are virtually no alternatives. So when some book by some old dead Japanese dude comes along and says otherwise, it's pretty hard to accept.

Yet a certain small and historically nearly insignificant group of frankly crazy-seeming people calling themselves Buddhists claim to have discovered that this ordinary and nearly universally accepted way of looking at things is absolutely untrue. Not only that, but they claim that any individual can see this for him- or herself if only that person is willing to do some work to transcend the ordinary view of things. And they say that if we throw away this false view of things, absolutely every aspect of our lives will become immeasurably better. We need to work to transcend the ordinary view, they say, because that view is so pervasive owing mostly to the fact that the vast majority of the world's population accepts it unquestioningly.

We can transcend this perspective, Dogen says, "when we come back to this concrete place." Notice he says, "come back" — as if we had somehow left the concrete place where we are right now. How can we ever leave where we are? But we do it all the time. In fact, most of us are sunk so deeply into our own mental images that we can barely even recognize where we are anymore. We need to learn to come back to a place we have never left. It's absurd. But that's the way it is.

"If we become familiar with action and come back to this concrete place," Dogen says, "the truth is evident that the myriad dharmas are not self." Becoming familiar with action sounds like a pretty easy requirement for understanding the truth of the universe. But becoming familiar with action can be tough. You'd think, for example, that becoming familiar with an action as simple as sitting on a cushion and looking at a wall — which is all that zazen really is — would be a snap. But try it sometime and see. And if something like that is hard to figure out, becoming familiar with the complicated actions of our everyday lives is about a bazillion times more difficult. So what are we to do?

"When we use the whole body-and-mind to look at forms," Dogen says, "and when we use the whole body-and-mind to listen to sounds," he says, "we are sensing them directly." Say what? But using the whole body to look or to listen is, again, not difficult at all.

You know how when you go to a really loud concert and you can feel Flea's bass hitting you right in the chest or Eddie Van Halen's high notes slicing right through your sinus passages? The truth is we always sense everything with our whole bodies. It's just that our ears are more sensitive to sound and our eyes are more sensitive to light. Nonetheless, light and sound always affect our entire bodies. Our senses aren't really as distinct from one another as we perceive them to be. And we can take what Dogen says here even further, since he often uses the term *the whole body* to mean the entire universe. What I call "me" may be little more than an organ the universe uses to experience itself the way we use our ears to experience the sound of Eddie Van Halen.

But, for Dogen, everything always seems to come back to that question he had as a kid. He wondered why Buddhists said we were already perfect but then recommended all these weird meditative practices so that we could realize this innate perfection. So if we only have to come back to right where we are, in other words, if we're always enlightened, why don't we notice it? Why are we so confused all the time, fighting, fussing, car-bombing each other and doing all kinds of nasty stuff based on the confused idea that our "self" is somehow real?

In "Genjo Koan" Dogen explains it like this: "When fish move through water, however they move, there is no end to the water. When birds fly through the sky, however they fly, there is no end to the sky."*

We can't notice reality any more than a fish can recognize water. No one can ever notice his or her own enlightenment. Like I said earlier, if you think you have realized enlightenment, then it's not

---

* Since this is a long quote, I've decided not to put it all in the text. But here's the rest of it: "But if a bird leaves the sky it will die at once, and if a fish leaves the water it will die at once. So we can understand that water is life and can understand that sky is life. Birds are life, and fish are life. It may be that life is birds and that life is fish. And beyond this, there may still be further progress."

really enlightenment, I'm afraid. And all those dudes out there who'll tell you they've realized enlightenment? Well, I'll let you be the judge of that. Bummer, huh? But, as Dogen says, "When buddhas are really buddhas, they do not need to recognize themselves as buddhas. Nevertheless, they are buddhas in the state of experience, and they go on experiencing the state of Buddha."*

Then he goes on to say, "This being so, a bird or fish that aimed to move through the water or the sky [only] after getting to the bottom of water or utterly penetrating the sky, could never find its way or find its place in the water or in the sky." This is a very important idea for any of you aspiring to really practice Buddhism. When you start thinking you just gotta, gotta, gotta get to the bottom of everything and experience whatever you envision as complete, unsurpassed, unqualified whiz-bang-with-cheese-on-top enlightenment, you're moving in the wrong direction. The enlightenment you're searching for when you search that way is always gonna be way off over there somewhere. Never here. Never now.

And just in case you missed the point about buddhas not necessarily recognizing themselves as such, Dogen says, "Do not assume that what is attained will inevitably become self-conscious and be recognized by the intellect. Realization is the state of ambiguity itself." The state of ambiguity — that messy, greasy, mixed-up, confused, and awful situation you're living through right now — is enlightenment itself.

Dogen ends the chapter with a short story that sums things up. It's one of those hot, sticky, humid days at the end of a long Japanese summer, and a Zen master is sitting in his room fanning himself with a paper fan. A monk comes by and asks, "The nature of air is to be ever-present, and there is no place that air cannot reach. So why are you using a fan?"

---

* He also puts it this way, which I like a lot: "There is a state in which the traces of realization are forgotten; and it manifests the traces of forgotten realization for a long, long time."

The master says, "You have only understood that the nature of air is to be ever-present, but you do not yet know the truth that there is no place air cannot reach."

The monk says, "What is the truth of there being no place air cannot reach?"

At this, the master just sat there fanning himself.

The mere fact that we are living in the enlightened state all the time does not absolve us from needing to have what Gudo Nishijima likes to call the will to the truth, just as the fact that there is air everywhere doesn't mean that there's no sense in fanning yourself when you're hot. The poor student is probably drenched with sweat and smells like a garlic-processing plant next door to a wastewater treatment facility. Yet instead of solving his real problem by doing something real, like fanning himself, he's asking about some idiotic theory of air being everywhere. This is the way we all are, though. We're far more interested in explanations of reality than we are in reality itself. The solution is to see the problem and take action — now. Start from just where you are, and do something. Without the practice of zazen all the theories in the world won't get you an inch closer to the mark. If you're really serious about Buddhism, don't just read about it. Do it.

Chapter 3

Proper Posture Required

Gosh-dang snowstorm! The last time I drove in one of these, Bill Clinton hadn't even met Monica Lewinsky yet. For the eleven years I lived in Japan I drove a car exactly once. And that was under severe duress. My boss there insisted I needed to know how to drive. I performed so badly that he gave up on the idea almost immediately. In Japan they have this amazing system most of us Americans have never heard of. It's called public transportation. You can get practically anywhere you want to go by trains or buses, which, incidentally, always run on time. Except when their drivers are in too big a hurry and crash them into apartment buildings. But we'll leave that for now. At any rate, you don't have to drive in snowstorms so bad that the view out the windshield looks like the opening credits from *Star Trek*.

I was on my way back from practicing with Agitated — not *the* Agitated, by the way, just Agitated — an Akron/Cleveland hardcore band that I was not a member of back in the day but that I'd been invited to play with, since their first bass player refused to do the show and their second bass player was now working for Associated Press in Dubai. Given the incestuous nature of the bands in those days, I could have been a member of Agitated back then. So it made sense to have me join for the reunion show.

The rehearsal went exceptionally well. Even though it was the first time the band had convened in more than twenty years, and even though they had a new guy — me — on bass, we all fit together pretty near perfectly from the first number. Unlike the members of Zero Defects, those of Agitated were far too scattered to be able to rehearse together before that night. Granted, songs like "Living like Garbage" and "Go Blue, Go Die" aren't exactly Mozart. But getting them just right isn't easy. We'd all been practicing to the same set of tapes, so we all knew our parts. It was just a matter of making them fit together properly.

Just like I had at the Zero Defects rehearsal the previous night, I got quite a buzz from playing. But it still wasn't quite like what happens when you do zazen. Zazen has a kind of power all its own. Dogen knew about that. In fact, every Buddhist practitioner knows about the power of zazen practice because they do it all the time. But the great Buddhist writers very seldom wrote about zazen specifically for this very reason: it was too obvious to state directly. The practice was always implied but very rarely stated. One of the truly unique and very, very cool things about Dogen is that he was very precise about just what zazen is.

So what exactly *is* this zazen stuff that Dogen goes on and on about? I'm glad you asked. There's a chapter in *Shobogenzo* called "Zazengi" (坐禅儀), which lays it all out. The *gi* part of it means "standard method," and *zazen* means "zazen." You figured that out, huh? "Zazengi" is one of the shortest and least poetic chapters of *Shobogenzo*. It's extremely straightforward, concerning itself strictly with the actual physical practice of zazen.

In them days the physical practice of zazen was something you generally learned directly from your master in a temple. But Dogen believed that zazen wasn't just something to keep temple-bound monks occupied when they weren't pruning the bushes or arranging funeral ceremonies. To him, zazen was for everyone, plain folks like you and me included. In fact, he even wrote a second version of "Zazengi" and called it "Recommending Zazen to All People."

This is an important point. In a short book called *Bendowa*, which sounds embarrassingly like "bend over" to me but actually means "A Talk on the Pursuit of the Truth," Dogen answers the challenge that zazen is just too difficult for ordinary people, who, instead, should do easier practices like chanting sutras. This is an argument you still hear today. I first heard it when I was in college and used to listen to talks at the Cleveland Hare Krishna temple. According to the folks there, seated meditation was a method that only great saints could ever hope to use to accomplish God Realization. Dogen didn't agree.

Okay, then. So how do you do it? First off, Dogen says you gotta find a nice quiet spot. Not too cold and not too hot. The room should be bright, he says. Zazen isn't something you do in the dark. "Cast aside all involvements," he says, "and cease the ten thousand things." I've seen wannabe Zen practitioners who get all hung up on phrases like "the ten thousand things." But it's just an old-fashioned Chinese way of saying "lots o' stuff." It just means to drop all your other junk and devote your zazen time to zazen.

For me, early mornings work best. When I was in college, I'd get up before all my housemates and do my zazen in that quiet time before everybody was up and about. I know. You wanna sleep. But once you get into the habit, you'll find that zazen is a really relaxing way to start off your day, and you don't really miss that extra sleep.*

Dogen says to sit on a round cushion called a *zafu*. Now, you young whippersnappers out there don't know how good you've got it nowadays. When I started doing this zazen stuff in the early eighties you couldn't just order a *zafu* online like you can now. Hell, in

---

* I'm presuming here that you aren't out carousing all hours of the night and that you're getting a decent night's shut-eye. Going to bed a bit earlier helps as well.

1982 there was no *line* to be *on*. In those days you had to make do
with whatever you could get. And that still works, in case you don't
want to invest in an official regulation-type *ʒafu*. I've used couch
cushions, bed pillows, folded-up towels, backpacks stuffed full of old
hankies,* and all sorts of other stuff. All you really need is something
reasonably firm that'll get your butt a couple of inches off the floor.

The hardest thing for me about doing zazen when I started out
was not the pain. It was the embarrassment. I was mortified that
someone might catch me sitting there all cross-legged and preten-
tiously meditating away. I used to break out in a sweat every time I
heard anyone moving around. It was especially bad if I'd had a girl
over and she caught me doing that stuff the morning after.

When I did get caught, people could be vicious. "So you're *meditating*, huh? Didja reach a higher plane?" they'd sneer. Or else
they'd think I was a nutcase. Some people really worried about it. I
knew a girl whose mom insisted that emptying your mind of
thoughts, like she'd heard meditators did, allowed demons to come
in and take over their bodies — as if the only thing keeping Satan
away is a nonstop stream of meaningless mental chatter. She must
have fantasized that one day I'd go all Exorcist on her daughter. Very
rarely did I meet anyone who thought the practice might be interesting or useful. But that didn't matter much to me. I found it useful,
and I wasn't about to stop.

Dogen recommends sitting in the full- or half-lotus postures as
the best way to fold up your legs. "To sit in the full-lotus posture,"
he says, "put the right foot on the left thigh and put the left foot on
the right thigh. The toes of each foot should be symmetrically
aligned with the thighs, not out of proportion. To sit in the half-lotus
posture just put the left foot on the right thigh." You can also put the
right foot on the left thigh for the half-lotus or even reverse the full
lotus.

---

* Okay, I made that one up.

While I very heartily recommend these postures as the best way to do zazen, you don't want to be stupid about it. You'll hear stories about folks who've messed up their knees in these postures. But most of these tales are from people who went overboard doing the posture in the face of intense physical pain or for many, many hours on end. Pace yourself. If the posture hurts your legs a bit, that's fine. Our leg muscles are generally really tight, and a little stretching does them a world of good — even though it sometimes hurts like heck. But know your limits. And watch for knee pain. That can be a sign of trouble. Your knees are not meant to bend sideways, so don't force them to. The necessary bending should come from a rotation at the hips, not the knees.

The essential thing is to keep your spine straight. Not unnaturally straight, mind you. The human spine has a natural curve to it that you shouldn't try to somehow undo. But Dogen says, "Do not lean to the left, incline to the right, slump forward, or arch backward. It is essential that the ears are aligned with the shoulders and the nose is aligned with the navel." Don't use anything to support your back either, like a wall or the back of a chair. Zazen is essentially a balance pose, and balancing while leaning against something isn't really balancing.

Keep your eyes open — "neither wide open, nor half closed," our man says, just somewhere in between. Try to keep 'em focused too.

Now hold that pose. If you just absolutely have to scratch or fix your legs, do it with as little fuss as possible, and get back to the practice. The correct physical posture is the single most important part of the practice of zazen. Keep focused on that, and everything else will follow.

There's a Zero Defects song called "Proper Attire Required." We didn't play it at the show in December. I wanted to. But I got outvoted. Anyhow, it's a rant about music clubs that wouldn't let you come in unless you wore a tie. The song was a statement of defiance against the tight-assed mentality of voluntary conformism.

But when it comes to zazen, I'm pretty conservative. I've seen places where they let folks meditate in all manner of positions, including giving them comfy "meditation chairs" to lounge around in. I don't believe in that crap. Do your zazen right, or you're not doing zazen at all. So I have somehow gone from ranting against conformity to insisting on it where zazen is concerned. How come?

There are meditation teachers out there who'll tell you that it's not important what position you sit in, that it's what you do with your mind that counts. I don't buy it. Proper posture is an absolute requirement of zazen practice. Here's why: the posture is not arbitrary. It was not arrived at by accident, nor is it a mere cultural contrivance. I'm not a doctor.* But after years of doing the practice, I've watched the way my body and mind react to the correct posture. It's as if the nerves that run from our brain into our spines just work better when they're lined up exactly as Mother Nature intended them to be. We often talk about balance in zazen. But remember that Buddhism makes no distinction between body and mind. Physical balance is mental balance.

This is why I don't accept the idea that as long as you keep your mind supposedly "pure," it doesn't matter what shape your body's in. No matter how pure your mind is, you can't play baseball using musk melons for balls, you can't play "Highway to Hell" using the elastic from your mom's old brassieres for guitar strings, and you can't do zazen in the wrong posture. Well, I suppose you *could* do these things if you really wanted. But it wouldn't be baseball, it wouldn't be "Highway to Hell," and it would not be zazen.

I've met loads of people who want Zen to be an "anything goes" type of practice. Truth be told, that's what I thought it was when I first got into it. It's pretty common to mistake the Zen insistence that wherever and whatever you are right now is Reality itself for the idea that anything goes.

---

* I don't even play one on TV.

But anything does not go. Buddhism is about discovering the things that "go," that really work and make our lives and the lives of others better and happier, and the things that do not "go" and make us and others miserable. The fact that Zen Buddhism doesn't have any set lists of hard-and-fast rules that are supposed to work anywhere at any time for anyone at all does not mean that everything is okay. Right and wrong still exist.

A science writer named John Horgan, who we'll talk about more in a later chapter, says that "the effects of meditation often touted by Buddhists are unquantifiable" and that, according to studies, zazen is no better for your physical and mental condition than just plopping your ass down in a comfy chair.

I do not believe that. There is an astronomical difference between doing zazen and just lounging around in an easy chair. I've done both enough times to know. If you want to find out what the difference is, try some zazen and see.

Zazen is not a "spiritual" practice. It is the effort of mind *and* body, as much so as playing bass guitar or doing gymnastics. As with any physical practice, there are right ways and wrong ways to do it. Keeping the spine straight using your ability to balance the vertebrae on top of each other is the key to good zazen. Like I said, it's essentially a yogic balance pose. One of the best known of the balance poses is the Tree Pose, in which you stand up on one leg with the other foot up against the thigh of the leg you're standing on. When you do the Tree Pose, it's easy to know when you've lost balance 'cuz you fall over in a heap on the floor. With zazen, the clues are far subtler. But once you learn to spot them, you won't have any trouble missing them. Zazen is a balance between tension and relaxation. That's part of the middle way that old man Buddha used to go on and on about. Zazen is all about achieving physical as well as mental balance because they are the same thing. Stay straight, and your mind will settle of its own accord.

Posture is a state of both body and mind.

If you're too fat to do zazen, try losing some weight. If your legs are too stiff, try doing what I did and learn some yoga exercises to loosen those muscles up. Nothing worthwhile comes without effort. But make that effort, and you'll find it has tremendous benefits.

Chapter 4

Four Points of Zazen

One of my clearest early memories of Akron from when I used to go there with my dad from the suburb where we lived is the smell. As soon as you crossed the city limits, it was like you were breathing the fumes of a million burning tires. The perpetually cloudy skies turned a shade grayer from the tons of smoke Firestone, Goodyear, Goodrich, and Seiberling constantly pumped into the air.

By the time I graduated high school in 1982, that smell was already a thing of the past. But what was good for our lungs, as well as for the trees and the birds and the rivers and the lakes, was not so good for our wallets. The tire companies had been the economic backbone of the city. My dad moved down to Texas in 1984 when all the rubber jobs left town. People like me, who stayed behind, found life a lot harder. Yet it was those tough times that gave birth to the town's lively artistic scene, including its punk rock venues. Throughout the eighties the town continued to decay, until by the time I finally wised up and moved to Japan in 1993, downtown was a mass of boarded-up buildings and the abandoned skeletons of once-bustling department stores.

Things have gotten a whole lot better since then, though. The city built a minor-league baseball stadium where there used to be a row of dead shop fronts. One of the coolest new places in the refurbished downtown is a little tavern called the Lime Spider. A throwback to the early days of Akron's New Wave glory when Stiv Bators used to rub elbows with Chrissy Hynde and the members of Devo at the Bank, the Lime Spider features the best of the area's local original music scene.

The first show Zero Defects was scheduled to do was a one-song appearance at the Spider at a thing called Joey-okie. I should explain the concept. See, a couple of years ago, Jimi, the lead singer of Zero Defects, invented this thing called Bowie-okie. He got a whole bunch of bands together for a show in which they'd all share equipment and everyone had to play only David Bowie songs. Audience members were also invited onstage to sing their favorite Bowie hits. Bowie-okie was a pretty big success. So Jimi and the folks at the Spider branched out into doing other bands. They even got Jerry Casale, founder of Devo, to come back to Akron for the Devo-okie show they put on.

Joey-okie was supposed to be a tribute to the late Joey Ramone. So every band had to play a Ramones song. I was a little worried about this. As much as all the members of Zero Defects were committed Ramones fans, there is no way you would have gotten us to play a Ramones cover back in our heyday. The very idea of covering anyone else's songs was deeply offensive to our hardcore sensibilities.

Still, that was then and this was now. It was Jimi's event, and we all wanted to help him out. Plus, getting onstage before the big show on Saturday could only do us good. So we worked up a version of "I Don't Wanna Walk Around with You," from the first Ramones LP, that didn't sound anything like the Ramones. We played the first section the way we played the slow lumbering intro to our song "Where Are the Kids Tonight?" The second section we played at pure breakneck hardcore speed. Finally, we added the free-form freak-out section from the end of our always-reliable thrash party crowd pleaser,

"No More Control," to the finish of the song. Voilà! A Ramones cover Zero Defects could play without embarrassing ourselves.

The bill was jam-packed. Every band in town was there. And our segment kept getting pushed further and further back. It was after 1 a.m. before we were set to play. Now, 1 a.m. was nothing to me when I was eighteen, or even when I was twenty-eight. But I'd been living a modified Zen lifestyle for the past decade or so and rarely went to bed any later than midnight, and much earlier than that whenever I could manage it. I really like being up at the crack of dawn. I feel ashamed when I sleep in till seven these days, like I've missed half the day already. But you do what you gotta do. The fact that it was three hours earlier in California and that 1 a.m. felt like 10 p.m. to me helped.

Once we got onstage, though, all our rehearsing of that evening and of the two days before went right out the window. I couldn't hear what the guitar was doing, in spite of the fact that it was pumping out through two six-foot-tall Marshall stack amplifiers. All I could hear was a gigantic roar. So I did what bass players have done since the dawn of the bass. I just watched what the drummer did and played something that matched.

Still, the most important thing onstage, and in rehearsals, was not to think about what I was doing. I can't tell you how many times I messed up onstage just because I started thinking about what I was doing. The number-one question I get asked whenever I instruct people in zazen is, "What should I be thinking about?"

My answers are always short, because what you think about in zazen is really not very important. The only specific instructions Dogen gives in "Zazengi" about what to think while doing zazen are "Good is not considered. Bad is not considered. It is beyond mind, will, or consciousness, and beyond mindfulness, thought, or reflection." But most people aren't satisfied if you just stop there. They wanna know what they should do inside their heads while doing zazen. People in Dogen's day were no different, so he addressed this point throughout *Shobogenzo*.

As we saw earlier, Dogen's strategy was always to look at things from four points of view: the mental; the physical; the point of view of action itself, in which body and mind are combined; and reality, which is all-inclusive. Dogen's four fundamental points for zazen related to these four points of view are:

1. 非思量, pronounced *hi-shi-ryo*, which means "nonthinking."

2. 正身端座, pronounced *sho-shin-tan-za*, which means "sitting upright making the body right."

3. 身心脱落, pronounced *shin-jin-datsu-raku*, which means "dropping off body and mind."

4. 只管打座, pronounced *shi-kan-ta-za*, which means "just sitting."

The word *hishiryo* — as well as its synonyms *fushiryo* (不思量) and *mushiryo* (無思量) — means "nonthinking." It comes from an old Zen story that goes like this: A guy walks up to a Zen master and asks, "What are you thinking in the mountain-still state of zazen?"

The master doesn't get pissed that his sitting's just been so rudely interrupted but instead tells the guy, "I'm thinking the concrete state of not thinking."*

The guy says, "How in the bejesus can you think what is not thinking?"

The Zen master replies, "It's different from thinking" (非思量, pronounced *hishiryo*).**

So what's the concrete state of not thinking? There's an episode of *Star Trek*, the older, cooler one with Captain Kirk, in which one

---

* 思量箇不思量底, pronounced *shi-ryo-ko fu-shi-ryo-tei* for those of you following along at home.

** For you linguists out there who get off on this kinda thing, the Zen master first says *fu-shiryo* (不思量), then says *hi-shiryo* (非思量). *Shiryo* (思量) means "thinking" or "consideration." The prefix *fu* (不) is usually translated as "un" as in *hitsyo* (必要) "necessary" and *fu-hitsyo* (不必要) "unnecessary." The *hi* (非) prefix is a stronger denial and often shows up in words indicating criminal activity, such as *higouhou* (非合法) "illegal" and *hikokumin* (非国民) "traitor." Don't say you never learned nothin' from one of my books.

Doctor van Gelder of the Tantalus Penal Colony has invented this machine called the Neural Neutralizer, which drains the mind of all thought. They put some guy under there, and he immediately turns into a mindless vegetable with this awful grimace on his face. On seeing this, Captain Kirk makes an impassioned speech about how terrible it must be to have your mind turned totally blank like that. Ghastly!

People who are new to the practice have all kinds of weird ideas about the state of nonthinking. Some people envision it as some kind of trippy spaced-out sorta thing. I've even heard the term *mushiryo consciousness* thrown around as if it was some way-cool and mysterious altered state. Some folks, like that girl's mom I told you about who was worried about my becoming taken over by demons, are even scared by the idea.

But it ain't like that, folks. In fact, it feels real nice to stop thinking. And it's not nearly as difficult as people want to make it seem.

You just kind of *think not thinking*.

It's like this: If you start *really* paying attention to your own thought process — I'm talking here about the process itself and not just the contents of the individual thoughts that make it up — you'll notice that thoughts don't just go on and on continuously. There are little spaces between them. Most of us tend to habitually try and fill these spaces up with more thoughts as fast as we possibly can. But even the best of us can't fill them all, so there are always little gaps.

See, you might say that there are two basic kinds of thought. There are thoughts that pop up unannounced and uninvited in our brains for no reason we're able to discern. These are just the results of previous thoughts and experiences that have left their traces in the neural pathways of our brains. You can't do much to stop these, nor should you try. The other kind of thought is when we grab on to one of these streams of energy and start playing with it the way your mom always told you not to do with your wee-wee in front of the neighbors. We dig deep into these thoughts and roll around in them

like a pig rolling in its own doo-doo, feeling all that delicious cool-
ness and drinking deep of their lovely stink.

To practice "thinking not thinking," all you need to do is ignore
the first kind of thoughts and learn how not to instigate the second
type. This is easier said than done, of course. But get into the habit,
and it begins to come naturally.

When you start doing this, you'll begin to notice that your
thoughts never just appear all at once fully verbalized. They start out
much more nebulous, and you sort of shape them into stuff you can
tell your friends or write down in a book or whatever. If you don't
understand what I'm talking about here, just put this book down for
a second, get out a pencil and paper, and try to write down whatever
it is you're thinking about right now.

Did you try it? Even if you were just thinking, "The guy who
wrote this book doesn't know what the hell he's talking about," it's
pretty interesting how difficult it can be to just turn your nebulous
thoughts into something solid like that.

Now try to look at the natural spaces between thoughts. Learn
what it feels like just to stop generating more and more stuff for your
brain to chew on. Now see if you can do that for longer and longer
periods. A couple of seconds is fine. Voilà! Thinking not thinking!

One thing about thinking that few of us ever really, uh, think
about is the fact that thinking actually takes a certain amount of effort. We often hear the word *ruminate* used in reference to going over
stuff in our heads. The word *ruminate*, though, literally refers to what
cows do when they barf up half-digested food and chew it some more
before swallowing it again. That's kind of an apt analogy for what we
do in our heads. Only with cows, this activity performs a useful function in digestion. In human beings its usefulness is a little more
doubtful.

The trick to not thinking is not adding energy to the equation in
an effort to forcibly stop thinking from happening. It's more a matter of subtracting energy from the equation in order not to barf the

thoughts up and start chewing them over again. This is easier said than done, of course, like most things worth doing. But work on it for a while, and eventually you'll get the hang of it.

And if you find you just can't do this on certain days, no problem. Everyone has days like that. Everyone. Me, you, Dogen, the Dalai Lama, all of us. Effort is far more important than so-called success because effort is a real thing. What we call "success" is just the manifestation of our mind's ability to categorize things. *This* is "success." *That* is "failure." Who says? You says. That's all. Reality is what it is, beyond all concepts of success and failure.

Next Dogen addresses the physical side of the matter using the phrase *sho-shin-ta-za*, meaning "right posture and regulated sitting." Just pay attention to how you're sitting, whether you're leaning to one side or the other. Watch your shoulders. When I first started, my shoulders were always drifting up toward my ears. My teacher would come along and push them down for me, and I'd be really surprised. I'd had no idea I was all hunched up like that.

There is one spot where your spine will balance perfectly on top of your hip bones without any effort on your part. It's a little different for every person and can change from one day to the next. You find this spot the same way you learn to ride a bike without falling over. You just have to fall over again and again and again. There's no point in beating yourself up when this happens. Just get back on the bike again.

The next point Dogen talks about — dropping off body and mind — sounds a little oddball to most folks. But he's just referring to the area of action itself. The concrete state of action is where body and mind function as one. Again, it's nothing strange or mystical. Body and mind always function as one. You're just used to looking at the two sides as separate things.

The only way I could play the bass line to our cover of "I Don't Wanna Walk Around with You" that night was to drop off both body and mind. Mind had to go, in the sense that I couldn't think about what I was playing, and body had to go, in the sense that I couldn't afford to be bothered by any extraneous concern over my physical state. I just needed to do it.

Of course, what Dogen was going on about was way deeper than playing bass in a punk rock band. Still, in many important ways it is a manifestation of the same thing. Yet, to be certain, zazen is a much more direct way to catch the truth than bass playing will ever be.

Zazen, in spite of its apparent lack of activity in the usual sense, is the purest form of action. It's action reduced to its barest essentials, the action of simply sitting there and paying attention. If you don't believe keeping still is action, try it sometime. It takes a lot of effort.

But what about those weird words he uses to describe it? I mean, what could be more far out, trippy, and mystical sounding than the idea of dropping off body and mind? I used to envision it as some magical state in which I would just suddenly disappear right off my cushion, like something from a Siegfried and Roy routine — only without the getting mauled by a tiger part.

But Dogen was talking about something much more immediate and real. There are a lot of other ways you could express this same idea. Gudo Nishijima likes to say it's the balance of the autonomic nervous system. Or you could say it's the balance between thought and feeling. When the two opposing sides are perfectly equal, they cancel each other out, thus causing both body — the material side — and mind — the spiritual side — to appear to drop away. Dropping off body and mind is recovering your natural state, the state that is your birthright and that you have somehow forgotten.

The state in zazen is, in and of itself, the dropping off of body and mind. And this goes for whether you're thinking not thinking or thinking about that waitress at Hooters — provided you get back to your proper position when you become aware you've been doing that. It doesn't matter much whether you notice your balanced state or not. The physical position itself *is* the balanced state of body and mind because body and mind are one and the same.

In Buddhism we make no distinction between mental and physical. This is very hard for lots of people to grasp. I know it was for me. Our habit of making a clear distinction between body and mind is so deeply ingrained that most of us take it to be irrefutable. Every religion in the world is based on the seemingly self-evident fact that body and soul are absolutely distinct. But Buddha looked closely at the matter and discovered, quite to his surprise, that this was not the case at all, that, in fact, there is no division between body and mind, no division between self and the outside world. You can see this for yourself, too, if you have the courage to look. The reason we say that the physical posture of zazen is enlightenment itself is because of this total lack of distinction between body and mind, spirit and matter, self and the outside world.

Finally, Dogen addresses reality itself when he says that zazen is *shi-kan-ta-ʒa,* or "just sitting."

But "just sitting" doesn't mean just sitting in the sense of "just sittin' around." To really understand "just sitting" in the sense that Dogen intended, look at the Chinese characters he chose to express the idea. *Shi-kan-ta-ʒa* is a compound word consisting of four characters. The first compound, 只管 (*shikan*), is normally pronounced *hitasura* in modern Japanese and means "earnestly" or "intently." The first character in the second compound, 打, is commonly pronounced *utsu* in modern Japanese and means "hit" or "strike." The final character is 座, which just means "sit." Together the characters evoke the image of sort of hitting your cushion as you sit and really meaning it, man. It's an image of real action taking place.

When you get right down to it, just sitting is the reality of the situation. No bells and whistles, no mystical trances, no enlightenment or daft attempts at "self-improvement." Zazen is just sitting there.

So what the hell is the point of just sitting? There's another old Zen story, which Dogen cites in the chapter "Zazenshin" (座禅箴), which means "A Needle for Zazen." Even though the title conjures up images of sneaking up behind people doing zazen and poking them in the butt, actually *needle* is used here as a colloquialism meaning a teaching that's sharp like a needle.

Anyhow, the story goes like this. A guy's sitting zazen, and his teacher walks up to him and asks, "What are you trying to do?"

The guy says, "I'm working on becoming a buddha."

So the teacher picks up a loose tile off the floor and starts polishing it on his sleeve. "What are you doing that for?" the student asks.

"I'm trying to make this tile into a mirror," the teacher says. In those days mirrors were made by polishing pieces of metal — not tile — till they gleamed.

"How's polishing a tile on your sleeve gonna ever make it into a mirror?" the student says.

The teacher says, "How's sitting in zazen ever gonna turn you into a buddha?"

This story is usually interpreted as an admonition that trying to become a buddha through doing zazen is as futile as trying to make a mirror by polishing a tile. But, as usual, our buddy Dogen rejects the common understanding.

He says, "It may be that even the eternal mirror and the clear mirror are made into mirrors by polishing a tile. If we do not know that mirrors derive from polishing a tile, we are without a Buddhist patriarch's expression of the truth."

The eternal (or ancient) mirror is 古鏡, pronounced *kokyo*, and the clear mirror is 明鏡, pronounced *meikyo*. It doesn't really matter which is which. They're both just terms ancient Buddhists used to talk about the mind, which they often likened to a mirror. Most of us these days imagine the mind to be like a computer whose function is to analyze reality. But to the ancient Buddhist philosophers the mind was supposed to function like a mirror that reflects clearly what is set in front of it without distortion. We do this by allowing intuition to operate freely. We polish our ability to appreciate this intuitive sense every time we do zazen. And, though we are buddhas from the very start, the polishing still has undeniable value. Remember Dogen's question about why we need Buddhist practice even though the Buddhist masters all say we're perfect just as we are? Here is yet another answer to that question.

To drive home his point about the need for practice even more, Dogen brings up another allegory. "If your cart doesn't move," he asks, "is it better to prod the cart or to prod the horse?" Of course everybody knows there's no use prodding the cart, so you should prod the horse. But, being his usual contrary self, Dogen insists that it sometimes makes more sense to prod the cart.

Obviously, then, Dogen was nuts.

Of course I don't think so, or I wouldn't be writing this. But there are people who have used these two absurd-sounding arguments to try and prove that Dogen didn't have a clue. But take a closer look, and the meaning becomes clear.

Dogen says that the secular world has plenty of ways to prod the horse but "lacks any method of prodding the cart." The horse refers to our intellectual, mental side. There are plenty of methods out there that help people get motivated by offering rewards or punishments. Since rewards and punishments exist in the future, these are methods of "prodding the horse" or of stimulating our brains to churn out positive or negative future scenarios that we can work toward or avoid. But in the here and now all that future stuff is just a dream, an intellectual fantasy.

In Dogen's view zazen is a method of prodding the cart. It addresses the physical side first. And when the physical body is right, the mind naturally follows suit. He doesn't deny the existence of the component of "prodding the horse" in zazen, though. He says, "There should be fist beating fist and should be horse beating horse." And though this sounds like a single-sentence treatment for a made-for-TV movie in which Mr. Ed wails on Francis the Talking Mule, it actually refers to taking real action here and now, or *just doing it*, as the sneaker ad used to put it.

Taken together, Dogen's four points add up to a portrait of zazen as real action in the here and now. He isn't concerned with some future state of enlightenment. He isn't concerned with addressing whatever wrongs we may have committed in the past. We cannot act in the past or the future. We can only act right now.

So when you do zazen, the focus should be on the practice itself, not on what it's gonna do for you or whether or not it's worthwhile. Even thoughts about whether you're doing it right are meaningless. If you find your posture slipping, straighten up. If you find your mind drifting, pull it back. Do that over and over for long enough, and it becomes a habit. And if it doesn't, don't worry. Just keep on keeping on. Eventually zazen gets easier. After a while you'll even learn to enjoy it. You'll start doing it because you want to do it.

But to reach that point, you have to start from where you are right now.

Chapter 5

Zazen by Alone

One of the best things about being back in Ohio was that I was not a Zen master there. When I was with that group of people from the old hardcore scene, I was just the bass player from Zero Defects. Some of them knew I had a book out. But most of them didn't care. To them, my book was about on the same level as the Offbeats's CD or Vince Rancid's tattoos, just another piece of art done by someone on the scene. We all respect each other's art — in fact, it was only on this trip that I realized how much Zero Defects and the Offbeats have always been each other's biggest fans. But we all know what it's like to do some piece of art, especially the type of art you have to do all by yourself because no one else is interested. So we're hardly in awe of each other for doing the same stuff we can do ourselves.

My being some kind of a religious leader made some of my friends a bit wary at first. I was really happy that I could still face those guys without being embarrassed about what I was doing these days. I mean, if I'd gone the way of certain supposed "Buddhist masters" — whom I won't name — and turned myself into an industry with hundreds of fawning disciples at my beck and call, I wouldn't have been able to look any of those people in the eye. In that sense, I suppose, the Ohio hardcore crowd functions a little bit like a *sangha*, a group of fellow believers who all help each other maintain their shared values.

It's pretty exhausting to play the role of Zen master. Some people dream dreamy little dreams of one day becoming a Zen master. As for me, I mostly hate being one. People project all kinds of things onto you. You cannot possibly live up to their expectations. A lot of the questions I get asked at my talks can be boiled down to just two categories. One is, "Will you take responsibility for me?" The other is, "Are you as enlightened as I think an Enlightened Being ought to be?" The answer to both of these is, of course, "No."

People are always looking for authority figures. An authority figure is really just a person to whom we can transfer responsibility for our own actions. Sure, I sent all those people to the gas chambers, but I was just following orders. The members of al-Qaeda can do what they do because they believe their religious leaders have the authority of God to take on the responsibility for their reprehensible actions. The Manson Family thought that spiritually enlightened Charlie would take the blame for the terrible things they did. But it was all bullshit. No one but you will bear the responsibility for all the things you have set in motion. Anyone who tells you otherwise is lying.

There are as many variations on the "Will you take responsibility for me?" question as there are people who ask it. More, in fact, since the same people will often rephrase the same question thousands of different ways. People like this demand answers about how they ought to live. There is an endless supply of guys and gals who are ready to give such answers. But I'm not one of them. I have no idea how you should live beyond the advice that Bill and Ted gave the people of the future in their *Bogus Journey*: "Be excellent to each other." There's really nothing else I can offer.

Then there are those who try to test your level of enlightenment according to their own vision of what Enlightened Beings ought to be like. People like this can be really, really tiring. They ask weird-ass questions that, I suppose, must sound like koans to them. One guy at a lecture of mine in Boston stood up and challenged me to tell him the difference between "being and to be." The best I could come up with was that one was an infinitive form and the other was a gerund. That pissed him off because he thought I was playing around with him. I actually worried that he was gonna run up and start punching me. But, honest to God, that was the best I could do.

Ever since I started writing and doing talks I've attracted a seemingly endless stream of people who want to challenge my enlightenment. But for any of you who happen to be reading this, I said it in my last book, and I'll say it again here: I am not now, nor will I ever be, Enlightened. And even though I've said that more times than I can count, there are still a couple of blogs right now devoted almost solely to debunking my enlightenment. I'm sure a few more will pop up before this book gets published. If you enjoy reading that sort of thing, go right ahead and read them. But if you see I'm coming to your town to do a talk, do me a favor and go see a movie instead, okay?

There are plenty of schools of meditation that play right into this demographic. See, 'cuz Enlightenment Challengers really want to be defeated. They want Big Daddy Zen Master to put them in their place. I know there are a ton and a half of supposed Zen master types who have a good time playing this role.

I know both these types of seekers for Enlightened Masters because I was one of them. When I met Tim, my first Zen teacher, I challenged his enlightenment. He told me he was not enlightened. Then I tried to get him to be responsible for my life. He refused. I tried the same thing with Nishijima Sensei. Same reaction. I sometimes wonder why I stayed with those guys. Somehow, I guess, I knew they were right. And since I'm no genius, I also assume that everyone else knows what's right and what's not, too. That's why I won't cut anyone any slack.

But let's say you're not like I was when I started. You're not looking for some authority figure to take on responsibility for your life, and you're not looking for someone whose enlightenment you can challenge. You just want to start doing a little bit of zazen and see where that leads. Where do you begin? Well, you could Google Zen and the name of your hometown and see if any interesting-looking places pop up. But let's say you don't get any hits. Or you do get a few, but they're all those Instant Enlightenment–type places, and you don't really want to be taken for a ride like that. What to do? Can you practice Buddhism without a teacher? Can you do zazen — as Japanese people just learning English tend to say — by alone?

In a little book called *Practical Advice for Studying the Buddhist Truth* (学道用心集, pronounced *gakudo yojin shu*) Dogen says, "If you cannot find a true teacher, it is better not to study [Buddhism] at all." Ouch.

Buddhists are pretty darned adamant about needing a teacher to study Buddhism. In fact, it's a long-standing matter of Buddhist tradition to say there was a mythical teacher who supposedly taught Buddha about Buddhism in another realm somewhere before his birth on planet Earth. Ooh, spooky! No one I know takes the story literally. But this tradition was established just to make sure that not even the Big Man himself got away with not having had a teacher. It makes the point that Buddhism is not something you can just sorta pick up on your own or gather from reading books.

If you're an intelligent person, you're probably thinking, "Obviously these Buddhist teachers insist that you gotta have a Buddhist teacher, 'cuz otherwise Buddhist teachers would be out of work." I mean, the practice is a totally individual matter, right? It's just you sitting and looking at a wall. What possible need could you have for a teacher?

Notice, though, that Dogen never said don't do zazen without a teacher; he just said don't study Buddhism without one. Although doing zazen is a form of studying Buddhism, it won't do most folks any harm to sit zazen on their own. Just don't get too gung ho about it. Don't push yourself to have some kind of enlightenment experience. If you don't have a teacher — or even if you do, actually — just make your zazen practice easy. I put in an hour each day, which is fine for pretty much anyone. If you can't manage that, a half hour in the morning before work can be a very good thing. Even five lousy minutes a day is far better than not doing it at all. Eventually you should seek out a teacher. But there's no reason you can't start off doing zazen by yourself.

Why, then, does Dogen say that you shouldn't study Buddhism without a teacher? To answer that, let's look at one example of what happens when people who've never had a Buddhist teacher set themselves up as experts in Buddhism. The February 21, 2004, issue of Tokyo's English-language *Daily Yomiuri* newspaper featured an article about a Japanese Zen priest named Shinzan Miyamae, who counsels former members of the Aum Shinrikyo cult. The Aum cult, as some of you may recall, was the lovely spiritual organization — a Buddhist sangha dedicated to saving all living beings whose leader was a close personal friend of the Dalai Lama, they claimed — that, in 1995, attempted to give a head start to the apocalypse their leader Shoko Asahara had predicted by gassing the Tokyo subway system with a nerve toxin developed by the Third Reich. Twelve people died in the attack, and many more were injured in the mayhem that broke out in the packed subways that morning.

Miyamae Sensei has made it a point to read up on the "spiritual writings" of the Aum leader, Asahara. In his books Asahara recounts the experience of the mystical awakening that led him to form his organization. After this enlightenment experience Asahara had no need for a teacher of any kind because, he said, he had completely freed himself of his physical body during deep meditation. When Miyamae Sensei read about this, he was struck by the similarities between what

Asahara had described as his moment of awakening and some of his own experiences of disembodiment during his training as a Zen monk. "I wasn't afraid of death," says Miyamae in describing one of those experiences; "I felt as if I could do anything."

Unlike Asahara, however, Miyamae Sensei had a teacher. When he told his Zen master about what had happened to him, the master admonished him, saying, "You may get all sorts of experiences while training, but you must not linger on them." That brought Miyamae back down to earth. I also had similar experiences, one of which I talked about in my first book, *Hardcore Zen*. In my case I'm absolutely certain that had my teacher not told me how utterly dorkified my little "spiritual awakenings" had been, and how I was hardly even unusual, let alone unique, for having had such an experience, I could easily have decided that I was the latest incarnation of God. Unfortunately, poor Mr. Asahara never had anyone to say something like that to him.

I've noticed that when you scratch the surface, you'll find that just about all the crackpot "spiritual masters" of whichever lineage you choose to look at either don't have a teacher or have, for one reason or another, "broken away" from their teacher to form something they believe is somehow purer, somehow truer to the original ancient source, or whatever other excuse they like to use to cover up the fact that they probably never understood what their teachers were talking about to begin with. On the other hand, there seem to be very few people who've studied and stuck with a qualified teacher in an orthodox school of thought who've gone totally off the deep end. There's something about having a bit of social control over the situation that helps keep people from getting really nutty and declaring themselves the One True Savior of the Universe. It's kinda the same thing my hardcore friends did for me. Being part of a group of people who are down-to-earth helps keep you from flying off into the stratosphere. And being part of a group that's already in the stratosphere...? Well, the Aum cult showed us where that leads.

It's not hard to understand why you need a teacher. You need to have a mirror to fix your hair or apply your lipstick properly. It's certainly physically possible to do these things without a mirror, and there are no laws against it. But you'd have no real idea what you actually looked like until you walked outside and everyone started giggling at you because you'd smeared lipstick all over your nose. A good Buddhist teacher can be your mirror. The teacher, in turn, learns to use his or her students as a mirror in a similar way.

It's not enough to depend on the distorted reflections provided by your friends, by society, by your peers, and so on. Face it. Are most of the folks you know honest enough with themselves to be perfectly honest with someone else? The criteria most people use to judge what's acceptable and what's not are pretty warped. That's why our society as a whole is so plagued with problems. A decent Buddhist teacher has an entirely different set of criteria.

So what are the criteria for judging if a Zen teacher is the real deal or not? Dogen says, "Generally, when looking for a true master, don't worry about age or experience. A true master is just someone who has realized the true teachings and received certification of a true master. Knowledge of words is not important. Understanding is not primary. A man* of extraordinary power and unrestricted mental vigor, who transcends his own opinion, who does not linger in states of emotional consciousness, and in whom practice and understanding meet in equilibrium — this is just a true master."

As for teachers who are not true, Dogen said, "Some of them teach others to seek enlightenment that is different from a concrete mental state, and some of them teach others to look forward to life in another world. Delusion, confusion, and wrong ideas spring from these teachings."

It's tough to get much more specific than that about what to look for in a real Buddhist teacher. In the end it may come down more to

---

* Or woman, of course. Dogen cites numerous great female Zen teachers in his writings.

instinct than anything else. When you find a good teacher, you'll have a gut feeling that he or she is right. But be very careful not to follow your emotions, because a deeply ingrained emotional response can often feel like intuition when it's really nothing of the kind. Examine your reaction quietly. Don't worry about your likes or dislikes. I intensely disliked Nishijima Sensei when I first encountered him. Yet I knew somehow that what he was saying was right, even if I hated it. That doesn't mean you'll have quite the same reaction. But be aware that just 'cuz you like what someone says, that doesn't necessarily mean it's doing you any good.

But Dogen's practical advice isn't just about finding a teacher. He gives ten pieces of advice:

First, he says, you gotta establish what he calls the "will to the truth," meaning you have to have the courage to face up to what's really true, whether or not it suits you. This means that you need to turn away from the idea that you're going to gain anything from the practice, and from any desire for fame and profit — including, or perhaps even especially, so-called spiritual profit and fame. "If you forget yourself for a while," he says, "and do your practice in private, you will become familiar with the will to the truth."

Number two is, "When you meet and listen to the authentic teachings of Gautama Buddha, be sure to learn them through practice." In other words, don't just read about them; do them. Buddhism is a philosophy of action.

Just in case that message wasn't clear enough, Dogen's next piece of advice rephrases it: "To enter into Buddhism, always rely upon practice." He says, "We establish practice just in our delusion." Meaning, we start from where we are right now. It's easy to want to put off your practice until you think you've established some kind of understanding. But that's just more of your own ego-based bull. "If we analyze every step of our practice as a step toward enlightenment, our feet will not be able to make contact with a single speck of real dust." Only by practicing in our delusion, Dogen says, "can we be free forever of our old delusions, seeing the terrible serpent [we thought we were seeing] was in fact nothing more than a creeping vine." All the stuff in our lives that has us so cheesed off is really nothing at all.

"Buddhas do not make intentional efforts for this to happen," he says; "it happens when they are activated by the moment of the present." You get it when you allow the universe to act through you without hindering what it wants with your own petty needs and wishes.

In number four he phrases this another way: "Do not practice Gautama Buddha's teachings with the intention of getting somewhere." We practice Buddha's teachings for the sake of practicing them. Yet if we practice sincerely, the resulting balance of body and mind is extraordinarily peaceful and pleasant. "Until the body and mind are pleasantly balanced," Dogen says, "experiencing the truth may be painful." But in the balanced state of mind, whatever comes to pass can be experienced with ease and calm. Or, as Henry Rollins said, "Sometimes the truth hurts and sometimes it feels real good." It all depends on your outlook.

With his fifth piece of advice Dogen talks about finding a true master. He warns that a bad teacher, even if he or she teaches Buddhism, is like a bad doctor. "Even when the medicine is good," he says, "unless the doctor tells the patient how to take it, it may be more harmful than poison."

Next up he talks about what we should know in practicing zazen. "People today," he said way back in 1234, "say that we should practice what is easy to practice. But these words are not Buddhism at all. Even if we chose to practice something as easy as lying on a bed it would eventually become tiresome." And if folks eight hundred years ago were looking for an easy way out, what about people in the twenty-first century, with all their "instant enlightenment" techniques? I even know of a supposed Zen master who promises enlightenment in a single afternoon.

The tough thing about Buddhist practice isn't so much the postures or the twisted-up legs. What's hardest is the effort to establish and to keep the balance of body and mind. In Dogen's words, it's harder to establish this balance than it would be to grind your own bones into powder. Youch! "The Buddhist truth," he says, "is beyond thinking, discrimination, supposition, reflection, perception, and understanding. We spend our lives dallying around in these things, so if the Buddhist truth exists within them, why haven't we realized it yet?"

And, as if he hasn't rubbed it in enough already, piece of advice number seven is that "anyone who hungers to practice Buddhism and transcend society should, without fail, practice zazen." Again and again he comes back to this one point. Buddhism is not Buddhism without the practice of zazen. Read every book you can find on the subject of old man Gautama and his teachings, and you still won't get one lick of good out of it unless you put those teachings into practice.

Next he writes about the conduct of Buddhist priests who practice zazen. "They remain at no fixed place," he says, "with nothing to attach to either in mind or body." And this doesn't just go for priests; it goes for everyone who establishes the practice. "Someone who is pursuing the truth," says Dogen, "is already halfway to the truth. Don't give up until you get there."

Number nine says, "Direct yourself at the truth and practice it." The truth is always with you at every moment, or, as Dogen puts it, "the Buddhist truth exists under the foot of every human being." It's not something far away, abstract, or difficult. It is the uncomplicated and direct truth of what is right here, right now. Truth is not removed from your day-to-day existence. God, way up in heaven on his big gold throne, is just an idea. That itch on your left ass cheek right now is the truth. It's way bigger than God could ever hope to be.

"Belief in Buddhism," Dogen says, "should be the belief that we ourselves originally exist inside the truth." When he says "originally exist," he doesn't mean it in the sense that maybe sometime in the distant past we existed there but we don't anymore. He means that the truth is our roots. The truth is the basis of our existence. We would not even be here if it were not for the truth. It's not something far away and mysterious. It is so close at hand and so obvious that you have to make a very deliberate and sustained effort to miss it. Which is exactly what most of us do all the time. "If a person genuinely believes that they are already in the Truth, they may even know the origins of delusion and enlightenment."

Finally, in item ten Dogen talks about "taking a direct hit here and now." Ow! There are two ways to regulate body and mind, he says. "One is to visit a master and listen to his or her teachings." And the other? Can you guess? "To make efforts in zazen." Both these ways are important to the practice of authentic Buddhism. "When we practice zazen," says Dogen, "our practice and experience are securely grounded."

"Without changing this body and mind which we have had from the past," he says, "we can say that we are in the here and now and we can call that a direct hit. It is not getting some new state." Look at what you really are right now.

Chapter 6

The Colors of the Mind

I had more to do in Ohio than just play punk rock and make a documentary about it. I had also agreed to do a book signing at a place in the Cleveland suburb of Lakewood called the Bela Dubby Gallery. The signing was to be combined with an exhibition of photos taken during Cleveland's punk rock heyday. It had been snowing like mad for the past week or so, and it was all the salt trucks and snowplows could do to keep the city's major thoroughfares passable. This did not bode well for a book signing, but I soldiered on anyhow.

The book signing ended up being just like the record-signing scene in the movie *This Is Spinal Tap*, in which the band sits there all day and no one ever shows up. A grand total of three people came to get my John Hancock. One was Dave Swanson, the ex-drummer for Dimentia 13 and now leader of his own band, Rainy Day Saints. One of the Offbeats also stopped by. And finally, one person I had never met came up and asked me to sign her copy. Luckily, she knew where to get some food in the area, 'cuz I was starving, and I knew there'd be nothing to eat at the club except maybe some stale potato chips. So much for the life of a Zen superstar.

If I dislike the life of a Zen teacher so much, you might wonder why I do it. Actually, I don't really dislike it. I have fun. And I'm actually glad I don't get too many followers since crowds of people tend to make me nervous. The main reason I write books and give talks, though, isn't because I think I have anything really wonderful to say. It's more because I've looked at the so-called spiritual scene and think it's incredibly awful. Hardly any of the books on the subject of Buddhism out today are even worth the paper they're printed on. But I know that Buddhism really is a good thing.

It's the same thing that drove me to be a part of Zero Defects and to make my own records. I knew that rock music could be amazing stuff. Yet the people out there who were supposed to be doing rock and roll in those days were, for the most part, putting out pure garbage. Certainly there was nothing on commercial radio that I could stand listening to. Just like the far too many so-called Spiritual Masters on the scene today, rock-and-roll musicians were more interested in playing to the lowest levels of mass stupidity in order to make the biggest bundle of money possible than they were in providing anything that resembled what I knew rock and roll had the power to be. There *were* a few people doing good things, just like there are some really genuine people on the so-called spiritual scene. But there were not enough, and their voices were virtually drowned out by all the schlock.

The worst thing about all those crap spiritual masters out there is the way they deliberately mislead people. I know I sound like a crank. But I won't cut any of these people the least bit of slack. They cheat and lie, and they are well aware of it. But when you get right down to it, if you're misled by a bad spiritual master, you have only yourself to blame. That sounds pretty harsh, I know. But it's true. Dogen has a little story that helps explain why that is.

A few hundred years ago a dude named Gensa, who later went on to be one of the great Buddhist teachers, was still a young monk. One day he gets fed up with the temple where he's studying. He figures he'd be better off getting out and seeing what the rest of the world has to offer. Maybe another temple will have whatever it is he's been looking for. Or maybe he'll just give up on temples altogether. As he's heading out the gate, he stubs his toe on a big ol' rock. He's hopping around in terrible pain, bleeding from under his toenail, going, "Ow! Ow! Shit! Piss! Damn!" And he thinks, "I've heard that the body is an illusion. So where the hell did all this pain come from?"

All at once he gets it.

Later on, his teacher, a guy named Seppo Gisan, asks him what's up, and he says, "I just can't be deceived by others."

Seppo really gets off on this statement. "Is there anyone who doesn't have these words?" he says. "But who else can speak them?"

There you have the key to understanding Buddhism. That one sentence, "I can't be deceived," says all you need to know.

When people say stuff like "I can't be deceived," the emphasis is usually on "I." They're usually saying something like, "Maybe all those other people out there can be deceived, but nobody can make a fool out of *me*!" But that's not what Gensa means here. "I" here is absolutely universal. It refers just as much to you and me as it does to Gensa himself. He's not bragging. He might even be a little bit sad when he says, "I can't be deceived."

You're probably thinking, Why would he be sad about that? I mean, he's enlightened, right? And enlightenment is supposed to be the happiest thing that can ever happen to a person — just like Disneyland is the Happiest Place on Earth® — right? Otherwise why strive for it? But think about it for a sec. Imagine a situation in which you suddenly realize with absolute certainty that you can never blame anyone else for anything that happens to you. You can't even blame your circumstances since you know those, too, are of your own making. You can no longer tell yourself that if only this or that happened, then you'd find perfect happiness. Your future has entirely vanished, along with your past. It must be just a little sad. But it's sad in a different way from usual sadness. It's a sadness that knows what sadness really is. It knows that there is no merit in taking hold of sadness, so it lets the sadness drift by. Still, it's not as if sadness isn't part of the equation.

The idea that we can be deceived is an illusion created by our amazing ability to think. Real deception never happens. We pretend to be deceived. We even fool ourselves into actually thinking we believe we've been had. But it just doesn't happen. When Gensa stubbed his toe on that rock — in other words, when he suddenly came face-to-face with the undeniable fact that he was living in this world and not in the world he created in his mind, in which the body is an illusion* — he understood that he could not be deceived.

This was not some unique, miraculous event, something that could only happen to an advanced student like Gensa, either. As his teacher says, "Is there anyone who does not have these words?" Is there anyone, anywhere in the world who does not come face-to-face with the real facts of the real world every moment of every day? But, says Gensa's teacher, who else but Gensa can speak them? In other words, why, oh why, do we keep insisting that we live in some other reality far removed from the one we encounter all the time? Why is it that any time someone says something true, we act like he or she has some magical supernatural power far beyond that of ordinary human beings?

There's a very good, very practical reason people want to believe that they can be deceived by others. See, when you've been deceived, nothing you do is really your fault. Just like the Nazis, you can plead, "I was only following orders." Maybe folks will even believe you. I won't. But that's just me. As far as I'm concerned, pretending you've been deceived — making believe that reality hit you smack in the face and you still didn't notice it — is nothing more than a way of abdicating all responsibility. You might get away with it because this world is run by people who also want to be able to use

---

* Ah, but yes, Grasshopper, according to Buddhist theory, the body *is* an illusion. Yet it may be that the words "the body is an illusion" and the real illusory nature of the body are not the same at all.

that excuse themselves if it ever comes down to it. People like you. People like me.

But it's a lame excuse. No decent Zen teacher would ever accept it. I used to come to my teachers with variations of that one all the time. "I was deceived! I'm in delusion! Please help me. Please tell me what's really true!" It was just another way of saying, "Please take responsibility for me."

"Nobody's tricked you, you moron," they'd say. "You know what the truth is. Stop being such a bonehead, and take an honest look at yourself." Gensa didn't need a Learned Zen Master to tell him he was in pain when he stubbed his toe that day. And you don't need anyone to tell you what your life really is either. You sure as heck don't need this book. I cannot possibly tell you anything you don't already know. You probably agree, since, if you're like most people, you think I'm an idiot. But you probably also think that somewhere out there in the land where books are written is someone way cooler and tons more spiritually advanced than me who *can* tell you something you don't already know. Keep right on looking. The publishing industry loves you.

If you can understand that you can't be deceived, you can understand pretty much any of these old Zen stories. Which leads nicely to another story Dogen talks about in *Shobogenzo*. It's all about giving up the idea that you can ever be deceived and discovering the truth for yourself.

Master Seigen Gyoshi asks his disciple Sekito Gisan, "Where have you come from?"

Sekito says, "From Mount Sokei."

Master Seigen holds up his whisk and asks his student, "Is there anything like this on Mount Sokei?"

Sekito says, "Nope. Not even in India."*

---

* He says India because Buddha was from India, so it means not even in Buddha's experience. In other words, Sekito's own experience was no different from Buddha's.

Master Seigen says, "You've never been to India, have you?"

Sekito says, "If I went to India, that whisk would be there."

Master Seigen says, "Stop talking about India and say something about your own experience."

Sekito says, "Can't you say something concrete? Why do you leave everything up to me?"

Master Seigen says, "It's not that I refuse to say anything. It's just that if I did, you might not be able to understand things for yourself in the future."

You can see the idea of wanting to be deceived pretty easily in this story. When Sekito asks his teacher to say something concrete instead of leaving it all up to him, he may think he's being really bold, telling his teacher that if he's so damned smart, why doesn't he just answer the stupid question? Why doesn't his teacher take responsibility for figuring out what's what so that when the student screws up he can blame it on the teacher? It's a tactic lots of students try with Zen teachers. Maybe he hopes that if the master answers him, then that will settle everything from there on. But really he's just asking to be deceived.

Master Seigen refuses to answer. No matter how right the master's explanation might be, it's still the master's explanation. Each person has to understand the universe for him- or herself. No one else's description will ever do — no matter who it comes from. It wouldn't matter if God him- or herself came down from the sky and explained it all to you. You still wouldn't be satisfied. Master Seigen was a great teacher and probably could have articulated his own understanding pretty clearly. But he had faith in his student's ability to discover it for himself. He did not want to deceive him.

If you find a Zen teacher who won't explain anything to you, you should be extremely grateful. There are plenty of "spiritual masters" out there who would gladly fill your head with all kinds of explanations. A certain "spiritual master" I met in my teens certainly tried. He could answer everything. This was when John Lennon had only been dead a couple of years, and I remember someone asking this "master" where Lennon was now. "John Lennon," said the spiritual master dude, "was reincarnated as a tree." Seriously. He really said this. Apparently once the head honcho of his sect went to visit Lennon's house, and Lennon — then in his *Two Virgins* phase — answered the door stark naked. Therefore he was an exhibitionist. And exhibitionists get reborn as trees. 'Cuz trees like to stand there naked and have people admire them. Case closed. Next question?

If you want to be deceived by stuff like that, there's plenty of it out there. But I don't. And Master Seigen was a cool enough guy not to try and fill up his student's head with explanations, even good ones.

But you don't even need someone else to deceive you. It's way easier to deceive yourself by believing your own thoughts. And the most fundamental of these deceptive thoughts we accept as true is the idea of self. The idea of the unreality of self is one we've taken up before, and it's one we'll take up again, just like Dogen did throughout his written work. In the *Shobogenzo* chapter titled "Buddhas Alone Together with Buddhas"* Dogen talks about that. He says, "The colors of the mind, excited by a flower or the moon should not be seen as self at all, but we think of them as our self."

Now, Dogen was a Japanese monk who lived in a temple way out in the woods in the middle of the mountains of rural Fukui Prefecture in the 1200s. Even today, Fukui Prefecture is a quiet little backwater. Pretty much the only reason people go there these days is to look at Dogen's temple. Living in a place like that, far from the amusements of the big city, without even cable TV or a Gameboy to keep him occupied, Dogen was turned on by stuff like looking at flowers and the moon. He was, shall we say, easily amused.

These days wannabe Zen dudes and dudettes get all hung up on

---

* Chapter 91, 唯仏様仏, pronounced *yui-butsu-yo-butsu* for those keeping track at home.

images of flowers and water and trees and all that, and too often that stuff blinds them to any real understanding of their own situation, which usually isn't anything at all like the kind of life the Zen monks of old experienced. Heck, it isn't even anything like the life the Zen monks of today usually lead. I haven't been to a rural Japanese temple yet that didn't have a VCR and one of those minisatellite dishes on its roof. Today we could say, "The colors of the mind excited by a CNN report on the Middle East situation should not be taken as self." Or even, "The colors of the mind excited by a noisy and belligerent book whose writer claims to be a 'Buddhist' should not be seen as self." In other words, whatever it is that grinds your crankshaft, be careful you don't start looking at your reaction to that stimulus as your "self."

Take a look at that bunch of stuff that you call your personality or your "self." Is it really anything more than a collection of set reactions to things that excite your brain cells in one way or another? We tend to take it for granted that something lies behind all our opinions, beliefs, ideals, memories, and whatnot, some source from which they spring. We call that thing "self" or "soul" or "personality." Nearly all our religions and philosophies are based on the assumption that this "self" is a real thing. But is there really any basis for such a belief? Or might our beliefs be just beliefs, without some entity called "self" behind them and somehow creating them?

Human beings have amazingly developed brains, and for that reason we easily confuse thought and reality. But when you get right down to it, even our biggest, deepest, most astoundingly brilliant thoughts are nothing more than thoughts. And thoughts are nothing more than electrical activity, changes in the organic chemistry of the brain. Big fat hairy deal.

Yet we constantly take the colors of mind to be much more than they are. Think about how it is when you go see a Bruce Willis movie, not *Breakfast of Champions* or *The Story of Us* but one of the good ones where he plays a guy who saves the world from international terrorism in his bare feet. By the end of the movie your heart is pounding, you're all sweaty, and you've spilled your popcorn all over the person in front of you. Your body reacts precisely the same way to manipulated images of Bruce Willis in simulated danger as it does to real danger — even though you are clearly aware the whole time not only that you are in absolutely no peril but that even Bruce was never in the least bit of danger and probably got paid more for that one movie than you'll ever make in your entire life. But our brains and nervous systems accept such manipulated images exactly the same way that they accept real situations.

Yet you react to all this mental stuff — stuff that might happen someday, stuff that happened but you wish it hadn't, stuff that hasn't happened yet but you hope will happen one of these days, stuff you dread because you know if it did happen you'd just die. You react to it all the same way a cassowary reacts when it's being chased by a wombat. Nature equipped you with buttons intended for emergency use only, which were supposed to be pressed maybe ten or fifteen times throughout your life, yet some of us are mashing down on these buttons every single day. Why? Because it's exciting! And, admit it, one of the main reasons we get so stressed out in life is because we'd rather be stressed out than — God forbid! — bored.

All this stuff threatens that imaginary thing we call our "self." We may say it threatens our future. But what is the future other than your imagination? It isn't here. You don't really know what will happen or how you'll feel when it does. You could regret your past actions. But what does that help? You can't change them.

Instead of just living moment by moment, we're stuck in all these twisting, swirling loops of thought — the colors of mind, as Dogen calls 'em — that have our bodies reacting in all kinds of ways they don't need to in response to situations that not only do not exist but never could exist.

We create this thing called "me," which we believe thinks and feels and experiences. We live in abject terror of the day that thing will come to an end. And when we're not dreading that, we're petrified that this "me" might someday find itself in some horrendous situation. We make all sorts of efforts to protect this thing above all else. We buy it gifts. We reward our "self" for doing good things like sticking with a diet. We show our "self" off to the world and hope that others envy it. We want it to become rich and famous, to live in a beautiful house with a bodacious wife or a hunky husband (or both maybe, I don't know). Every minute of every day we look for new reasons to make believe it exists and that it is important.

But it doesn't, and it's not.

It's a phantom, an illusion. This thing you've elevated to God-like stature does not even exist. It's just another thought. No bigger or realer than any of your thoughts. It doesn't even stick around very long. The thought of self appears and disappears just like any other thought. But we like that particular one so much that we always seem to come back to it. It's not even that you have to get rid of this "self," either. What's there to get rid of? You simply need to see it for what it is. Yet this is much harder than most of us realize.

See, you are not what you think of as "you" because you are everything.

You are everything because there is nothing else you can be. You are reading yourself. There's really nothing else that could possibly be happening. There is nowhere else to go.

And, by the way, when you see that everyone is you and you are everyone, you'll also come to understand that everyone in the world is just as dumb as you are. This goes for your boss, and your peers, and the president of the United States of America. They're all just a bunch of dummies. Just understanding this will alleviate a lot of the stress you feel. It's hard to worry what other people might think when you realize their thoughts are just as dopey and meaningless as yours.

Chapter 7

Kill Your Anger

As Zero Defects was getting ready to play its first show in twenty years, my mind drifted back to the last time we played. (Cue cheesy, twinkly sound effects as the scene dissolves to a misty flashback. . . .)

Akron, Ohio, February 1982. It's way below freezing outside. But in here it's so hot I feel like I'm going to melt into a puddle on the floor. I stand, legs akimbo, sticker-encrusted Fender Musicmaster bass in hand, on the two-inch platform that serves for a stage at the Dale, the tiny Irish-themed pub near Akron University that has somehow been duped into hiring a bunch of hardcore bands for the night's entertainment. Every dilapidated muscle in my undernourished body is flexed and ready for action. "Drop the A-Bomb on meeeeeeeeeeee!" Jimi Imij, shaven-headed lead singer of Zero Defects, shrieks as drummer Mickey X-Nelson counts in the beat and Tommy Strange and I attack our guitars. A mass of furious fuzztone erupts from the amplifiers, and the pit comes alive with surging bodies smashing into each other like a forty-car pileup. Eighteen seconds later the song is over. Like when a cease-fire's just about to be called off, an uneasy calm falls over the crowd for a few tense seconds until Jimi shouts, "Die Before More of This!" the title of the next song. We launch into another feedback-laden aural assault, and the crowd is free once more to pummel each other bloody.

Back then it seemed like it was all about anger. We were pissed off at the senile B-movie actor who'd somehow been elected president. We were mad as hell at the Bible-thumping lunkheads who wanted to curtail all forms of free speech. We were enraged at the mind-numbing complacency of a generation of vacant-eyed mall rats — our so-called peers — who didn't seem to notice that we were being cheerfully led straight down the path toward global Armageddon. And hate? We hated hate. There was nothing we hated more than hate. We loved hating hate.

Yet at the same time I was screaming my lungs out at hypocrisy, greed, and bad fashion, I was also discovering Zen Buddhism, a philosophy that said the very best thing you could do for world peace was to sit with your legs twisted up like a pretzel and stare at a wall. You could hardly find two more seemingly contradictory philosophies. Even so, I never felt the desire to leave behind my punk rock ways in order to follow the path of Zen. At their core punk and Zen share some key features. They're both about action in the present moment, about doing something right now, and about taking responsibility for your life. But the real reason the punks believed we had to vent our anger was that we hadn't followed our own philosophy of totally rejecting society all the way to its logical end. We were still reacting to anger the way society told us to.

I got an email the other day from a guy who'd read my first book. "Can a Buddhist listen to angry-sounding music like heavy metal and hardcore punk?" he asked. "I have read that a Buddhist is supposed to let go of their anger, not suppressing or expressing it, but kind of disabling it by recognizing it. Would this mean that anger, although not to be suppressed, is something we should avoid expressing through art and music?"

The writer worries about listening to angry music. But is supposedly "angry music" really angry? In Zero Defects we used to describe our music as angry. But appearances to the contrary, the music itself actually wasn't angry at all. When we were writing it, rehearsing it, and playing it onstage, there was never any anger involved. When on occasion there was actual anger involved in our performances — like maybe Jimi had broken all of Tommy's guitar strings again and hadn't bought replacements — we couldn't play for shit. Jimi may have written "Drop the A-Bomb on Me" as a means of dealing with his anger at Reagan's nuclear policies. But you can't actually write a decent piece of music — not even when it's hardcore punk — during a fit of anger. To express what we were feeling, we had to learn how to leave our anger behind and just play.

Because there's a difference between "angry music" or "angry art" of any kind and real anger. Anger doesn't make music, not even angry music. Music comes from a completely different place.

Music should be honest, and what we were expressing in Zero Defects was our honest view of the world. That's much more important than trying to force yourself to make something you think is "happy music" when you don't actually feel very happy because you have some idea that "happy music" — or "happy" whatever kind of art you want — will make the world a happier place. For me, so-called angry music has never aroused feelings of real anger — quite the opposite, in fact. I'd have been far angrier in a world where you could only hear so-called happy music. "Angry music," exposing as it did its author's truest feelings, let me know I was not alone in my own feelings of frustration. Far from making me angry, it made me feel as if there was something positive I could do with my feelings.

But let's look at the questioner's other point, about how one "should" deal with anger according to Buddhism. He says he's heard anger shouldn't be suppressed. Actually, though, my teacher, Gudo Nishijima, advises his students to always suppress their anger. When I first heard this, it sounded not only absurd but positively unhealthy.

Everyone knows you don't bottle up your anger; you have to let it out, or else you explode.

But then I began to look at anger a little more carefully. This I had ample opportunity to do because for most of my life I was one of the most hotheaded people you could ever have hoped to meet — or, better still, to have avoided meeting. When I really observed my anger, it became apparent that it wasn't some substance that built up inside me that I could "let out" and be rid of. There was nothing into which anger could be bottled. That something I called "me" and that something I called "anger" were completely indistinguishable. I started to see that the process of "letting anger out" was actually the process by which more anger was produced.

When you suppress your anger, though, you've got to do it in the right way. Suppressing anger is not the same thing as what most folks call "keeping it inside." For most of us, "keeping anger inside" is the act of reinforcing anger internally. To really suppress anger, you have to suppress the urge to enjoy the beautiful juiciness of it all.

It's hard for most of us to admit, but when you start paying attention you'll notice that you actually enjoy being angry. There's this wonderful rush of self-righteousness to it. Because, obviously, you can't be angry about something unless you know you're right and the other person is wrong. You are angry because you want to be angry. Always, always.

So what do you actually *do* to suppress anger? I'll tell you what I do. Or at least what I try to do, since I fail sometimes. Not as often as I used to, though, because unlike any other method I've found for controlling anger, this one actually works because it addresses the real problem in a realistic way.

The main thing is to avoid acting on any angry impulses that might pop into your head. No matter how justified you might know yourself to be, an angry action will only invoke another angry response, both in the person you're dealing with and in yourself. These actions and responses scramble your brain and make it impossible to act in any kind of efficient way to solve the problem at hand.

In a little book called *Shobogenzo Zuimonki*,* which compiles a bunch of Dogen's short talks as recorded by one of his closest students, Dogen puts it this way: "It is not good to overwhelm another person with argument even when he is wrong and you are right. Yet it is also not right to give up too easily, saying, 'I am wrong,' when you have every reason to believe you are right. The best way is to drop the argument naturally, without pressing the other person or falsely admitting that you are wrong. If you don't listen to his arguments and don't let them bother you, he will do the same and not become angry. This is something to watch carefully."

That's pretty straightforward advice, I think. But we can go a bit deeper. The next step is to see anger for what it really is. And that's the tough part.

See, if anger isn't some substance that gets bottled up inside us, what is it?

Since meditation is all about understanding the state you're in here and now, and since I was often consumed with black rage as I sat on my black cushion, I've often focused my attention during zazen practice on understanding the real source of anger. It took a long time for me to see anger for what it was, and when I did, I was truly shocked.

See, I always used to believe that anger was somehow something apart from myself, that "I" experienced "my" anger. But as my practice deepened, it began to dawn on me that this was not the case at all. It wasn't that I could eradicate those things about myself I'd labeled as negative qualities while leaving the good stuff intact, like cutting off the rotten parts of a carrot left in the fridge too long and cooking the rest. The source of anger, hate, fear, and all the rest of it was the

---

* This is not Japanese for *Shobogenzo for Sea Monkeys.*

same as the source of that collection of ideas and habits I had mistakenly called "me" for most of my life. To end anger once and for all, I had to die completely. Not commit suicide but something much, much more difficult.

If you're serious about transcending anger, you have to be prepared to give up everything. I'm afraid most people, including those who say they're Buddhists, are not at all serious about doing this. We've invented a million clever methods of building up our egos while pretending to tear them down.

When you get angry, you need to ask yourself where anger comes from. Not just your anger right now, about whatever it is that might be pissing you off, but anger itself. What is it? Can you really say it's caused by whatever it was that set you off? Did that idiot who cut you off on the freeway — or whatever — really *produce* your anger? Or is the real cause of anger something deeper? What is the need we so often feel to prove to everyone around us that we are right and they are wrong? Why is it important to us that others agree with what we believe? Where does that desire come from? Why do we do that? Does that help? Or does that just begin a chain reaction that will inevitably lead to more anger?

Watching the recent debates surrounding the war in Iraq — war being the ultimate expression of human anger — I began to notice that neither the warmongers nor the peaceniks had the slightest clue about what the real situation was. None of them has the courage to look deeply into themselves, to find the source of war itself — which is ultimately the same as the source of anger — and to rip it right out of their guts. Because that is more difficult than marching with picket signs or firing guns and dropping bombs. It's far more repulsive to us to really face up to who and what we actually are than it is to face the prospect of fires and bombs and blood and misery. We would gladly choose war any day of the week over that. Quite literally. You can get all self-righteous and pretend that there's a big difference between the anger you feel at some warmongering politician or general and the anger those guys feel toward whomever they've labeled as "the Enemy" this week. But is there? You need to find out. You really, really do.

It isn't just anger and the other so-called negative states that are the problem. It is that whole collection of things you call your "self." The very same force that makes it possible for you to gush all over a fuzzy little puppy dog with icky sticky syrupy sweet love is the force that makes it possible for you to hate with passion and lash out with anger. There is no love without hate, no happiness without depression. It's like a roller coaster. If you go up, you're gonna have to come back down. You cannot destroy hate with love. Nishijima likes to say that in order for a person to be balanced, love and hate must be exactly equal.

Now wait a minute! A Buddhist master advocating hate? Isn't that what a KKK master or an al-Qaeda master is supposed to do? But the hate he describes is a very different variety of hate from that preached by the world's hate mongers. That kind of hate is a perversion of true hate. Real hate is that part of you that sees itself as eternally separate from the rest of creation. Real love is that part of you that sees everything as a seamless whole. The truth of the situation, though, is right smack-dab in the middle. Once you open your eyes, it's impossible to see things any other way.

Hate can be your teacher. Anger can be your guide. See your anger for what it is, and you can see yourself for what you are.

Watch how your anger begins, and see how it grows. When I did this myself, I discovered that anger always starts out very, very small. It's always based on the difference between how I think things should be and how they actually are. Within this gap the fiction known as "me" appears and reacts. To protect this fiction, I begin to justify my anger, to build a convincing case to prove to myself that I have every right to be angry. I do this, I found, because the very existence of this fiction of self is based on its supposed ability to feel anger. To let go of anger is to let go of my sense of self. And that, my friends, is very, very, very difficult.

This all happens very quickly, so it's important to stay on top of it. To suppress anger in this way means you do not allow yourself *any* excuses. You cannot accept *any* of the justifications for anger that your ego coughs up at you, no matter how reasonable you make them sound. Even the absolute, incontrovertible certainty that your anger is 100 percent utterly and absolutely without a shred of a doubt justified is not an adequate excuse to allow yourself to feel anger.

When you see all this happening, the very last thing you'll want to do is put aside your anger. Trust me. I'm an expert. I fought hard against it, like an alcoholic fights against the realization that the only way to stop being an alcoholic is to just stop drinking. I knew clearly that the only way to stop being an angry person was just to stop being angry. Right. Now. But doing it, that's a whole different ball game.

When you know for certain you're right in the face of circumstances that are undeniably "wrong," *that's* when you have to really look hard at what's actually happening within you. Your habit of reacting with anger has been built up over long years of reinforcement from a society gone terribly wrong. You allow yourself to be angry because all the people you've ever known have reacted to their anger that way. Pretty much everyone you've ever heard of in every culture in every country in the whole wide world reacts to anger that way. All your education, both formal and informal, has told you very clearly that this is the way human beings are supposed to react to anger. We can't help it! Even the law admits that! Could it be perhaps that society is made up of people who are all clinging to a comfortable fiction and who draw support for this unfounded belief from the fact that so many others believe it too?

I'm making this sound much easier than it really is. But remember, I'm compressing twenty-some years of hard work into a mere few pages. With practice this stuff gets easier. But you'll never completely lose your desire to get mad at things.

What helps a lot, though, is when you start seeing how well this works. I'll give you a for instance from my own life. The other day

I was driving somewhere with my wife. For reasons I can't recall, we were both feeling a little snippy that day. As happens in these circumstances, we started to argue.

I wish I could recall exactly what was said or even what we were arguing about because it would make for a better story. But I can't, and of course as is typical of these arguments, none of it mattered anyway. At any rate, at some point in the argument my wife said something, and I thought of the perfect comeback. Now, that is a very rare occurrence. Remember that episode of *Seinfeld* in which George is in a meeting and a co-worker makes some joke at his expense? George is too steamed to respond, but hours later he thinks of the perfect comeback. So he spends ages trying to re-create the same situation so that he can use his comeback.* That's a feeling I can understand very well.

Well, this time I came up with the perfect comeback right there on the spot. But just as I was about to say it, I saw the chain of events it would catalyze. The fact that my comeback was so sharp and witty would do nothing to drive home whatever point I was trying to make. It would only make Yuka more pissed off that I was being a smart-ass. The argument would continue, and bad feelings would linger. So I caught myself, and I stopped. I let the world's greatest snappy comeback fade off into the distance. In a few seconds it was gone forever, its moment having passed.

And you know what happened? The argument stopped. No one won. No one lost. It just ended, and we got along a whole lot better the rest of the day.

What I did was to let go of my self. I dropped "me" out of the equation. When there is no "you," there is nothing for "you" to get angry about and no one outside yourself to get angry at.

---

* "The jerk store called, and they're running out of you!"

Chapter 8

Zen and Stress Management

One of the questions Dogen never had to answer but that comes up all the time for Zen teachers these days is, "Is Zen practice a good way to manage stress?"

Eastern meditation became popular in the West at the very time when the concept of stress was just getting started. It wasn't until the mid-1950s that the term *stress* was coined.* By then, modern corporate business culture had given rise to levels of stress not seen since our Neanderthal ancestors had to deal with ways of avoiding becoming lunch for bands of marauding Parasaurolophus.** Physicians and psychologists were starting to see illnesses that had never been described previously and that seemed to have no clear physical cause. They concluded that people were worrying themselves sick over what were essentially imagined dangers. The fight-or-flight responses that

---

* Endocrinologist Hans Selye claims he came up with it in 1956.
** I know, Neanderthals probably were not ancestral to modern man, and the Parasaurolophus was an herbivorous hadrosaur that became extinct sixty-five million years before the first Neanderthal appeared. But *When Dinosaurs Ruled the Earth* was still a great movie.

were activated in our Australopithecus ancestors whenever they were set upon by an angry Chasmosaurus* were now being activated by wholly nonphysical causes like deadlines, mortgage payments, and the looming threat of nuclear annihilation.

These days we're so accustomed to the concept of stress that it's hard to imagine a time when the idea didn't exist. Retroactively, we could certainly say that people in Dogen's time must have suffered from what we would define as stress. Samurai retainers must surely have lost sleep over whether they'd be forced to commit ritual suicide for some arcane offense. Even Buddhist monks must have worried about getting hit with the "stick of education" used in some temples in those days to correct bad posture. But the causes and conditions of stress were so different in those days that it doesn't make much sense to compare them.

Rather than going by Dogen on the matter of stress, let me just give you my take on Zen and its effectiveness as a stress-management technique. Most of my life I've been a fairly stressed-out guy. But, at the same time, I always had a hard time admitting that. For one thing, I grew up in a middle-class white suburb. I was always under the impression that people from that kind of background couldn't possibly experience real stress. I mean, unless they had, like, abusive parents or a terminal disease or something. My understanding was that true stress was something you only got when something seriously awful occurred. Anything else was just a case of being whiny.

I was wrong, of course. But that's what I thought. So I was never able to acknowledge that the migraines and the pizza-face acne I suffered from in my teens and twenties were brought on by stress. At one point I even convinced myself, incorrectly, that the headaches were the result of an allergy to corn.**

So, seeing as how I didn't believe I could possibly be suffering

---

* An herbivorous ceratopsian of the upper Cretaceous.
** It's a long story.

from stress when I first got into Zen in college, I was not specifically looking for something to help control it. Nor was Zen ever sold to me in those terms. Although you will often see hawkers of various meditation techniques touting meditation as a method of managing stress, you very rarely hear of Zen teachers advising people to take up the practice for that reason. Yet I think Zen practice may be the most effective way to reduce stress.

There's a caveat, though. There are techniques that can help really stressed-out people find a bit of calm rather quickly. Zen isn't one of those. It doesn't work the way things like relaxation tapes or self-hypnosis do. In fact, it's pretty common for people to end up getting more stressed out when they first start Zen practice. Which is why a lot of therapists and even Zen teachers caution against using zazen as a way to cope with stress.

But that's in the short run. In the long run Zen is a far more thorough way to manage stress than any of those other techniques. And the reason for this is the same reason that it's a fairly poor way to manage stress in the short run.

There are times when zazen can make you more aware of tensions you hadn't noticed before. This sometimes leads people to believe that zazen has increased their tension. But it hasn't really. When you do zazen it's like taking the lid off a boiling pot. All the stuff that's bubbling away under that lid comes rushing to the surface and might even start bubbling over if you don't turn down the heat. By bringing things to the surface, zazen enables you to see very clearly what you need to work on. That in itself can be stressful. This is one of the reasons Zen doesn't really work as a short-term solution to being stressed. Plus, it's not enough just to see what you need to work on. You've actually got to work on it.

Other methods of stress management can give you a way to calm yourself down a bit without making any real committed effort to work on the things that are actually causing your stress in the first place. Those other methods are like clamping an even heavier lid on the pot so you can't see what's wrong. But most of us would rather do that than turn down the heat. That's because turning down the heat means turning away from our ego-based sense of self, something most of us take to be the most important thing in the whole wide world.

In my case, when I finally admitted I was a ball of stress and got right down to the real cause of that stress, I discovered that *I* was the source of it. It never came from outside, from my boss or my girlfriend or my parents or my economic circumstances. It came from my habitual ways of responding to those things. Now, when I say "habitual ways of responding" that sounds pretty easy. Sounds like I just needed to develop some new habits, right? Exactly. But that's not quite as easy as it sounds.

In Buddhist terms, what you call your self or your personality is just a collection of habits. You believe this collection of habits is a real thing, though. You may even believe it's your immortal soul. But it isn't. The reason it's not is that there is no such thing as a self, a personality, or an immortal soul. When I say the problem was my habitual responses it's like saying the problem was my immortal soul. And what I had to do to solve that problem was to toss away my immortal soul. Sounds a little harder now, doesn't it? If I said that to the wrong crowd, they'd probably want to burn me at the stake. That's how tough it is to face the real issue at hand.

Let me give you a concrete example of how Zen practice has helped me deal with stress. The company I work for is in the character business. We create characters — mostly variations of our popular superhero character Zone Man and all the gigantic city-stomping Godzilla-type monsters Zone Man battles to keep the world safe each week* — and exploit them through TV shows, movies, and, most

---

* Actually it's not called Zone Man. I'm not gonna use the real name in this book because it raises all kinds of issues of copyright and trademark and what I, as an employee, ought to or ought not to say. I just don't feel like dealing with that stuff. Maybe when you read the rest of this story you'll figure out why.

important, merchandise. Our company does not produce any of this merchandise. We just make the Zone Man TV shows and films. We don't make the Zone Man watches and Zone Man toothbrushes and Zone Man novelty condom packages. That's an aspect of the business that surprised me at first, and I still have to explain it constantly even to people in the business, who ought to know how these things work. Each year we launch a new Zone Man character, and this character and his ancillary monsters and spaceships and suchlike are tied in with various licensing deals with a network of other companies.

In Japan there's this thing called a *nengajo*. The word is usually translated as "New Year's card." But that doesn't really explain it very well, especially since we in the West don't usually give people cards on New Year's. A *nengajo* is a special kind of postcard. If you place a postcard with the word *nengajo* written on it in red in a mailbox any day from around the end of November through the end of December, the post office will hold that card and deliver it on the morning of January first. In Buddhist Japan, New Year's Day, not Christmas, is the big winter holiday. It's not a big party scene like we have in America. It's a dignified day of rest when families gather. Shops and businesses are generally closed for about three or four days before and after, just to make sure you have nothing better to do than hang out with uncles and aunts you haven't seen for the previous eleven months. No other mail is delivered during the holidays, so the New Year's morning *nengajo* delivery is pretty special.

One year our sales department decided to combine these two events, the launching of the new Zone Man character and the traditional *nengajo* delivery. The newest Zone Man was to be announced on January 1 via a busload of *nengajo* sent out to the press, our business partners, and to specially privileged (read: fully paid-up) members of the Official Zone Man Fan Club.

This *nengajo* in and of itself was nothing new. We send one out every year, as does pretty much every other business in the country. What was special that year was that the *nengajo* showed the name and photograph of the brand-new Zone Man character — Zone Man Galacticus — which was not to be revealed until January 1. The problem was that no one had bothered to tell me about this marketing plan.

I work for the international division and, as such, deal with people in countries where they do not have *nengajos*, most of whom — and this goes for Asian countries as well — regard Christmas as a much bigger deal than New Year's Day.* So we in the international division normally get our *nengajo* early and send them out as Christmas cards.

That year, as usual, we got our allotment of *nengajo* around the second week of December. They sat on a table in the office for several days before I took a look at them and thought it was about time I got around to sending a few out. Otherwise they weren't gonna make it overseas in time for Christmas. So I wrote out the addresses of a couple of our most loyal fans in America, pasted on some stamps, and sent them out. I was about to do a few more, but some other work came up.

Maybe a week later I got an urgent call to come down to the sales department offices. When I got there, they showed me a computer screen on which an American Zone Man fan site was opened to a page showing the image from the front of this year's *nengajo*, a full-color photo of the Zone Man Galacticus in all his plastic-faced glory. "What is this?" they said. A little confused, I said it was our *nengajo*. "How did these guys get it?" I sent it to them, I said, feeling fairly proud of myself for getting us a bit of extra publicity yet still wondering why they looked so concerned. This certainly wasn't the first time some overseas fan site had displayed our *nengajo* before the first of the year.

---

* In China and other countries with large Chinese populations, Chinese New Year, which usually falls sometime in February, is much bigger than either Christmas or January 1. Once again, don't say you never learned anything from one of my books!

"This is a terrible problem," they said. "Have them remove that image immediately!" They had to explain it to me before I got what the problem was. The sales department's whole marketing strategy depended on the post office not delivering any of those cards until the first of January. That way suspense would build and build until the grand reveal. I had blown everything.

This was a major disaster as far as the company was concerned, and everyone, every single living being in the building, was going absolutely ape-shit. Luckily for me, the guy who ran the web page in question was still awake when I called — it being late at night U.S. time by the time the poop hit the fan in Japan — and the offending image was pulled within a few minutes. But, of course, things could not be left at that.

I was told to report to a special meeting of all the heads of every department in the company, as well as the president himself, to discuss the matter. The meeting was to convene at 2 p.m. It was about 11:30 a.m. Word of what had happened got around the company with amazing speed. No one would speak to me. Some were mad as hell. Others realized it was not in their best interests to be seen consorting with a known criminal. There was nothing to do but wait.

Now, here's the weird part. I knew that I was supposed to be nervous, tense, perhaps even panicked. But, try as I might, none of those emotions would arise. And I did try. I was more worried about the fact that I wasn't worried than I was about the meeting! But the whole thing felt a bit comical, cartoonish. It was like watching a poorly done soap opera and not being able to get involved with the story no matter how hard it tries to pull you in.

I don't mean to sound like I was aloof, arrogant, or even indifferent. I knew I had done a bad thing, and I was sad about that. I should have paid more attention, should have asked questions. I regretted my actions. I felt sorry for the people who were put in a difficult position by what I had done. One woman in the sales department was on the verge of tears when she was bawling me out about it. At the same time, though, I knew that, practically speaking, I had done everything I could do to fix the problem. The image was off the website, and the person who'd put it up in the first place had promised not to put it back up until the first of the year. There were no other cards in circulation, since I hadn't gotten around to sending out the ones I'd been meaning to send. There literally wasn't anything else to do.

At first I couldn't understand why I was so calm about everything when everyone else was running around like their heads were on fire. If anyone should have been upset, it should have been me. Who knew what was gonna happen in that meeting? I could lose the job I'd dreamed my whole life of doing and with it my visa status in Japan and be forced to hastily move back to America. What would happen to my wife if that happened? Where would I go? I'd already invested a lot of years in that company and had no real marketable skills. Would I have to go back to Akron and be a starving musician again? There was a lot riding on this meeting. So why the hell wasn't I worried about it?

It took some time before it sank in that all that wall gazing I thought I'd been wasting my time on all those years was actually paying off in a practical way. In *Hardcore Zen* I wrote about an incident that happened a few years before this one in which I'd confronted a massive panic attack one night in a Zen temple in Shizuoka. That was the first moment in my life when I'd faced fear itself. FDR was more right than he ever dreamed of. The real thing we fear isn't whatever it is that's supposedly scaring us. What we really fear is fear. Once you find the true source of your fear, there's not a whole lot that can scare you anymore. While there will never be the magical Enlightenment Experience that fixes all your problems forever and ever amen, as your practice deepens, things that once seemed terribly important reveal themselves to be hardly even worth your attention. And things you thought were hardly worth your attention reveal themselves to be the most important things of all.

I remember sitting in the park that day eating my lunch and thinking, how can I eat at a time like this? I should have had dry mouth and nausea instead of a healthy appetite. Yet I finished off my sandwich and headed back to what was sure to be my doom.

The meeting was deliberately designed to be as demeaning as possible. The Japanese have had so many centuries of experience designing situations to reinforce hierarchies, to make the small feel small and the important feel important, it's no problem at all for them to whip up the most psychologically degrading situations imaginable at a moment's notice. I was actually kind of impressed by it.

The room next to the president's office that usually served as the executive meeting room had been rearranged so that the tables formed a semicircle. At the center sat the company president flanked by the heads of each department arranged in a precise manner so as to show who ranked where in the company pecking order. The head of my department and my boss were seated off to the far left to show that they were in almost as much trouble as me since a superior must be held responsible for the actions of those under his command. Me, I didn't get a chair. I had to stand in the center of this semicircle to answer for my crime. Everyone else in the room had a cup of tea in front of them, but no one even offered me anything to drink. The president launched into a long speech about the seriousness of what I had done. When he paused at the end, I began to speak. "No," I was told. It was not my turn yet. First my superiors would have to explain how they had allowed this to happen. My department head, a veteran of the World War II Imperial Japanese Army, knew just how to respond, taking full responsibility for my actions and offering himself in sacrifice.

Again, I was most impressed by the performance. Yet I could not bring myself to feel any of the shame and guilt that they were all trying to heap on me, nor did I experience even a twinge of fear. I felt like I was acting in a play. In fact, I had to call on my experience in the high school drama club in order to try and display the emotions

I was clearly supposed to be feeling. I did my best impression of shame and disgrace. When my turn to speak finally came around — they made me wait as long as possible to build up the tension — I gave a brief and most humble apology. It worked. I was not fired.

As it turned out, not a whole lot of people had seen that web page in the brief time the forbidden picture had been available for viewing. The marketing plan was not nearly as damaged as had been feared. In fact, that character went on to be one of our most successful properties.

Had I been adept at some stress-management technique other than Zen, I may have gotten through that simulated public execution without projectile vomiting or soiling myself. I might have been able to stave off panic with soothing images or with regulated breathing. I have no doubt these things have a certain degree of usefulness. But Zen had served me much better. It wasn't that panic arose and I successfully quelled it. Instead, panic never even arose. And that is far better.

But it takes a lot more time and a lot more effort to get to this place. As it should. If there's any single point I don't mind repeating until you're sick to death of it, it's that there are never any shortcuts. You've got to be willing to give up the root cause of your stress. This is not an easy thing to do because the root cause of your stress is that imaginary thing you call your "self."

Giving up your self isn't really such a big deal. You're not really giving up anything at all. You just have to see your illusions for what they really are — illusions. It's like noticing that the serial killer you thought was hiding behind the curtains is really just your little sister. It's no more devastating than that.*

But you've been growing and nurturing this particular set of illusions for a very long time. You protect it the way a mama bear

---

* Unless your little sister happens to be a serial killer, of course, but I think you get my drift.

protects her cubs. You'll tear anyone to bits if he dares threaten it. If he tells you it's not real, you think he's insane. Or worse, you think he's some kind of mystic with insights you could never aspire to. That's a good one. The perfect excuse not to do anything at all!

Unfortunately, doing nothing isn't an option. You always have to do something. As for me, I had a punk rock show to do.

Chapter 9

Buddha Never Metta Man He Didn't Like

D oes anyone remember the old punk rock episode of the TV show *Quincy*? *Quincy* was this early-eighties cop show starring Jack Klugman as a police coroner who investigates murders. In one episode he looks into the death of a young girl who got stabbed during some intense slam dancing at a punk rock club. Basically the plot is just an excuse to point out the supposed dangers of punk rock. At the end of the show Quincy and his girlfriend are dancing to some lame-ass pop pap and Quincy says, "Why would anyone want to listen to music that makes you hate when you could listen to music that makes you love?" Yech.

Yet in spite of the fact that all of us were in the business of making "music that makes you hate," there was a lot of love in the room at the Beachland Ballroom on the night of the big hardcore punk reunion show. It's great to see old friends you haven't seen in a very long time. All the many arguments we'd had in the past didn't seem very relevant anymore. Back in the day there was a huge split in the hardcore community over whether or not punk rock had to be political. It was a really stupid issue, and I'm not sure where it came from.

But the two poles back in 1983 were Zero Defects, who were decidedly political, and Agitated, who were decidedly not. I'd pretty much forgotten this until I got hold of a copy of *The New Hope*, the compilation LP that Tom Dark, lead singer of the Dark, put together back in the day.

Each band got to make its own page in the booklet that accompanied the record. The Zero Defects page is full of printed lyrics about Reagan and the Bomb* and decorated with Native American–inspired images of each band member. On the other hand, Agitated's page contains a note telling all the political-minded bands of the day — including MDC, the Dicks, the Dead Kennedys, Crucifucks, and a whole list of political hardcore bands — to fuck off. And yet here I was twenty years later playing bass for both bands. When the offer to play with Agitated came up, I never even thought of it as being the least bit ironic, though back in the day I might have been seen as a traitor to the cause.

Nowadays we all love each other, and ain't it wonderful? The atmosphere at the show was incredibly positive and uplifting. The interviews I conducted for use in my documentary all went extraordinarily well. Which is not to say that it was never wonderful twenty years ago. But I think one of the reasons I stepped away from punk was because it was uncool not to have a pessimistic, gloomy outlook toward life in general. Although I was generally pretty pessimistic, I couldn't get into just hating everything all the time the way a lot of folks in the scene did. I didn't want to dwell on the negative aspects of life all day long.

On the other hand, I had firsthand experience of what happens when you try to force yourself to think positive all the time. Back then I lived in a house in Kent they called the f-Model House because a few members of the band the f-Models lived there, and they used

---

* Actually, we were never cheesy enough to write a song specifically about Reagan, but almost everything we played was somehow "political."

it as a practice space. By the time I moved in, the f-Models were in a state of disarray that eventually led to their breakup, but the house still bore their name, as it did for several years until some developers bought it and made it into a cute duplex for nice families to live in. That's progress, I guess.

One of the other people who lived there when I did was a girl whose name I can't recall. But I'll call her Debby, since she had a very Debby-ish personality. For all I can remember, maybe her name really was Debby. So apologies, Debby, if your name really was Debby.

Debby was a psych or sociology major or something like that. She lived in the room next to mine. Debby was on some kind of a positive-thinking kick at the time. So she was always smiling, always cheerful, always ready to lend a helping hand. I can't tell you how well this went over in a house full of gloom-and-doom punk rockers. But no matter how much we took advantage of her and made fun of her, Debby remained bright and chipper as ever.

Debby was hard at work at the time on a book she planned to call *Butterfly*. I'm not sure if it was gonna be a novel or an autobiography or what. But I gathered that *Butterfly* was going to be uplifting and positive and would serve as Debby's cheerful gift to a gloomy sourpuss world.

Debby had all kinds of ways of psyching herself up to get down to the serious business of getting this book together. At one point she took a big felt-tip marker and wrote "Butterfly 1983 Yes!!!!!" in giant letters on the wall next to the fridge. She must have thought that writing stuff on the walls was okay because it was a punk rock house. But, in fact, we had been specifically trying to avoid abusing the place in that way, having seen how horrendous other punk houses looked as soon as they started letting everyone write stuff all over the walls. I think Debby was doubly bummed out that we didn't like her attempt at decoration.

Anyway, sometime after this — and I don't think it was directly related, but it might've been — I came home and, when I opened the door to my room, I noticed that something inside the door was making a rattling sound. Although the house was old enough that all the doors inside should have been made of solid wood, the door to my room was a newer, cheaper one made of two slabs of plywood with some slats of even cheaper wood in between to add thickness. After investigating it further, I realized that all those slats had been broken, although the door itself did not appear to be damaged. That was weird.

I went around the house asking if anybody knew what had happened. It took a while, but Debby finally sheepishly owned up that it had been her. At some point, when she'd been home alone, she could no longer contain her rage beneath a mask of forced positivity, and she had kicked the living crap out of my door.

While I had actually sort of admired Debby's attitude before then, the incident served as an object lesson that you can't be happy in life just by willing yourself to experience only those states you regard as positive. This was a bit before I encountered Zen. But when I did, I was kind of surprised to learn that in the practice of zazen they didn't make a distinction between supposedly "good" and "bad" thoughts, and they also didn't draw a line between so-called positive and negative emotional states.

I had trouble with this idea for a very long time. Yet while the notion of promoting supposedly "positive" emotional states while eliminating "negative" ones is one of those ideas that sounds good on paper, it tends to work out extremely badly in the real world. Buddhism doesn't try to promote positivity over negativity. Buddhism is about balance. And in the state of balance, right action presents itself at every moment. The results, while they might be called "positive" or "good," have nothing to do with the confused emotional states we usually label with those words.

To get a feel for this, let's look at that one emotional state most universally accepted as positive: love. Everyone loves love. Love is all you need, said the Beatles and then, of course, there was Arthur Lee and Love.* But what did our man Mr. Buddha have to say on the subject?

You won't be surprised to learn that there's a story about that. Once upon a time a bunch of monks asked Buddha if they could go practice in a forest. The Buddha said, "Fine by me." So they did. Each monk picked a tree and parked himself under it and started meditating. After a time the monks began to believe they were being hassled by invisible demons that lived up in the trees and wanted the monks to stop all that meditating and get out of their forest. The monks asked Buddha what to do, and he said, "Tree demons, huh? Ho-kay, why don't you try having loving thoughts toward your . . . um . . . *tree demons?*"

The full text of what he told them that day is still recited by Buddhist monks as a sutra known in Sanskrit as the *Metta Sutra*. The word *metta* itself is hard to translate and is usually given as "loving-kindness." "Benevolence" may be a better translation, since it's a little less drippy sounding. Anyway, it goes something like this:

> This is what should be accomplished by the one who is wise,
>   who seeks the good and has obtained peace:
> Let one be strenuous, upright and sincere, without pride,
>   easily contented and joyous;
> Let one not be submerged by the things of the world;
> Let one not take upon oneself the burden of riches;
> Let one's senses be controlled;
> Let one be wise but not puffed up;
> Let one not desire great possessions even for one's family;
> Let one do nothing that is mean or that the wise would
>   reprove.
> May all beings be happy.
> May they be joyous and live in safety.

---

* You hipsters who think hardcore punk was invented in 1980 oughta go check out Arthur Lee and Love's "Seven and Seven Is" from 1966.

All living beings, whether weak or strong, in high or middle or low realms of existence, small or great, visible or
invisible, near or far, born or to be born, may all beings
be happy.

Let no one deceive another, nor despise any being in any
state; let none by anger or hatred wish harm to another.

Even as a mother at the risk of her life watches over and
protects her only child, so with a boundless mind should
one cherish all living things, suffusing love over the entire world, above, below and all around without limit;
so let one cultivate an infinite goodwill toward the whole
world.

Standing or walking, sitting or lying down, during all one's
waking hours let one cherish the thought that this way
of living is the best in the world.

Abandoning vain discussion, having a clear vision, freed
from sense appetites, one who is made perfect will never
again know rebirth in the cycle of creation of suffering
for ourselves or for others.

This sutra is where all the stuff you hear in Buddhist books and magazines about "loving-kindness" comes from. But since this book
is about Dogen and his philosophy, it's interesting to note that
there's not a single reference to the *Metta Sutra* in the whole of the
Shobogenzo.

So you gotta wonder why. I mean, love is an important thing in
pretty much every religion. How could a religious thinker like Dogen
completely ignore it? Was he just some kind of a mean old ogre who
hated love?

But rather than talk about love, Dogen talked about compassion.
Chapter 33 of *Shobogenzo* is titled 観音, or "Kannon," which is the
Japanese name for Avalokiteshvara, the Bodhisattva of Compassion.
Kannon is supposed to have zillions of hands and zillions of eyes,

The poster for the 1968 movie *The Green Slime*. Is this the type of being Dogen had in mind when describing the characteristics of the ultimate in compassionate bodhisattvas? Read on.

sort of like the multieyed, multitentacled space monsters from the old Japanese sci-fi flick *The Green Slime* (see above). Anyhow, in the chapter about Kannon Dogen relates the following story.

One Zen master walks up to another and asks, "What does the Bodhisattva of Great Compassion do by using his limitlessly abundant hands and eyes?"

Now, if the guy asking this were me, I'd be hoping for a really cool answer, like, "He grabs helpless young girls with them and drags them screaming back to his lair."

Disappointingly, though, the other Zen master says, "He is like a person in the night reaching back with a hand to grope for a pillow."

The first Zen master goes, "I understand. I understand."

The other Zen master asks, "How do you understand?"

The first Zen master says, "The whole body is hands and eyes."

The other Zen master goes, "Nice. But I only give you a B+ for that answer."

The first Zen master says, "That's my answer. What's yours?"

The other Zen master goes, "The thoroughly realized body is hands and eyes."

Mmmm. Okay. But, again, it's not quite as nutty as it sounds. When you reach back for a pillow in the night, the action is totally unconscious. Someone is suffering from a stiff neck, and someone does something spontaneously to relieve that suffering. Forget about the way we usually conceive of both of these "someones" as being the same person. Just look at the action itself. It's totally spontaneous. There is no thinking involved. Something needs doing, and it gets done. When it's finished, no one even remembers it. There are no medals given out, no pats on the back from the master, no ticker-tape parades. In fact, there's no evidence it ever even happened. All truly compassionate action works exactly like this.

It's damned tough to practice that kind of compassion. But I can give you a little bit of incentive. No matter how unacknowledged your act of compassion, the universe always notices it. And the universe has a very long memory.

What's under discussion here is what Buddhists call *prajna*, or intuitive wisdom. It's a kind of wisdom that isn't limited to the things that lump of gray meat you carry around in your head can make sense of. It's a kind of wisdom that pervades the whole body and, by extension, the whole universe. This is why the second Zen master makes a point of emphasizing the "thoroughly realized body." He's indicating that your body — the one that burps and farts and gets itches in unmentionable places — includes and is included by the entire universe. Compassion is real action based on this kind of intuitive wisdom.

Besides writing about compassion, Dogen also wrote about what makes for good interactions between people, another topic much related to the idea of loving-kindness. He devotes a chapter of *Shobo-genzo* to what he calls "The Four Elements of a Bodhisattva's Social Relations" (chapter 45, 菩提薩摩四摂法, pronounced *Bodaisatta-shishobo*).

The title sounds a little off-putting, I know, like some kind of weird guidebook for a snooty group of socialites that you know is never gonna invite the likes of you and me to join. Actually, though, Dogen manages to address some extremely practical and universal guidelines for social conduct in this little chapter.

Traditionally, the four elements of a Bodhisattva's social interactions are free giving (布施, pronounced *fuse* in Japanese, which is a translation of the Sanskrit word *dana*); kind speech (愛語, pronounced *aigo*, or *priya-akhyana* in Sanskrit); helpful conduct (利行, pronounced *rigyo*, or *artha carya* in Sanskrit); and cooperation or identity of purpose (同事, pronounced *doji*, or *samana arthata* in Sanskrit).

The idea of free giving is a toughie, and, tellingly, it's the one Dogen spends the most time trying to explain clearly. And the Sanskrit word *dana*, from which it is derived, is a huge buzzword in Buddhist circles these days. It's usually used to refer to the money you give to Buddhist teachers to help them continue their work, though far too often this tradition of *dana* is badly abused. I once watched a supposed Buddhist master mooch a scrumptious Indian dinner and — I kid you not — skydiving lessons and a luxury boat cruise around Southeast Asia off his students under the guise of accepting *dana* from them.

To get back to Dogen's definition of free giving, though, you might tend to equate free giving with charity. But too often we place ourselves above those to whom we wish to be charitable. Our "giving" then becomes just another way to enhance our self-image. And just as often, we place ourselves below those to whom we give our charity, thinking, for example, that a charitable contribution to some spiritual master will gain us merit in the spiritual world or that a gift of *dana* to some Zen master might speed us on the way to enlightenment — and, believe me, folks, there are lots of teachers who play right into this one (see above). But when we do this our so-called giving becomes just another form of greed.

Real free giving isn't like that. Dogen describes it this way: "We give ourselves to ourselves, and we give the external world to the external world. The reason is that in becoming giver and receiver, the subject and object of giving are connected."

In true giving, self and other disappear. It's not that *we* give *something* to *someone*. The one who receives our gift is just the reflection of our self. In fact, even the thing that we give is also our self, no matter what that thing might be. You don't need to get all mystical about this idea, either. Just try to really put yourself in the place of the person to whom you're giving something, and see how it transforms everything.

In Dogen's view the meaning of giving goes way beyond what most of us conceive of as giving. He says that even "earning a living and doing productive work are originally nothing other than free giving." Normally we think that we work for our ugly, stupid, pain-in-the-ass boss making the crappy stuff our company produces to sell to suckers who don't have anything better to do with their money for just one reason: so that we can get our paycheck at the end of the week and go out and spend it on stuff we want.

Okay. Hopefully you're not quite as cynical about it as all that. Though I know at times when I used to work brain-deadening file clerk jobs for Kelly Temporary Services just to keep myself in Kraft Macaroni 'n' Cheese® and Top Ramen® for another week, I really did pretty much feel that way about what I did for a living. I knew what I was working for, and it had nothing to do with any kind of free giving. It was slave work, and my slave driver was the need for the Almighty Dollar.

It's sad that most of us work without much feeling of free giving involved. But Dogen points out here that working for a living is originally done for just that purpose, as a means of giving freely of ourselves for the sake of others, which is the most joyful experience a human being can have.

Any job you do contributes somehow to the welfare of all of humankind. Maybe a little, maybe a lot. It doesn't matter. For example, I wrote up a synopsis of the TV series *Zone Man 80* this morning, and it made my co-worker Jimmy's job of selling the show to a Brazilian TV station that much easier. How does that rank with Nelson Mandela freeing South Africa from apartheid or Mother Teresa saving Indian kids from cholera? You know, it doesn't really matter to me. I just need to do what I do and not worry about comparing myself with anyone else. When you get into the idea that helping a million people overcome some great catastrophe is wonderful but helping the guy next to you fix his pencil sharpener is trivial, you run into all sorts of trouble because you will never measure up to your ideal.

All the various forms of work that exist today are nothing more than extensions of the original jobs our remote ancestors did, like planting and harvesting crops, building shelters for our tribe, generally making the world more comfortable for ourselves and those around us. To be sure, some of the jobs we do today are dire corruptions of this idea — like being a Mafia hit man, for example. Still, even such work is often done as a highly confused way of attempting to help make the world better for everyone. Not that I'm recommending it. Still, even those people doing things we deem to be "evil" probably feel their jobs are of some benefit to someone.

The reward you get for the work you do, even if it's financial, is the natural outcome of your efforts. In the end it's impossible to understand how this works. The rewards for doing work flow as they will.

The attitude of free giving itself is, in Dogen's view, something very basic and essential in our nature. He says, "It is because we are originally equipped with the virtue of free giving that we have received ourselves as we are now."

Now, stop a minute and look at what he's saying here. He's claiming that what we really are isn't men and women capable of giving and receiving. What we really are, in his view, is the action of giving and receiving itself made manifest. "Free giving" grows itself a body, and it looks an awful lot like you. What a bizarre idea! Yet in many ways it makes a whole lot more sense than our ordinary way of looking at things. We usually conceive of ourselves as individuals who alternatively compete and cooperate with each other to ensure our own benefit and survival. But Dogen is suggesting that this isn't the case at all.

Our most basic functions, like breathing in and out, are really the act of giving and receiving. We give carbon dioxide to the plants of the world and receive oxygen in return. As far as the planet as a whole is concerned, our existence as a breather-inner of oxygen and breather-outer of carbon dioxide is way more important than our existence as, say, a file clerk or a member of the Screen Actor's Guild or a writer of lousy books about Buddhism.

Next, Dogen tackles the idea of kind speech. Kind speech is rendered in Chinese characters as 愛語, which is pronounced *aigo* as in "*aigo* to the store to pick up some bagels" and can also be translated as "loving words." I prefer the term *kind speech* since it's far less gooey.

"Kind speech," Dogen says, "means, when meeting living beings, first of all to feel compassion for them and to offer caring and loving words. Broadly, it is there being no rude or bad words." This is a big relief to me since so many people complained about all the rude and bad words in my previous book. Actually, what I think Dogen's getting at here is that it isn't the specific words you use that are good or bad; it's the intent behind them. Dogen himself wasn't above using rude words in his own writing, saying, for example, that the Buddhist dharma was "sometimes the sound of a fart or a whiff of shit."* There are instances when saying "you suck" — as Dogen often does say to his contemporaries — might be the kindest thing you can do. Just be careful when you're being kind in that way!

* This in a chapter called, of all things, "The Dignified Behavior of Acting Buddha"!

He goes on to say that "in secular societies there are polite customs of asking others if they are well. In Buddhism there are the words 'Take good care of yourself!' and there is the disciple's greeting 'How are you?'" This is a very important point, so don't just gloss over it. Even trite phrases like "take care" and "how are you?" are of great importance to Buddhists. It's easy to get all intellectual about it and believe that there's no value to such clichéd phrases because most people don't really give two cow pies how you are or whether or not you take care of yourself. Yet this kind of stuff should never be overlooked. Talk nice to people.

The next point Dogen brings up is helpful conduct. The Chinese characters for helpful conduct are 利行, which are pronounced *rigyo* and come from the Sanskrit *artha-carya*. The Sanskrit word also carries the meaning of "helpful conduct" or "beneficial conduct." Dogen says, "Helpful conduct means utilizing skillful means to benefit living beings, high or low; for example, by looking into the distant and near future and employing expedient methods to benefit them."*

Skillful means is 善巧 in Chinese characters and is pronounced *zengyo*, as in "after *aigo* get some bagels I *zengyo* buy some cream cheese." The phrase originates in the *Lotus Sutra*, where there is a story of some children who are trapped in a burning house. The kids are too dumb to understand that they should get out of the house so that they don't end up crispier than a couple of Kellogg's Coco Krispies®, so their dad tells them that all kinds of cool stuff is waiting for them outside, and they run out to get it.

Please be careful here. The concept of skillful means — or *upaya* to hipster Buddhists who know the Sanskrit for it** — refers to doing the absolute best you can with what you have. The point isn't that the

---

* Don't get all New Agey here. "Looking into the future" just means imagining what might be necessary an hour from now, or a year from now.

** True Buddha-nerds call everything they like "skillful" and everything they don't like "unskillful."

guy got his kids out of the burning house by deceiving them so it's therefore fine and dandy to deceive others as long as there's some sense of a "greater purpose" behind your lies. The real point is that the father in the story acted spontaneously, intuitively, doing the best thing he could think of at that moment to save his kids. He didn't dick around trying to figure out some brilliant foolproof plan of action; he just *did something*. The fact that it worked does not erase the fact that he lied to his kids. He'll still have to face his kids' disappointment that there was no stuff outside after all and their resentment at the fact that he considered them too dumb to grasp the truth of the situation. It's a big mistake to see the story as saying that using skillful means is license to deliberately lie to those you think of as beneath your lofty level of understanding.

To illustrate the benefits of helpful conduct, Dogen brings up a legendary story of a kid who helped out a sick sparrow and as a result his descendants received high positions in the Chinese court. "He was motivated solely by helpful conduct itself," he says. "Stupid people think that if we put the benefit of others first, our own benefit will be eliminated. This is not true. Helpful conduct is the whole Dharma."

Yep. It's the old "good karma" thing. Do something nice for somebody, and it comes back to you. It sounds all idealistic and drippy, I know. But it really is an observable fact once you learn how to observe clearly. Notice that Dogen points out that these people did not do their good actions for the sake of some reward later on. They just did them. That's the important thing. If you find that you cannot help but think "maybe I'll get some good karma for this" as you're walking an old lady across the street or whatever, that's no problem either. Just do what's right, and don't worry too much about such thoughts.

Finally, Dogen tackles the idea of cooperation. The Chinese characters are 同事, which are pronounced *doji*. The two characters stand for "identity" and "task." So the word literally means "sharing the same aim" or "being in the same boat." The Sanskrit term for those of you keeping score at home is *samana-arthata*. "Cooperation," says Dogen, "means not being contrary. It is not being contrary to oneself and not being contrary to others."

Real cooperation means being true both to yourself and to those with whom you share a purpose. And with whom, you may ask, do we share a purpose? The only answer to that, for a Buddhist, would be "everybody." We don't exist just to serve ourselves or our families or our nations or even our species. Our real mission in life is to be of service to everyone and everything we encounter. Another great Buddhist writer, Nagarjuna, says that the universe does not exist for many aims but for only one.

Dogen says that we should not be contrary to others, which is pretty much the standard definition of cooperation. But he also says we shouldn't be contrary to ourselves. Often we think there is a choice. There are situations in which it seems we have to decide whether we'll be contrary to others or contrary to ourselves. But Dogen doesn't recommend doing either.

Finding this middle ground requires that we give up both the idea of self and the idea of others. This is very nearly impossible to accomplish unless we have a strong grounding in zazen practice. At least I know I couldn't begin to achieve anything like it without the practice. Zazen can help you become clearer about what this whole notion of "self" as contrasted with "others" really is. It's one thing to read that the self is nothing more than a convenient fiction. But to actually come into contact with why this is so is something quite different.

Now, that's pretty much Dogen's take on what we usually call positive emotions. Talk about compassion and social conduct isn't all warm and fuzzy like religious teachings about love can often be. But it is immensely practical. And that's what interested Dogen, not what is emotionally satisfying, but what is real and useful.

Chapter 10

Cleaning Up Your Room

Right from the opening screech of "Drop the A-Bomb on Meeeeeeeee!!!!" I knew the show was going to be just fine. By the middle of the second song, our lead singer, Jimi Imij, was doing backward somersaults across the stage. And he's five years older than I am! I was worried he was gonna hurt himself. Then when he started doing flying kicks, I was worried he was gonna hurt me. And he did. He kicked me a good one in the left hand. When I went up to the mic and thanked him for almost breaking my hand, he just scowled at me and said, "That'll make you play more punk rock!" Someone in the audience yelled, "Break his neck!" That's when I knew I was home.

My perception of time always gets kinda weird when playing hardcore. Every song is so short, yet you have to pay way more attention to what you're doing than when playing stuff at a normal tempo. The effect is that even a twelve-second song ends up feeling like a three-minute one. And a two-minute song feels like it goes on forever. By the end of a twenty-minute set you're totally exhausted. And I had to go back out there again right after and play with Agitated.

The set with Agitated went great too. I always loved those guys, in spite of what they'd written in the New Hope compilation booklet. It was an honor serving with them. Still, in that band I was more like a hired hand, so the pressure wasn't turned up as high.

Then came the comedown. See, we're not big enough to have roadies or any of that. So we had to do all the cleanup work by ourselves. That has always been the biggest drag for me as far as playing rock and roll is concerned. Everybody else gets to go home and crash. But the band has to stay there another hour or more just packing all the stuff up and making sure everything's settled. Plus, because I was making a movie as well, I also had to run around and catch people to do interviews with them and then clean up all the camera equipment. I've always hated cleaning up after myself, not just after rocking out but any time. I am, by nature, a consummate slob. But the more I've come to embrace Buddhism, the more I've come to see that that is no way to live.

Here's the way cleaning up my room went for most of my adult life, when I was a struggling indie-rock artist before I moved to Japan. First I'd have to kick away enough of the garbage on the floor so that I could stand in one corner and take the whole thing in to see what needed doing. Inevitably my room would be like Baghdad the day after George W. decided he needed to teach Saddam Hussein about democracy. There'd be copies of *MOJO, Maximum Rock-'n'Roll*, and *Outre* magazine strewn across the floor. There'd be pawnshop guitars with the pickups held on by yellowing Scotch tape leaning at random angles against mounds of stained T-shirts. There'd be stacks of month-old Domino's boxes with the cheese stuck on the inside beginning to look like something from a third-grade science experiment, next to empty cans of Jolt Cola and V8 — y'know, from the days when I decided to "eat healthy." I'd look at all this and think, "There is no way this will ever, ever, ever be clean." It was an impossible situation. Just organizing all the stuff would take hours, if not days or even weeks. Plus, there were all kinds of other things I could be doing with that time. I could be writing, recording, practicing guitar, or just taking a nap. I mean, even if I made my bed — okay, my mattress on the floor — it was just gonna end up back in the same state after I slept on it later anyway. What was the point?

But the clutter was always so depressing to look at that I'd start thinking of ways to make the room look clean without all the drudgery of actually cleaning it up. There had to be some expedient means of going from messy room directly to clean room without all the toil and slog in between. Like, if I had the cash I could hire a maid to come in and clean it once a week. But I was always broke, so that wasn't an option.

Or I'd think, there's gotta be something that would make the place look not quite so messy so I could get a taste of what a clean room was like before I actually cleaned it. Y'know, to see if it might really be worth all the trouble — what you might call an "opening experience" of cleanliness. If there was just some way to get that experience, it might enlighten me to the world that those with truly clean rooms experience all the time. Like maybe I could just shove everything into the closet. Then the mess would be in *there*, where I wouldn't have to look at it, and not over *here*, where I was. After that maybe I would make the real effort to clean up later on. You know, in the future. Some other time. Not now.

But there's a big difference between the experience of a room in which everything's been shoved into the closet and the experience of a room you've actually cleaned up.

It took me ages and ages to finally come to terms with the obvious solution to the problem, which was staring me in the face the whole time. You clean up your room by simply getting off your ass and cleaning it up.

It's only when you stop worrying about the final goal, the idealized vision of the perfectly clean room, only when you forget about trying to find ways to avoid what needs to be done, that you can actually get down to doing what really needs doing. It's then that you start to see the real miracle. Every little thing you do makes the room just a little bit neater. Throwing away one old pizza box makes your room one old pizza box cleaner. Making your bed makes your bed look nice for a few hours before you wreck it again. And that's something. Try it sometime. I did, and I was amazed. Dusting off the Godzilla toys sitting on the computer makes for less dust on the Godzilla toys on the computer. Eventually all those little things add up. One day, when you put away the last piece, you might suddenly notice that your room's gotten clean. But the process was anything but sudden.

Don't worry if you can't get it all done on the first day. Or the second or third or fiftieth or fifty-thousandth. Just do what you can do right now.

The trouble with lots of folks who get into Buddhism is that they approach Buddhist practice the way I used to approach cleaning up my room — and the way I first approached Buddhism, too, by the way. We compare the goal of Perfect Enlightenment — whatever we imagine Perfect Enlightenment to be — to our messy mental state in the present moment and decide it's completely hopeless. There is just no way to get from here to there. Nothing we ever do is gonna transform this garbage-filled brain of ours into the perfectly calm state of purity and inner peace we envision the Great Enlightened Masters to possess.

Or else we look for shortcuts, something that's going to remove a few steps in the process, expedient means to get from point A to point Z without bothering with points B through Y, which are really boring anyhow. Or maybe we want to have some kind of opening experience, a free sample of this product called Enlightenment, to see if we want to spend our time and money on it.

But there are no shortcuts. For me there's only one way to do Buddhist practice, and that's to slog through it the same way you slog through cleaning up your room. In *Shobogenzo Zuimonki* Dogen likens real Zen practice to the way you get wet if you walk through fog. You don't notice it as it's happening. But walk through that fog long enough, and you'll get thoroughly soaked.

So do what needs to be done right now. Then do the next thing. And the next. And the next. Dust off that pile of old Van Halen records without worrying about whether that action in and of itself is going to end up making the entire room look like the bright and spotless room in your imagination. Do that and then dust off something else. Do what you can, and do it now. Eventually, if you do enough of that, your room gets clean. It may happen quickly, or it may happen slowly. It all depends on how much you messed up your room to begin with and how willing you are to deal with that mess. And those are the *only things* it depends on. Not on whether or not you've chosen some miracle room-cleaning method, not on whether you've had a taste of cleanliness (however dubious), not on whether you've discovered the Highest Room Cleaning Master in the Universe to tell you what needs cleaning and how it should be done.

If you want to learn to play the flügelhorn, you have to be prepared to really suck at it for a long time before you actually get any good. It's the same way with Buddhist practice. When you first start doing zazen, thoughts and ideas and memories of yesterday's lunch and plans for tomorrow's cleaning of the sump pumps are going to be whizzing around in your head. You're going to hate staying still like that. It'll hurt your legs and your back. You'll be sitting zazen one day with a group of very serious people, and you'll just *know* for absolute certain that if you don't stand up at that very moment and sing the chorus to *Enter Sandman* at the top of your lungs, you will definitely, definitely die. And the only thing you can do when stuff like that happens is to just sweat it out. That's the way it is with every skill worth pursuing. It's a pain in the ass for a very long time until you become any good at it at all. And this is true for everyone, whether they were born in the foothills of the Himalayas fifteen hundred years ago or in Reno, Nevada, in 1985.

It's easy to become paralyzed in your practice when you focus on the so-called results. But there really are no "results" in the real world. There is only what is, right here and right now. You can compare what's here and now to your memories of the past, connect the dots in your head to come up with a logical reason for how you got from there to here, and then call *this* the result of *that*. But that's just something in your mind. What's here and now is not really the result of anything. It may be just the accumulation of things that have happened.

Buddhism is a philosophy about just doing things bit by bit until the work is done. Ah, but the work is never really done. That's the beauty of it. You'll be doing it all your life, and you will never stop improving at it the same way even a master violinist keeps practicing, keeps learning, continues getting better and better without end.

But it's the most wonderful thing in the world to do that because the most boring experiences in your life are the boring experiences of God himself experiencing the most boring aspects of God himself — which he created because he wanted to know the experience of true boredom. How could anything be better? How could you want anything more than that?

Everything starts from right here. If you can't see what's right in front of you, how are you going to do anything about it? How are you going to recognize your enlightened state if you can't even recognize the state you are in right now?

But it's incredibly tough to pursue a practice that says that if you spend tons of time and energy on it, your reward is . . . nothing! I mean, who wants to waste their time on that? You can feel like a schmuck for doing it. So let's take a look at that fact, shall we, and try to work out why it may yet make sense to follow a practice that offers you nothing for all your hard work.

Chapter 11

Evil Is Stupid

We finally got all the gear packed away at the Beachland at about three in the morning. I loaded up my car and made my way back toward Mickey's place in Akron, where I was staying. Just my luck, it had started snowing again about an hour earlier. I hate driving, and I hate driving through snow even more, and I hate driving through snow at three in the morning even more than that. But you do what you gotta do.

The snow was so heavy there were times when I couldn't even guess whether I was in the right lane or the left. But at least I didn't lose the road altogether. I made it back safe and crashed on the bed rather than on the highway. I had to set the alarm because my first Zen teacher, Tim, had his classes on Sunday mornings at Kent State University, and I wasn't about to miss that.

Tim's style is different from Nishijima's in a lot of ways, yet in a lot of ways it's very much the same. Neither of them pays much attention to matters of ceremony or to the standard form that a Zen class is supposed to take. They've both boiled it down to just the essentials of the practice itself. But while Nishijima's lectures tend to be a bit scholarly and focused on particular works of Zen literature, Tim just wings it. So one day he might be talking about Dogen, and the next he might give a lecture on the latest Freddy Krueger epic and why it doesn't measure up to the previous ones. You never know. But that's what makes it fun. And I'm always amazed at how he can keep the focus on Buddhism no matter what the overt topic might be.

It was kind of ironic that one of the other guys who showed up that day happened to have come along because he read about Tim in my first book. The guy had been doing Buddhist practice for a little while, maybe a couple of months, maybe a couple of years, I can't re-call. But he'd reached the point where it was getting kind of frus-trating. He felt like it just wasn't going anywhere. He was thinking about giving it up entirely. But he'd come along to the class to see if maybe it might not be worth pursuing just a little bit further.

I know the feeling well. I got totally fed up and gave up on Bud-dhism any number of times during my early years of practice. But I kept coming back. Most of the time, I wasn't quite certain why I came back. But I did.

Recently I had the pleasure of reading an article by a guy who went the other way. After getting fed up with it, he finally decided he wasn't gonna deal with this Buddhist crap anymore. The article was called "Why I Gave Up Buddhism," written by a science writer named John Horgan. After reading this article I have far more re-spect for Horgan — whose book *The End of Science* I enjoyed a few years ago — than I do for a great many of the people out there sup-posedly speaking on behalf of Buddhism.

Horgan says that the Buddhism he encountered "cannot be rec-onciled with science or, more generally, with modern humanistic values." He says, "To someone who sees himself and others as un-real, human suffering and death may appear laughably trivial. Zen lore celebrates the sadistic or masochistic behavior of sages such as Bodhidharma, who is said to have sat in meditation for so long that his legs became gangrenous."

The idea that Buddhists see themselves and others as "unreal" is a common misconception. It's based on a faulty understanding of the Buddhist concept of emptiness or, in Sanskrit, *sunyata*, which is represented by the Chinese characters 空, pronounced *ku*, meaning "empty," or 無, pronounced *mu*, meaning "nothingness."

Dogen talks about this confusion in a chapter called "Space," or 虚空, pronounced *koku*. There he tells a story about two Zen masters. One Zen master says to another, "Do you understand how to grasp space?"

The other Zen master says, "Yup."

The first Zen master says, "Okay, then, big shot, how do you grasp it?"

The other Zen master grabs at the air with his hand.

The first master says, "That's not how you grasp space, you poser!"

The second Zen master says, "Okay, then, if you're so smart, how do you grasp it?"

The first Zen master grabs the second one's nostrils and pulls them just like Moe used to do to Curly.

"Eep! Eep! Eep!" the second Zen master yelps. "That hurt. But now I think I get it."

Wiping one of the second Zen master's boogers off his fingers, the first Zen master says, "Directly grabbing hold like this, you should have got it from the beginning."

Horgan might see this as another example of Buddhism celebrating sadistic behavior, but he'd be missing the point. The point is that the first Zen master thought of "space" or "nothingness" as something opposed to "somethingness." In other words, he held the nihilistic point of view. So, for him, the idea of grasping space or understanding nothingness was like grabbing for something unreal. Think about it a minute, though, and you'll see the problem. The first Zen master tried to grasp nothingness by grabbing the air. But the air isn't nothing. It's something. It's air. As Dogen points out, "the Universe has no gaps to accommodate 'space.'" In other words, Dogen understood something scientists would confirm a thousand and some years later, that even what we call "empty space" isn't really empty at all.

To illustrate his point in a very concrete way, the first Zen master grabbed the other one by the nose and yanked. The "emptiness" referred to by Buddhists isn't unreality. Emptiness is reality itself when we see it as it is, which is to say, when we see it as "empty" of our concepts about it — and that includes the concept of emptiness. By pulling the second Zen master's nose, he was saying to the guy, "You are emptiness too, douche bag!"

Real Buddhists do not see human suffering as trivial. They devote their whole lives to the cause of relieving it. But they do so in an unusual way. Buddhists relieve the suffering of others not by going out and doing good deeds for everyone — though they often do get off on doing good deeds for people — but by maintaining their own balance. It's only when we are balanced that we can do any good for anyone else. Otherwise we act from confusion instead of true compassion.

Horgan, though, characterizes Buddhism as a philosophy touting that "detachment from ordinary life is the surest route to salvation" and that "life is a problem that can be solved, a cul-de-sac that . . . should be escaped." He cites Gautama Buddha's leaving behind of his wife and baby to pursue a life of meditation as an example of a man escaping life.

Lots of people hate this episode in Buddha's life. I've had reservations about it myself. But this is just one example. Many other Buddhist masters have chosen to stay with wives and families. The fact is, we can never really know Gautama's personal situation completely, so it's foolish to make judgments. We do know from historical records that this was not a decision that Gautama took lightly. He thought long and hard about it before he actually left. And I, for one, am very glad he made that decision. Had he chosen to stay at home and be a good dad, the whole philosophy of Buddhism might never have emerged. And don't forget, Gautama's son and even his wife eventually entered the Buddhist order, so even they must have come to understand why he left.

I've said it before, and I'll say it again: Buddhism is emphatically not about running away from this world into some beautiful cosmic la-la land where nothing matters and nothing can ever bother you again. It's about seeing your real troubles, your real trials, all your real difficulties and real joys as they actually are, without the overblown drama we usually ladle on top of them.

Horgan says that "all religions, including Buddhism, stem from our narcissistic wish to believe that the universe was created for our benefit," while "science tells us that we are incidental, accidental." He continues: "This is not a comforting viewpoint, but science, unlike religion, seeks the truth regardless of how it makes us feel." He says that Buddhism is "not radical enough to accommodate science's disturbing perspective."

Actually, though, Buddhism has no arguments at all with science, no matter how disturbing its conclusions may seem. This stands in stark contrast to most other religions and is one of the things that first attracted me to Buddhism. The scientific view is perfectly true, Buddhism says, as far as it goes. But science can only go so far.

To illustrate this, let's say you're walking down a deserted street at nine o'clock one winter's night. You come across a girl, about ten years old, sitting on the curb. She has no coat and is shivering and crying her eyes out. Now, you could explain that scene in terms of emergent phenomena, or in terms of chemical reactions taking place within the body of a highly developed animal, or in terms of sociological theory. But is that really all there is to it? Is that the Truth of the matter? Do our words and symbols really encompass all that life really is? When you can explain something even extremely thoroughly and with pinpoint accuracy, have you really understood it? Lived it? And if this is clear in terms of the little scene I described above, how can we be so bold as to say that something as big as the whole universe is utterly without meaning? That we and our experiences are simply incidental, accidental?

The universe is more than just facts — more, even, than the sum of all the facts that make it up. The universe *is* meaningful. The universe is meaning — as well as matter. The two are not different. What we call matter is meaning, and what we call meaning is matter. In purely scientific terms that little girl may indeed be nothing more than a lump of carbon-based matter. But to say that's all she is would be wrong. By the same token, the universe may indeed be described as a mere collection of molecules and atoms thrown together more or less at random. But that's just one side of the coin.

The thing that really gets Mr. Horgan's knickers in a twist is what he sees as the Buddhist belief that "enlightenment makes you morally infallible — like the pope, but more so." I don't blame Horgan for taking issue with this idea. It's yet another in a seemingly inexhaustible list of truly stupid ideas that are all too often presented as "Buddhism."

Enlightenment does not make anyone morally infallible. Fuggedaboutit! Enlightenment, if we can even say there is such a thing, comes when you can no longer deceive yourself with the excuse that you didn't know any better when you do fall off the moral wagon. You are still fully capable of acting like a complete and utter butthead, and like everyone else you will suffer the consequences of such behavior. Gudo Nishijima is fond of quoting a Buddhist master who, when asked what the point of Buddhism was, answered, "Just do good and avoid doing bad." When the questioner complained that even a three-year-old child could have told him that, the master said, "It's easy enough for a three-year-old child to say, but even an old man of eighty [the master's age at the time] has difficulty practicing it."

You'll often hear it said that Buddhists don't believe in good and evil. But what does that really mean?

In college I majored in philosophy for one whole semester. Can't recall much. But I do remember that whenever a new philosopher was introduced in class, one of the main things we were expected to look at was his or her take on what the profs all called the Problem of Evil. We don't know quite what evil is — its inexplicability is part of the philosophical Problem of Evil — but as products of Western culture most of us have no doubt that something called Evil exists.

There's a tendency among Western people interested in Buddhism to try and shoehorn the concept of evil into the philosophy, often by citing the idea of karma as an example of Buddhism's view of the Problem of Evil. But this is a complete misunderstanding of the idea of karma. The Sanskrit word *karma* literally means "action." The concept of karma includes the idea that action always produces results. According to Buddhist theory the laws of cause and effect are not just limited to the physical world. They apply equally to the realm of mind. So we can say there is a moral law of cause and effect.

When people hear that Buddhism embraces the idea of moral cause and effect, they have an unfortunate tendency to want to insert some kind of deity figure into the picture. Horgan takes issue with the idea of the law of moral cause and effect as it's been presented to him. He says it implies "some cosmic judge who, like Santa Claus, tallies up our naughtiness and niceness before rewarding us with re-birth as a cockroach or as a saintly lama."*

But there's no more need to involve a deity in the matter of moral cause and effect than there is to invoke the God of Rain as an explanation of thunderstorms or the God of Stupid Hair as an explanation for David Beckham's latest do. Astronomers use telescopes to observe distant galaxies otherwise invisible to the naked eye, and Buddhists can use zazen as a tool to observe the real circumstances of their lives in ways that might otherwise be impossible. In so doing they come to see the workings of moral cause and effect as an undeniable fact.

---

* I love that line.

That story I told in chapter 7 about the perfect comeback I had for my wife would be a good example of this. The practice of zazen had allowed me to see exactly why saying what I'd wanted to say would have been the wrong thing to do. Morality for Buddhists isn't just about big things, the "moral issues" our editorial columnists wring their hands about. Buddhist morality includes everything we do. You can never know just how far-reaching the effects of your actions might be. That snide remark you make to the clerk at the grocery store might be enough to put her in such a foul mood that she fails to pay attention to a red light on her way home and ends up dead. You've got to be very careful. Always.

So what the heck is evil, anyhow? I think most of us would agree that evil is the worst type of bad you can imagine. Evil stands apart from its surroundings. No matter where you put it, evil will always be evil. Evil can never change. Evil is undeniably evil, universally evil.

Often evil is personified in the form of Satan, a dude who is supposed to be so super-duper bad that nothing he ever does could be the slightest bit positive. What's more, he makes perfectly nice people do bad things. It's somehow comforting to believe that evil exists in the form of some being outside ourselves who can force us to do bad stuff. This way we can absolve ourselves of responsibility for the wrongs that we've done.

We can all list famous evildoers of history, most of them bloodthirsty tyrannical despots. Yet only cartoon villains cackle with glee while rubbing their hands together and dream of ruling the world in the name of all that is wicked and bad. Hitler, to choose a guy most of us regard as most certainly evil, believed deeply in the Problem of Evil. In his twisted mind the Problem of Evil resided within one particular race of human beings. Eliminate them, and you get rid of the Problem of Evil, thereby doing a tremendous service for all humankind. How kind of Hitler to work so tirelessly on behalf of all humanity!* Our modern-day terrorists believe exactly the same thing.

The idea of moral cause and effect really shouldn't be so surprising. You know, for example, that if you roll a bowling ball straight down the lane, when it hits the pins at the end, it's gonna scatter them every which way. Why is it so hard, then, to understand that if you roll some loud, angry thought into your brain, it's gonna scramble all the rest of the stuff in there every which way? Whenever your mind is disturbed, it affects everything you do. And whenever you do something you know is wrong — and Buddhist theory says you *always* know when you're doing wrong — your mind becomes overactive, and you end up making mistakes you wouldn't have made if your brain weren't so scrambled up. And because of those mistakes things start going wrong in your life, and you begin to reap the dubious "rewards" of your previous behavior.

So even with the idea of karma, Buddhism doesn't address the Problem of Evil. But be careful here. The idea that good and evil really don't exist creates some problems when it's not clearly understood. Take a look at this letter I received from a guy who'd read my first book:

"While studying Zen I have come to feel unity in all forms, life and death are equally perfect, good and evil are equally perfect, everything is one. Since good and evil are equally important and perfect, why do we only show *love* and *compassion* to everything, why not show *hatred* and *evilness* to everything? Could one be an enlightened individual even if he was a nun-raping murderer? These thoughts kind of scare me because these are the thoughts that crazy, murderous lunatics have."

Of course such ideas are the kinds only lunatics believe. To believe such ideas is the very definition of lunacy. Just having ideas like

---

* For those oblivious to the completely obvious, I am being sarcastic here. Okay?

that is another matter. Bad ideas are fine until you start believing them. Recognizing that ideas like those are crazy and not believing them is an exceptionally healthy thing.

There's a tendency to think that Buddhism is about leaving this world of distinctions for some nebulous ill-defined imaginary someplace where everything is all the same. But actually the idea that all is one *and* the idea that everything is separate are equally important. Reality includes both. What is needed is the balance of both views, and that's tough to find.

To adopt the Buddhist view doesn't mean getting all blissed out and saying everything is one. You need distinction. You need to know the difference between your ass and a hole in the ground, between Hostess Ho Hos® and dog turds, between your boyfriend and your sister's boyfriend. Distinctions are very important.

Contrary to popular belief, Buddhism is not about doing away with all distinctions. It's about seeing distinctions for what they truly are. That does not mean you throw them away and start eating dog turds instead of Hostess Ho Hos®. Like I said, you gotta be careful! Dogen goes into this idea of real difference as opposed to false difference at length, and we'll get into it a little later in the book.

Just because there is no absolute immutable eternal substance we can call evil does not mean that right and wrong do not exist. Right action is doing what needs doing right here and right now. Wrong action is doing what doesn't need doing. Knowing the difference requires mental and physical balance. To become more balanced, you need . . . you know what I'm going to say by now, I think.*

I suspect that much, perhaps even all, of the "evil" that is done in the world is done as a kind of test, as a way for the "evildoer" to try and prove to him- or herself that he or she really is separate from the rest of creation. If you poke your little sister with a pin, she screams,

---

* The practice of zazen. Duh!

and you laugh. She felt pain, and you felt pleasure. This proves that the two of you are eternally separate. At least you think it does. But the rule of the universe never lets any action go without some reaction. So she smacks you a good one right across the jaw. Instant karma!

You may be inclined to say it's nonsense to believe that all "evil" will one day be "punished" — as it were — by the laws of moral cause and effect. You can probably think of all kinds of examples of people who do evil deeds and live to a ripe old age without ever feeling their effects. But do such people really exist? I have my doubts. When I look at my own life I see very clearly that the law of moral cause and effect works perfectly, 100 percent of the time. It's impossible for me to suppose that there may be other people out there somewhere for whom the same laws do not apply. We do not know the full story of all these people who've supposedly profited from evil deeds without ever suffering the consequences. If we did, we might see something quite different from what we expect.

Dogen writes about what he calls "karma in the three times" in chapter 84 of *Shobogenzo*, titled "Sanji No Go" (三時業), which has nothing to do with anybody named Sanji refusing to go anywhere but in fact translates as "Karma in the Three Times," natch! In this chapter he says, "These words [of Buddha] 'Retribution for good and bad has three times' mean retribution is received in the immediate present, it is received in one's next life, or it is received latterly."

Now, please don't get too into the "next life" business here. Remember that a single human lifespan can be seen as consisting of a series of lives — as a bucktoothed schoolkid, as a masturbation-addicted friendless teenager, as a bass player for a punk rock group, as a maker of bad Japanese monster movies, as a writer of dubious "Buddhist" books, as a . . . well, you get the picture.

What Dogen's saying here is that the results of our actions don't always show up right away in some form we can clearly recognize. Often they're spread out over a very long time. It's also a fact that you are constantly acting and creating new karma for yourself, which can change the nature of the effects you feel from past actions.

The practice of zazen can help you gradually clear away the layers of mental noise that prevent you from seeing how the things you're going through now relate to the stuff you did in the past. It's amazing how ignorant human beings can be about the way we are fully responsible for what happens to us. I once heard a story of a Nazi concentration camp commandant who was shot in the stomach by a prisoner of his who'd somehow acquired a pistol. With his dying breath, he said, "What have I done to deserve such pain?"

We may shake our heads in amazement at such a story, but are we really all that different? We all have a tendency to feel that, in the words of the great philosopher Jerome Horwitz,* we're merely "victims of circumstance," that things just kind of happen to us. But do they really? Or are we just oblivious — often very willfully oblivious — to the ways we've created our own fate?

It's hard to accept the idea that you're responsible for the seemingly random circumstances of your life. But just try it sometime. Try accepting full responsibility for everything in your life, including seemingly random events you couldn't possibly have had any control over. Don't worry about *how* you were responsible for these things. It doesn't matter. Just accept that you are responsible, and see what happens.

It might sound like it would be depressing to accept that kind of responsibility. But do it for a little while, and you'll discover there's a surprising kind of power in looking at your life that way.

Let me tell you why that is.

---

* Curly from the Three Stooges.

Chapter 12

"Hyakujo's Fox"

An old Zen story relates to the idea of good and evil and what happens to evildoers. It's called "Hyakujo's Fox." I first heard the story from my first Zen teacher, Tim McCarthy, when I started studying with him at Kent State University. It was in a book I borrowed from him called *Buddha Is the Center of Gravity*, by a Zen teacher named Joshu Sasaki. Tim had studied with Sasaki for a little while, so I was interested in what Sasaki had to say.

Apparently the book had been put together by some of Sasaki's students somewhat against his wishes. It quickly went out of print, and although Sasaki is still alive and teaching in California, the book was never republished. Like Tim's main teacher, Kobun Chino, Sasaki was not fond of committing his teachings to paper. Some Zen teachers like writing. Some don't. Gudo Nishijima has published a buttload of books. I go back and forth. I keep writing books. But I'm not sure how valuable they really are. Maybe about as valuable as an average issue of *Mad* magazine.

At any rate, I've always been fond of this story, despite the fact that it took me years to have even the faintest idea what it was about.

Like a lot of Zen stories and poems and things that I encountered when I was young and that stuck with me for a long time, I had an intuitive sense of the story's value long before I could make any cognitive sense of it. That's the way Zen stories are supposed to work. It really doesn't matter if you ever "get" them intellectually.

Dogen must have been fond of the story of Hyakujo's fox because he devotes two chapters of his *Shobogenzo* to it. Each chapter seems to offer a completely contradictory interpretation, by the way. I told you Dogen's a frustrating guy. In fact, the story is so popular that it also appears in a bunch of other old Zen books, including *The Gateless Gate*, the classic collection of koans used by the Rinzai sect. Each translation is a little different. What follows is a version of my own, cobbled together from the one in Sasaki's book, the one in Nishijima's translation of *Shobogenzo*, and the one that appears in R. H. Blyth's translation of *Mumonkan*. Here goes:

Whenever Zen master Hyakujo preached a sermon, an old stranger was always there among the monks. When the monks left, so did the old man.

One day the old man didn't leave. Hyakujo asked him, "Who is standing in front of me?"

The old man replied, "I am not a human being. In the days of Kasho Buddha* I was the head of the monastery on this mountain. One of my students asked me, 'I know that all beings are subject to the law of cause and effect. But do people of great practice fall into cause and effect or not?' I replied, 'They do not fall into cause and effect.' Since then I have lived five hundred lives as a wild fox."

Let me jump into the story for a second here and tell you that in ancient China a wild fox was a symbol of deception. Foxes are supposed to be clever and devious even in our culture. But the first time

---

* A Buddha who is supposed to have lived about two million years before Gautama — and if you believe that one, I've got some beachfront property in Nebraska I'd like to talk to you about.

I read this story, I didn't get that. You probably did, though. Anyway, back to the story. . . .

The old guy continued, "Now, Master, will you please put another word in place of mine and deliver me from the bondage of being a wild fox? Is a man of great practice subject to the doctrine of cause and effect or not?"

The master said, "The working of the doctrine of cause and effect is as clear as noonday." Some translations say, "Don't be unclear about cause and effect." (We'll talk about this a little later.)

The old man had a great realization on hearing these words. He bowed and said, "I was already free from the bondage of being a wild fox and have been living behind this mountain. I am sorry to trouble you, but would you please perform my funeral according to the regular ceremony of a dead monk?"

The master instructed the head monk to tell everyone that after the meal there would be a funeral ceremony for a monk. The monks all said to each other, "What gives? We're all fine. No one is in the infirmary. What's the deal?"

After the meal, the master took them to a cave behind the mountain, took out a dead wild fox with his stick, and performed the ceremony of cremation.

That evening, the master told his students what had happened. His student Obaku asked, "The ancient happened to answer wrongly and was changed into the body of a wild fox for five hundred lifetimes. If he had given no wrong answer, what would have happened?"

The master said, "Come forward and I will tell you."

Obaku came forward and gave his master a slap. The master clapped his hands and laughed. He said, "You just expressed that Bodhidharma's beard is red. But it's also true that the man with the red beard is Bodhidharma."

How's that for a non-sequitur ending?

There are two key phrases in this story. The wild fox/ex–Zen

master says to his student, "They do not fall into cause and effect."
When he is asked to say something to take the place of these words,
Hyakujo says, "The working of the doctrine of cause and effect is as
clear as noonday," or, "Don't be unclear about cause and effect." I
like the translation that uses the word *noonday* because it's a cool
image and because it indicates that cause and effect is so bloody obvious you could hardly ignore it if you tried. But "don't be unclear"
is a closer literal translation.

Anyway, the two phrases in the original Chinese are a variation
on a string of four characters. First the fox/ex-master says, 不落因果,
which would be pronounced *fu raku in ga* in Japanese. A literal translation would be "not fall cause effect." Hyakujo then says, 不昧因果,
which would be pronounced *fu mai in ga* and literally means "not
unclear cause effect."*

As I said, in *Shobogenzo* Dogen seems to want to take two completely contradictory positions on these statements. In the chapter
titled "Deep Belief in Cause and Effect" he says that "[the expres-
sion] 'they do not fall into cause and effect' is the negation of cause
and effect, as a result of which people fall into bad states. [The ex-
pression] 'do not be unclear about cause and effect' shows deep belief
in cause and effect, and those who hear it can get rid of bad states."

That's pretty straightforward. When you try and negate cause
and effect, you lose because everything is governed by the law of
cause and effect. Most religions postulate the existence of beings that
are beyond the laws of cause and effect. God can bend his own rules
whenever he chooses; he can part the Red Sea, cause frogs to rain
from the sky, raise his son from the dead, and all the rest. His various
servants, angels, and whatnot have all kinds of wicked-cool powers
too. A host of modern-day gurus and fakirs claim to be able to break

---

* In modern Japanese the second character means "taste," so this might be read "no
taste of cause and effect." That's not what it meant in ancient Chinese. But it's kind
of cool, I think.

the laws of cause and effect as well. But Buddhist philosophy does not allow for any of that. Everybody is subject to cause and effect.

And just in case anyone was impressed with the fact that the fox/ex-master remembered five hundred lifetimes, Dogen says, "There are among human beings or among foxes or among other beings those who innately possess the power to see a while back into former states. But it is not the seed of clear understanding. It is an effect felt from bad conduct." Buddhists aren't terribly impressed with supposedly paranormal powers either. Even what we call paranormal is subject to cause and effect.

At any rate, in terms of cause and effect the verdict rendered by Dogen in this chapter seems pretty clear and easy to follow. The fox/ex-master was wrong, and Hyakujo was right. End of story.

But in the chapter called "Great Practice" Dogen says, "Great Buddhist practice is just great causes and effects themselves. Because these causes and effects are inevitably perfect causes and complete effects, they can never be discussed as falling or not falling, or as unclear or not unclear. If the idea of not falling into cause and effect is mistaken, the idea of not being unclear about cause and effect must also be mistaken."

Ack! I thought he said the answer "don't be unclear about cause and effect" was right and the answer "not falling into cause and effect" was wrong! Now he's saying both are wrong? What gives?

As I said earlier, Dogen's methodology is to look at things from four points of view. Sometimes he expresses all four points of view in a single chapter or even a single paragraph, as we saw in "Genjo Koan." Other times he sticks to one particular viewpoint for a whole chapter, only to express its opposite in another. He'll often follow that up with two more chapters containing two more distinct and contradictory viewpoints on the same subject. This is one of those cases.

In "Deep Belief in Cause and Effect" Dogen sticks mainly to the subjective interpretation. In this point of view the two statements about cause and effect are absolutely contradictory. This is the way things work in the world of thought. Thought works by distinguishing things from each other. Therefore, one must be correct and the other incorrect. Either the new Beck album sucks, or it doesn't. Either your Converse high-tops are black, or they're not black. But in "Great Practice" Dogen addresses the same subject from the point of view of action itself. These viewpoints are evident in the chapter titles. One is about belief, which is a subjective matter, while the other is about practice, which is action.

From the point of view of action, neither of the expressions about cause and effect can be called correct. If I hit the low E-string real hard and let it ring at the beginning of the Zero Defects song "By the Day," in terms of thought we can say that's the right note or it's not. But in terms of action, it is just what it is. BLARRRRRINNNNNNGGG!!!! This is because real action in the real world refuses to be limited to the boxes we try and fit it in. Real causes and real effects are not ever the same as our images of cause and effect.

Think about our poor beleaguered weather forecasters. The only ones who ever get it right are the ones who happen to live in places like Los Angeles and Las Vegas, where the weather never changes. Back where I come from, Cleveland's channel 8 had Dick Goddard, who used to make a running gag out of how often he got his predictions wrong. It wasn't that he was a poor meteorologist. It's just that there are so many factors involved in the weather in northeastern Ohio that it's impossible to predict it all that accurately.

The same is true of all instances of cause and effect. The human mind is simply incapable of factoring in everything that needs to be taken into account in order to truly comprehend the cause and effect relationships we experience. But that does not mean that things happen at random. It just means that what we call cause and effect and real cause and effect are two different things. Just like you can't drink your Kool-Aid® out of the word *cup*.

Okay, then, you may be asking yourself, what was all that stuff about red beards and foreigners and the guy slapping his master?

In "Great Practice" Dogen points out that Hyakujo's student Obaku says, "The ancient happened to answer wrongly and was changed into the body of a wild fox for five hundred lifetimes. If he had given no wrong answer, what would have happened?" However, says Dogen, Hyakujo never actually said that the ancient master's answer was wrong. "A mistake in the age of Kashapa Buddha is not a mistake in the age of Shakyamuni Buddha," he says. In other words, what is a mistake and what isn't a mistake depends far more on the situation than on the words themselves.

Let me give you an example that those of you who read *Hardcore Zen* might be familiar with. In that book I talked about attending my grandfather's funeral and how my grandma asked if I thought maybe Grandpa was here and that he knew we were all there to honor him. My immediate answer was, "Yes. Definitely."

In pretty much any other context, if someone asked me if dead people hang around and watch their own funerals, I'd almost certainly say, "No way! Dead is dead. Stop dreaming." But imagine if I'd said that to Grandma at the funeral. By the same token, I was not lying, nor was I just saying something nice to try not to hurt her feelings. Grandpa was right there with us, and that is a fact. Dead as a doornail, but enjoying the funeral along with everyone else. And if that seems contradictory, like I'm trying to have it both ways, then you're catching on. There's a story in which two monks are standing by a casket. One of them taps the casket and says, "Alive or dead?" The other says, "I cannot say." Real life and real death do not fit neatly into the categories we call "life" and "death."

Hyakujo's comment, "You just said Bodhidharma's beard was red, but it's also true that the guy with the red beard is Bodhidharma," just means six of one, half a dozen of the other. For some reason I didn't get that when I first read the story. You probably did.

Even so, in "Great Practice" Dogen even questions whether or not Hyakujo's response to the slap was a true manifestation of understanding. He's only willing to give the old guy a B grade on that one, calling it "80 or 90 percent realization." For him both Obaku's and Hyakujo's comments fail to express the whole truth. But, he says, "In a slap [by Obaku] and a clap [Hyakujo clapped in response] there is one, not two." In other words, although the real truth cannot be put into words, Obaku and Hyakujo's real action expressed the truth perfectly. Real action is always true action. But no matter what words you use to try and capture this, you will always fail.

Chapter 13

The Twelvefold Chain

The sequence of cause and effect surrounding the Zero Defects reunion show still wasn't complete. Back when the gig had first been proposed, I thought it was a bit of a waste for me to come all the way to Akron just for one show. So I lobbied for us to do a few more. The other guys in the band cast around for some places to play. But there just aren't that many gigs available for aging hardcore bands in northeast Ohio. And it wasn't like we were ready to commit to a tour without even knowing if the show in Cleveland was gonna go alright or not. But we did end up with one more gig, at a record store called Square Records in Akron's hip Highland Square district. Of course, you have to accept that what qualifies as the "hip" part of town in Akron doesn't really amount to much by big-city standards. But even if a town's only got enough trendies to fill up an average-sized sweat-box rock club, those trendies still need a place to hang out, and in Akron, Highland Square is the place.

Now, I gotta tell you, by the time that gig rolled around, I was starting to regret having pushed so hard for it. I'd also managed to leave the AC adapter for my camcorder behind at the Beachland

Ballroom the night before. There was no way to get it back. So, right after seeing Tim, I had to embark on a frantic hunt for a replacement. No small feat, since there are, like, a grand total of two places in the whole city that might stock a thing like that. Luckily, one of them had a universal battery charger that worked on the battery that came with my camera. So even if I couldn't plug in, at least I could run for an hour or so on that before recharging. I could finish up a few interviews.

It seemed like cause and effect was jumping out at me from all directions the whole weekend. But actually your whole existence is the working through of cause and effect. Buddha himself came up with a very famous formula for how this all works called the Twelve-fold Chain of Codependent Co-origination.* It's said that Buddha attained enlightenment on contemplating this twelvefold chain. Whether or not Buddha himself said this remains a point of con-tention among scholars. But it seems almost certain that he was the guy who came up with the list, unlike other such formulae that were invented by later teachers and then attributed to Buddha.

I can never remember all twelve gol-danged folds off the top of my head. But since this is a book, I can stop and look them up as I write. Dogen talks about them in a chapter called "Bukkyo" (仏教), which means "Buddhist Teaching." I'll give you the English first fol-lowed by the Japanese and then the Sanskrit (Sk.) so you can impress your friends. The twelvefold chain goes like this — ahem:

1. Ignorance (無明, Mumyo, Sk. *Avidya*), which is the cause of . . .

2. Action (行, Gyo, Sk. *Samskara*, also sometimes translated as "predisposition" or "impulses"), which is the cause of . . .

3. Consciousness (識, Shiki, Sk. *Vijnana*), which is the cause of . . .

4. Name and form (名色, Myoshiki, Sk. *Nama-rupa*), which is the cause of . . .

---

* Try saying that ten times really fast.

5. The Six Senses (六入, Rokuju, Sk. *Sad-ayatana*), which are the cause of...

6. Contact (触, Shoku, Sk. *Sparsa*), which is the cause of...

7. Feeling (受, Ju, Sk. *Vedana*), which is the cause of...

8. Love (愛, Ai, Sk. *Trsna*, also sometimes translated as "craving" or "desire"), which is the cause of...

9. Taking (取, Shu, Sk. *Upadana*), which is the cause of...

10. Coming into Existence (有, U, Sk. *Bhava*), which is the cause of...

11. Birth (生, Sho, Sk. *Jati*, also sometimes translated as becoming), which is the cause of...

12. Aging and Death (老死, Roshi, Sk. *Jaramarana*), which is the cause of...(go back to the top of the list).

The chain of codependent co-origination is best conceived of as a circle rather than as a line leading from A to B to C. Like any chain, you could start with any link and go all the way around till you got back to the one you started on.* As Dogen puts it, "Remember, if ignorance is the One Mind, then action, consciousness and so on are also the One Mind. If ignorance is cessation, then action, consciousness and so on are also cessation."

The first link is ignorance. *Ignorance*, as the word is used here, has a bit broader meaning than the ignorance that's talked about when somebody yells at you, "You's ig'nant! Fool!" It's not the same as being ignorant of who was president during the Spanish-American War or who is buried in Grant's tomb.** This doesn't stop loads of Buddhist newbies, like me as a young tyke, from misinterpreting things and trying to cure their ignorance of Buddhism by reading

---

* Or just stop at the link that your pant leg is caught in.
** Jim Backus.

every supposedly "Buddhist" book they can get their hot little hands on. Ignorance is much more than merely being unaware of particular facts. True ignorance refers to our remarkable human ability to completely ignore what's right in front of us, to absolutely deny the existence of things that are undeniably true.

If we look at our lives sincerely, it's easy to see the ways we all ignore what's completely obvious. Look at the way we push for our own way at the expense of others. Ask yourself if such actions ever make you any happier in the end. Look at the way you worry about the future, and then think about whether that worrying ever made your future any better or if it just excited your brain cells, thereby leading to a future full of more worry.

Face it, you, me, your uncle Phil in Chicago with the bad toupee, we're all pretty damned ignorant. But we can work on it really hard and after some practice learn to be less ignorant. To stop being ignorant, all you need to do is stop ignoring what's plain as day right in front of you.

The second link in the chain is action. *Action*, as the word is used here, has a far broader meaning than we usually ascribe to it. The third-century Indian Buddhist poet Nagarjuna says in his *Fundamental Song of the Middle Way* that action — what you do right here and now — creates the entire universe. Now, that's just weird. That's totally bass-akwards from the way we usually look at things. We normally believe that the universe was created a bazillion years ago and that when we act, all that's happening is we're just doing our own little individual stuff inside this big old universe that acts as little more than a stage for whatever goes on inside it. How can anyone claim that the silly little things we all do every day, like mowing the lawn or doing the dishes or complaining about our stupid boss, somehow *create* the universe?

When you first come across an idea like this, it sounds so bizarre as to seem entirely meaningless. But once you live with the idea for a while — and, more important, once you sit with it for a time — it turns out to be a far better explanation for what you encounter every day than the so-called commonsense view you carried around in your head before. Try it on for size and see. Watch how the things you say aren't just responses to situations; they create completely new situations — even when you think no one is listening. Watch how the little things you do — or that you leave undone — make a huge difference in the lives of everyone you come in contact with. Pay some more attention, and you'll see your own influence on the universe is endless. Literally endless.

Next up in the list we have consciousness. What's that doing there? I mean, how the heck can you possibly be ignorant before you're even conscious? Most of your garden-variety Eastern philosophies these days, just like the ones that existed in Buddha's lifetime, postulate the idea that "we are not this body; we are the pure consciousness which inhabits this body." Buddha didn't think so. To him consciousness was just one of the things that make up what we call a human being.

So what is this thing called consciousness anyhoo? Gudo Nishijima likes to say, "Consciousness is just an illusion." The first time I heard that it freaked me out totally. I mean, how could consciousness possibly be an illusion? For a lot of philosophers, consciousness was the only thing that couldn't be disproven. I think, therefore I am, dude! I only know I exist because I am conscious. But observe for a long time, and you'll see not only that we are *not* beings of pure consciousness inhabiting material bodies, but that consciousness itself is just an illusion.

Consciousness isn't some immutable substance that exists apart from that which it is conscious of. Think of it this way. The Ramones are what we call the combination of Johnny, Joey, Dee Dee, and Tommy. Now maybe you can substitute Marky for Tommy, or CJ for Dee Dee. But anything short of this combination is not the Ramones. In other words, there's no thing called the Ramones that exists independently of its four members. The Ramones are the point at which those four people intersect and interact. It's the same with consciousness. Buddhists don't postulate some thing called consciousness that sits there twiddling its thumbs until something steps up in front of it to be conscious of. Consciousness is just what happens when the stuff we call "mind" interacts with the stuff we call "matter." To conceive of it any other way is an illusion.

Next up are name and form. The brain operates by carving up the world into little pieces, each with its own name and form. We imagine that things can be separated from their environment. And while we may move around, for example, I recently relocated from Tokyo to Los Angeles — thus exchanging the world's coolest place to live for the world's most pretentious place to live — we are always *here* wherever *here* might be. We are never truly separated from our surroundings. So when you give something a name and imagine it has a specific form, you're really only offering your brain a handy reference point to work with. The real world does not operate that way.

Reality is not a bunch of individual things sitting around on top of some other thing called the universe. There is only one continuous and undivided whole stretching on through infinite space and infinite time. Our brains carve this up into bite-sized chunks that we can manipulate. But this manipulation we do in our heads is just a very poor model of what actually happens. That's why nothing ever goes according to plan, no matter how carefully you plan it out. Every action affects the entire universe in ways both obvious and subtle that we cannot possibly work into our calculations.

After name and form come the six senses. Sense number six has nothing to do with Bruce Willis or with any of the crystals and crap they sell at your local New Age shop. In the Buddhist way of thinking our brain is considered a sense organ, the same as our eyes, ears, nose, tongue, and skin. What the brain senses is the mental sphere of reality. So sense number six here is just your ability to detect thoughts and other mental phenomena.

Next up we have contact, which refers to sensory contact. In the Buddhist view contact occurs before "coming into existence" — which is four more steps away — even happens. Now, this one really sounds stoopid. Obviously the outside world exists first, and then we sense it. Right? But that's not the way Buddhists look at it.

This is just weird, weird, weird! Or is it? We'll come back to this in a little bit. I just want to bring it to your attention now so you can keep it in mind as we go along.

Feeling is next. Once contact occurs, there is an inevitable emotional reaction. We develop some kind of attitude or feeling toward that which we see as outside ourselves. Since we believe *it* is out there while we are over here, we believe we ought to have some kind of view, some attitude or feeling toward it.

Next up is love. While it is represented in Chinese and Japanese with the character 愛, which means "love" in both languages, the Sanskrit word is *tṛṣṇa*, which is a more general word and is related to the English word *thirst*. We're talking here about a kind of desire or thirst for that which we perceive as separate from us.

In other words, in this list love and desire are considered pretty much the same thing. What gives? I mean, isn't Buddhism all about destroying desire so that we can experience love?

That's the way it's being sold in a lot of those cheesy magazines and books about Buddhism these days. But it's not really like that at all. Remember that, in the end, words are just words. *Desire* is a word, and so is *love*. The word is never the thing it indicates. Every one of us has a different definition of the word *desire*, and how many breakups occur every day over the definition of the word *love*? So the old Buddhist masters used both words to try and get a sense of what it was they were talking about.

Love, or desire, leads to taking. You try and make that which is separate from yourself "yours." This is where the mistakes really start to pile up. To Buddhists, subject and object are really two facets of the same thing. That which you desire to incorporate into yourself was never apart from you to begin with. But most of us are very much caught up in the quest to make those things we desire into our possessions. You wanted this book, for example, so you made it into your possession by snatching it off the shelf at your local Book Barn and then running out the door as fast as you could.* By reading its contents you're making them part of your mental makeup. Or so you think. The funny thing is, though — and try getting your cranium around this one because it's really worthwhile — if these ideas were not part of your mental makeup to begin with, you'd never have been able to understand them in the first place.

What you perceive as words written on this page are just funny shapes that trigger images that already exist in your mind. What's more, they don't necessarily trigger quite the same images in your mind as the ones that were in my mind when I wrote the words. But they're close enough that we can communicate. Ultimately, though, the ideas in this book don't come from me or from Dogen or from Buddha. They come from you — from your previous experiences with similar words, from all the things your family and your teachers and the cartoon shows and commercials on TV told you about what certain concepts mean, and so on and on.**

It works that way with everything you desire. It's already part of you, but you see it as something other. We all do. I do. I'm sure even Buddha himself was not immune to slipping into this view from time to time. Of course, you can say that it's observably provable that Lucy Liu is not me, and therefore it makes perfect sense that I would desire for her to sit on my lap. Yet, on a deeper level, inaccessible to our usual senses, Lucy is me, and I am Lucy.† Knowing the real

---

* Okay, maybe you paid for it. I never know with the kinds of people who read books like this!

** So if you had these words already, why'd you bother stealing the book? This isn't just a joke [though I hope you didn't actually steal it]. It's a real question you might want to ponder for a while.

† And Lucy, if you're reading this, give me a call and we can get together and I'll explain it to you.

situation, even intellectually, can be a tremendous aid to understanding the difference between what is and what is not necessary in your life.

Be that as it may, taking then leads to coming into existence. Now, think about this for a second. It's what I was hinting at way back when we talked about contact. To the Buddhist way of thinking, all this stuff, everything we went through up till now — ignorance, action, consciousness, name and form, the six senses, contact, feeling, love, and taking — comes *before* coming into existence. I mean, how on earth can you *take* things and be conscious of them and have feelings about them and take action and be ignorant and all that before anything — including you — comes into existence?

Just think about how whacked-out that is! I mean, a Buddhist would say that first you sense the words on this page and then, after that, the book appears. Sounds like science fiction, doesn't it? Yet once you start to live with this idea a little, to see how things work when you look at them this way, you begin to see that it makes a whole lot more sense than the so-called commonsense view. But be careful. Buddhism is not a form of solipsism. Buddhists *do* believe in the reality of the outside world. It's not all just in your head.* Other people are real. When you stub your toe on a brick, that's a real brick, and your real toe is in real pain. Ah, but what, exactly, is pain? That's what you need to work on.

The last two links in the chain are birth, followed by aging and death.**

I see all those little lightbulbs going on over your heads. Obviously we're talking about reincarnation, you're thinking to yourselves. I mean, the whole sequence leads to birth, aging, and death and then back to ignorance again and eventually around the whole

---

*   In fact, to a Buddhist your head is part of the outside world, which is ultimately the same as the inside world.

** Or "aging, death, grief, lamentation, suffering, sorrow, and despair" for you completists and Swedish art film fans.

circle to birth and death? And there are, like, a whole bunch of steps before we even get to birth. So that must imply that there's like this cool, spiritual-type mystical realm that exists before we're even born, right? While there are plenty of writers out there who will explain it this way, I ain't one of them.

The problem is that once you get into any kind of a discussion about what happens after you die or before you were born, you've stepped out of reality and into the realm of speculation and fantasy. No two ways about it. The only people who've ever made statements about what happens after you die were people who themselves were not yet dead.

In his discussions about the twelvefold chain our buddy Mr. Dogen never brings up the idea of reincarnation. Instead, he relates all twelve links of the chain only to the present moment. He says, "While practicing these twelve causes, causing dependent origination to occur in the past, present, and future, we take causes one by one." Notice that he says we cause dependent origination — using the present tense, meaning we do this *now* — to occur in the past, present, and future. Now, maybe you can cause things to happen in the future. But how can you cause something in the past to happen now? Dogen believed in the instantaneous creation and destruction of the universe at every moment. To him these were not just things that occurred in sequence but that happened instantaneously as well.

How on earth is any reasonable person supposed to understand this? Dogen says, "Though we do not discuss a subject who reflects and an object which is reflected, we investigate them in practice." That is, although we do not believe in the existence of separated subjects and objects, we just investigate what these things we call "subject" and "object" really are in our actual practice, in our real lives. By doing so we see codependent co-origination at work. Just stay with me for a little bit here. Birth and death are not just things that happen once in each person's life; they are going on all the time. Every second of every minute of every day you are born and you die. Literally. Factually. Something goes through all those steps we just talked about, then ages and dies, and something new takes its place all the time. It's just an illusion you carry around in your head that you were born on a particular day a certain number of years ago and that you will die on a different day some time in the future. You exist now. That's it.

And speaking of birth, does everybody know what causes it? No, not the stork or the cabbage patch. It's sex. So even though Dogen cautioned us not to, let's talk about it a little.

Chapter 14

Sex and Sin

In the old days Zero Defects was known as a straight-edge band. Straight edge was a philosophical movement within punk started by Ian MacKaye of the Washington DC hardcore band Minor Threat. MacKaye says he didn't really intend for straight edge to become a philosophical movement. It was just his personal credo. But it was a good one, so lots of other folks adopted it. Straight-edgers did not drink, smoke, or do drugs. Some straight-edgers took it one step further and gave up sex as well. The idea was to get rid of the stuff that clouded your mind so you'd be able to focus on real life. A great idea.

Although Zero Defects was viewed as a straight-edge group, we really weren't, nor did we claim to be. The fact that we had a song denouncing drug abuse and that we sounded a lot like the DC straight-edge bands led folks to assume we were part of that movement. I, for one, really admired the straight-edge thing. And while I was a member of Zero Defects, I didn't drink or use drugs, and I've never smoked. As for the giving up sex thing, though, I wasn't really interested in taking it that far. Not that it mattered much. Zero Defects was not exactly the kind of band the girls threw their panties at. So, in the end, I usually had no trouble keeping all the rules of straight edge without really trying.

Since I've started speaking and writing about Buddhism, I've found that lots of people want to know about the Buddhist views on sex. It's difficult for me to say anything about the overall, worldwide view of everyone who calls him- or herself a Buddhist regarding the matter of sex. But I'll say what little I can here.

The first thing you gotta know is that in Buddhism there's no such thing as sin.

The most overt expression of this fact I know of is the Japanese attitude toward sex. A quick trip to any well-stocked Tokyo bookstore or video shop will bring this attitude graphically into view. Magazines full of pictures of nekkid ladies flash their lurid covers right there on the lowest shelves where kiddies browse. Bondage fetishists the world over know the most explicit S and M porn comes from the Land of the Rising Sun and the high-rise leather boot. One of Japan's funniest cartoon shows — *Crayon Shinchan* — features a five-year-old boy who's constantly trying to look up ladies' dresses or make awkward passes at his mother's cute friends. This isn't some ironic postmodern late-night cable show for adults, either; it runs in the early evening — prime children's viewing hours in Japan. It's now on TV in America too. But, tellingly, they show it way late at night when its main Japanese audience — little kids — is in bed.

All this because sex, in Buddhist Japan, has never been considered sinful.

For people from countries where we take it for granted that there really is such a thing as sin and that most sins involve s-e-x, the Buddhist-informed Japanese attitude toward sex can be really hard to grasp.* But the Buddhist attitude toward sex has nothing to do with any notion of sin and everything to do with following the Middle Way in all our activities.

---

* Heh-heh, I said "hard to grasp"!

People often misunderstand this idea of the Middle Way, thinking that the point of Buddhism is the utter destruction of all desire, including the desire to get one's rocks off. But you can't live without the desire to breathe and eat. And the human race couldn't survive if we did away with the desire for sex. Not that some people don't try their darnedest anyway.

In the *Shobogenzo* chapter titled "Prostrating to the Attainment of the Marrow," or 礼拝得髄, pronounced *raihai tokuzui*, Dogen gives us his take on this kind of thinking when he challenges the runaway sexism of many of his contemporary Buddhists. "Nowadays," he says, "extremely stupid people look at women without having corrected the prejudice that women are objects of sexual greed. Disciples of the Buddha must not be like this. If whatever may become the object of sexual greed is to be hated, do not all men deserve to be hated too?" The fact is that absolutely anything can become an object of desire. When I worked for the Summit County Board of Mental Retardation, there was a fellow there around whom you couldn't leave your shoes unattended lest you return to find a sticky present in them. God only knows how he came to believe shoes were the most sexually attractive thing in the world. But it takes all kinds.

Buddhism doesn't ask us to deny our natural desires. But it does ask us to regulate how we respond to them. And so there is a fundamental Buddhist precept against the misuse of sexuality.

In some forms of Buddhism there are explicit definitions of what exactly counts as "misuse of sexuality." For example, the *vinayas* — ancient rules for moral conduct among Buddhist monks and nuns — say that for celibate monks "intentional emission of semen, except during a dream, is an offense requiring a formal meeting of the Sangha [the order of monks]." The same rules state that it isn't a violation of a monk's vow of celibacy if he is asleep and therefore does not know that a woman is having sex with him.* In contrast to those

---

* I wonder if anyone ever actually tried to use this lame-ass excuse?

forms of Buddhism, the Japanese Zen tradition leaves the matter deliberately vague. In fact, Zen monks in Japan are free to marry or to conduct themselves in pretty much any manner they choose as regards sexuality, so long as their conduct doesn't cause too much trouble.

The Japanese Zen attitude toward sex gets a fair amount of criticism from Buddhists in other countries, though. A Taiwanese woman I know who learned I'd become a monk* after getting married said that my monk's status and newly shaved head were "just for show," like all Japanese monks, who she viewed as similarly degraded.

The origin of the tradition of married Japanese monks** goes back to the Meiji Restoration of the late nineteenth century. It was one of several measures enacted by the Japanese government to try and curb the political power of the Buddhist clergy.

What's allowing monks to marry got to do with curbing their political power? Quite a bit, actually. Celibacy tended to make monks seem slightly superhuman, perhaps possessed of powers above and beyond those of ordinary — married — people, including members of the government. Allowing monks to marry effectively humanized them, robbing them of some of their apparent holiness. As the Taiwanese lady I spoke to can certainly attest, many of us want to keep our holy men and women as holy as possible. We don't like our monks human.

Be that as it may, even the *vinayas*' regulations regarding the celibacy of monks don't classify any of these "offenses" as sinful in the Western sense of the word. They are not acts that go against the Will of God or of Buddha, nor are they applied to the population in general. A monk, by definition, is someone who has agreed to abide

---

* I tend to use the words *monk* and *priest* interchangeably. In Zen they aren't two different things as they are in the Catholic tradition.

** And nuns too, but I don't feel like writing "monks and nuns" over and over again. Those of you who can't stand this omission are free to pencil in the missing words. To me monks can be either male or female. So there!

by a certain set of regulations, just like members of the local Elks Club agree to wear those goofy hats. Showing up at the Elks meeting without your hat means you risk being kicked out of the club. Violating the precepts regarding sexual conduct means you risk getting kicked out of the Buddhist monks club.* Nothing more.

Even Japanese-style Zen Buddhists with their comparatively lax attitude on the matter do acknowledge, though, the obvious fact that sex itself is a thorny issue for human beings. Dogen didn't have a whole lot to say on the subject aside from the bit I quoted above. It's quite possible that he never had sex in his entire life, given the fact that he became a monk at age twelve in an era when Japanese Buddhist monks were traditionally celibate. We'll never know for certain either way. But given his character, I tend to believe he may very well have never gotten it on with anyone.

A very early piece by Dogen may reveal the origins of his attitudes toward sex as well as shed some light on how Buddhists look at sexual morality in particular and morality itself in general. It's called *Hokyo-ki*, 宝慶記, which literally means "Record of the Baoqing Era," referring to the Chinese designation of the time he spent in China (it's better known in English as *Journal of My Study in China*). This is a series of notes Dogen wrote while in China studying under his teacher Tendo Nyojo. Here he cites a list of proscriptions laid out by Nyojo for students first starting to study Buddhism:

Don't read or chant too much.

Don't overwork.

Don't eat onions.

Don't eat meat.

Don't drink too much milk.

Don't drink alcohol.

---

* Not the Buddhist club altogether, mind you, just the monk division.

Don't eat too many olives.

Don't eat fungi.

Don't listen to singing or music.

Don't watch dancing women.

Don't look at pornography or talk about sex.

Don't take medicines for mental diseases.

Don't pay attention to matters of fame and fortune.

Don't be associated with eunuchs or hermaphrodites.

Don't have too much candy.

Don't pay attention to loud noises.

Don't watch herds of pigs or sheep.

Don't stare at the ocean, bad pictures, hunchbacks, or puppets.

Always have clean feet.

Don't view big fish.

So if you want to be a good Buddhist, be sure to avert your eyes whenever you see a Sea World billboard with Shamu on it. I'm joking. Okay? I gotta be careful 'cuz I know there really are books out there that make absurd statements about what people of a certain religion should or should not look at.*

Reading this list, you get an idea just how different society was in those days. Like the thing about not eating olives. Even today, when you order a sandwich at Subway in Japan, they actually count the number of olives they put on so as to conserve them because they're very expensive. In Dogen's day they must have been extremely precious. So it's a bit like if a modern teacher advised you not to eat too much caviar or too many truffles. What's important here

---

* By the way, I know Shamu is a mammal, not a fish. It's a joke, fer cryin' out loud!

is to try and get a feel* for the general principles Tendo Nyojo is getting at here rather than dwelling on the specifics of what he says we should or should not do.

In contrast to Tendo Nyojo's specific concrete recommendations, most of our religions tend to encourage adherents to achieve various abstract ideals of sexual purity. While the idea of purity sounds good, the problem is that purity itself only exists in our minds. Nature knows no such thing. A purebred dog is a dog whose characteristics fit those determined by its masters. Left to their own devices, any "purebreds" will produce standard-issue medium-sized brown mongrel dogs in just a few generations. Purified water doesn't come out of any lake, river, or mountain spring. It's produced by humans who decide what should and should not be in those little plastic bottles. All examples of purity are the manifestations of some kind of synthetic ideal.

In fact, ideals are always matters of the human mind. And in the pure world we create in our mind, unsullied as it is by messy things like bodies with wee-wees and pee-pees attached, there is no sex.** So the divine beings we create in our heads should not boink. But do our ideals actually exist outside that lump of gray meat between our ears? When we project our expectations about what a Divine Being ought to be onto real people, what else can we hope for but bitter disappointment? The religious fantasy of sexual purity just replaces society's extreme views, which alternately commercialize and trivialize the matter of sexuality or turn it into something rarified and mystical with another set of equally extreme views of its wickedness and sinful nature. The real problem — the fact that we permit ourselves to act so extremely with regard to anything at all — remains unaddressed. To view sex as a vile act that the pure of heart dare not even dream of is, in its own way, just as unbalanced as spending all

---

* Heh-heh, I said "get a feel"!

** Well, okay, sometimes there's plenty of sex in our minds, but I think you know what I'm getting at.

your time, energy, and cash trying to get some hot man-meat or some tender nookie.*

To practice the Middle Way means to apply that view to all your desires. You can't establish real balance if you hold certain desires apart and say it's okay to go to extremes as long as those extreme actions are in the service of eradicating sexual desire. Constantly moving from one extreme to the other is what got your brain and body into the mess they're in right now. How can you expect to get at the root cause of your troubles by doing the very thing that caused them in the first place?

There's a big difference between not being a total sex freak and trying to live your life as a sexless robot. The Middle Way lies between these two extremes. The best thing to do is to deal with the sexual desires you have in the most reasonable way you can.

Because while sex isn't sinful as far as Buddhism is concerned, it is obvious to anyone who pays any attention to his or her life that improper sexual behavior can cause a mountain of trouble for oneself and others. One way to get around these problems is to do what Dogen did and simply refrain from sexual relations altogether. My own teacher gave up doing the dirty deed in his mid-fifties, but when asked if he could have done so earlier in his life, he replied, "Let me tell you clearly: that would have been absolutely impossible." Most Zen teachers I know of caution against attempting to practice total abstinence from sex since such a practice often ends up making people even more sex crazed.**

The next-best option for those who wish to refrain from abusing sex is having a long-term, faithful, monogamous relationship. Yeah, I know, that sounds really boring. But, as usual, the most boring option is usually the best one. Let me tell you why I think so.

The sixties and seventies, when Buddhism was first starting to catch on in a big way in the West, was also a time of great sexual freedom. Which may be why some of the earliest Buddhist establishments

---

* Or both if you're so inclined.
** No comment here about the often staggering levels of violence in those cultures in which sexuality is most highly repressed.

in America had so many sex scandals. The notion of free love, though it might look really good on paper — especially if that paper is the glossy center pages of *Penthouse* magazine — is far too idealistic and one-sided. As with all idealistic notions, it can work out very nicely in the realm of thought and art, but reality is quite another matter. It's easy to convince yourself that you and Ned and Edwina and Lucy and her sister Debra are all reasonable, responsible adults — modern in your thinking, clean of habit, and so on — and that if you all decided to start having an open sexual relationship, pairing, tripling, quadrupling, and quintupling as the urge strikes you,* it ought to work out just fine and dandy. But would it really?

The early-eighties punk rock scene I was part of in Akron emerged before AIDS started to be a big issue and before the sexual revolution of the seventies had quite wound down. So lots of people I knew in those days were experimenting with interesting sexual relationships. Envious as I often was, as far as I could see this practice drove all of them nuts. I'm sure the sex itself was fun, at least sometimes, but it led to all kinds of interpersonal weirdness that could make the atmosphere extremely uncomfortable at times when large groups got together. And, in fact, some of the people involved in these various groupings would tell me that, really, even the sex itself hadn't been as much fun as they'd imagined it would be. Real life rarely works out quite like the stuff they show you on the Playboy channel. In the end most of these folks found it far more pleasant to avoid all the nutty stuff and stick with one person.

Now, having said that a faithful, monogamous relationship is probably the best way short of celibacy to avoid misusing sex and causing lots of trouble for yourself and others, I don't want to step into the minefield that is the American obsession with finding the perfect relationship. For some reason I tend to get a lot of questions about how to find the perfect mate, as if a guy who writes books about Zen ought to be able to give advice about such things. The whole idea that

---

* They call it "polyamory" these days, but it used to be called "sleeping around."

we must all find that perfect, special someone, our "soul mate" or whatever the vogue term is now, is just another way we have of making up "if only" fantasies. You sit there and think, "If only I could find the perfect man/woman/stuffed antelope,* then I'd be happy," which gives you the perfect excuse to mope around and miss out on all the real joy your life is offering you right this minute.

Part of the Zen way is learning to enjoy the fact that you cannot possibly have all the things you desire. In the truest sense none of your desires, no matter what they are, can ever be fulfilled because nothing will ever be the way you imagine it to be. The trick here is to give up imagining how things are gonna be. Or, at the very least, to give up believing that the way you imagine things are going to be has anything to do with the way they really will be.

The fact that real life and fantasies are never the same isn't true just for sex. It's true about everything in life. Whatever your dreams are, erotic or not, if you manage to realize them, you'll discover the reality isn't anything like what you'd imagined. Some people find it frustrating to know that they'll never get it on with all the Dallas Cowboy cheerleaders at one time — or all the Dallas Cowboys at one time, or a mixture of both, take your pick. But you're probably better off not being able to live out your favorite fantasies because that way you'll never suffer the disappointment of finding out how thoroughly unlike your fantasy the real thing would turn out to be.

So no matter what kinky things you get up to in the bedroom, or the kitchen, or the local hockey arena, no Buddhist will consider you sinful. To a Buddhist these things are a waste of time at worst. But there's the rub.** As far as Buddhism is concerned, wasting time is the most heinous — sinful, even — thing a person can do.

Now, good sex and the perfect soul mate are things that we usually imagine will give us perfect happiness. So let's look a little bit at this whole notion of happiness, shall we?

---

* Different strokes, y'know.
** Heh-heh, I said "rub"!

Chapter 15

The Futile Pursuit
of Happiness?

I'm proud to say that the Zero Defects set at Square Records was one of the all-time great moments in the history of hardcore. We pummeled that audience into submission just like in the old days. You shoulda been there. The shop is just around the corner from drummer Mickey X-Nelson's house, where I was staying and where we'd been rehearsing. We just had to lug our stuff around the corner to the store and plug in and play. Of course, that was easier said than done, seeing as how there were a couple of inches of ice and snow on the ground. But we got it together pretty quickly, and off we went.

It was a whole different atmosphere playing in Akron as opposed to playing in Cleveland. Even though Cleveland is only thirty miles away, it still doesn't feel like home. Doing shows anywhere in Akron, to me, is always like doing a show in my own living room. My bass came unplugged during "Where Are the Kids Tonight?" But it was fine. We were playing to a very forgiving crowd.

The whole thing was a really happy experience. Like I said earlier, even though hardcore punk is supposed to be "angry music," it always made me really happy to hear and especially to play. I was happy to see those guys again, happy to be playing again, happy to be alive. I was a pretty happy guy the whole weekend.

Happiness is an interesting phenomenon. A guy who read my first book* sent me an article he found in the September 7, 2003, issue of the *New York Times*. It's by Jon Gertner, and it's titled "The Futile Pursuit of Happiness." The article's about a guy named Daniel Gilbert, a professor in Harvard's department of psychology. Gilbert, along with his pals psychologist Tim Wilson of the University of Virginia, economist George Loewenstein of Carnegie Mellon, and Daniel Kahneman, a psychologist and Nobel laureate in economics, get their happiness by studying happiness. This group has developed some interesting ideas about happiness, some of which confirm what Buddhists have been saying about the subject for a couple thousand years. While I'm not sure Gilbert and friends have quite the right take on the problem, it's really gratifying to see scientists take any kind of interest in this sort of thing. It's a terribly important matter that human beings have rarely looked into very deeply.

The studies these gentlemen conducted basically involved finding out how people anticipated they would feel if certain events happened, then interviewing them afterward to see how they really felt. Mostly they did this in the form of controlled laboratory studies using situations deliberately devised by the researchers. They also did some field studies based on real events in people's actual, non-laboratory-controlled lives. According to the article, "Gilbert found that we overestimate the intensity and the duration of our emotional reactions — our 'affect' — to future events." In other words, when anticipating something that might happen to us in the future, we tend to think those things are going to be either much better or much worse than they usually turn out to be.

"The average person says, 'I know I'll be happier with a Porsche than a Chevy,'" Gilbert explains. "'Or with Linda rather than

---

*   Rick Matz; thanks, Rick.

Rosalyn. Or as a doctor rather than as a plumber.' The problem is, I can't get into medical school or afford the Porsche. So for the average person, the obstacle between them and happiness is actually getting the futures that they desire."

Gilbert comes close to the Buddhist view right there, but he still misses the real point. As a Buddhist I would say that the obstacle between us and happiness is the *future itself*. In other words, the real obstacle to our happiness is the way we place our notions of the future and our notions of the past between us and what we are actually living through right at this very moment. This moment sitting here in my Chevy is dull and ordinary, we think, but maybe someday I'll have a Porsche and that'll be really rad! But what happens when we get that Porsche? What I've discovered in my own life is that no matter how thoroughly I satisfy any of my desires, they never stay satisfied very long. Just like in the lyrics to "Hell Hole" by Spinal Tap:

> The window's dirty the mattress stinks
> This ain't no place to be a man
> Ain't got no future, ain't got no past
> And I don't think I ever can
> The floor is filthy the walls are thin
> The wind is howling in my face
> The rats are peeling, I'm losing ground
> Can't seem to join the human race.
>
> Chorus:
> Yeah, I'm living in a hell hole
> Don't want to stay in this hell hole
> Don't want to die in this hell hole
> Girl, get me out of this hell hole.
>
> I rode the jet stream, I hit the top
> I'm eating steak and lobster tails

The sauna's drafty, the pool's too hot
The kitchen stinks of boiling snails.
The taxman's coming, the butler quit
This ain't no place to be a man
I'm going back to where I started
I'm flashing back into my pan.

Chorus:
It's better in a hell hole
You know where you stand in a hell hole
Folks lend a hand in a hell hole
Girl, get me back to my hell hole.

It seems that no matter what we're doing right now, it's never the thing we really want. The thing we really want is always somewhere off in the future, when we finally get rich, or get laid, or get enlightened.* Or else it's buried in our past, the first time you kissed Billy-Bob Rubinowitz under the bleachers at the high school stadium, or the first time you got all the way to the center of a Tootsie Pop without biting, or maybe that time a few years ago when you thought you'd gotten enlightened — why can't you get *that* feeling back? Whatever thing we use to define happiness for ourselves always seems far away. So we look at people we envy and say to ourselves that if only we had what they have, we'd be happy.

But just think about those moments in the past that you classify as truly happy. What's the difference between those moments and this one right now? Could it be that that day you kissed Billy-Bob under the bleachers was a rare moment when you were fully present, staying just with what was happening right at that very moment?

---

* What I really want right now is to have this book published instead of having to sit here writing the stupid thing. But wait! That's what I said when I was writing my first book!

You weren't worried about the past. You weren't thinking about the future. You weren't thinking about anything at all. You were just totally and completely *there*. Billy-Bob's lips on yours, his tongue gently sliding against your retainer...I'll shut up now.

Yet, most of the time, even when we find ourselves living through moments we consider truly happy, there's always that nagging feeling in the back of our minds that sometime — in the future, of course — this happiness is going to end and things will be dull and ordinary again.

Gilbert's fellow researcher Loewenstein gets a little closer to the heart of the problem when he says, "Happiness is a signal that our brains use to motivate us to do certain things. And in the same way that our eye adapts to different levels of illumination, we're designed to kind of go back to the happiness set point. Our brains are not trying to be happy. Our brains are trying to regulate us."

There's a lot to be said for this idea. But I still think they're sailing right past the real point. Most of us tend to divide our lives into these big peak moments of enormous happiness or horrendous sorrow on the one side, and everything else in between those moments, which we consider to be mundane, boring, and unimportant, on the other. In doing so, we miss out on almost our entire lives. If our brains are trying to regulate us, as Loewenstein, I think, quite rightly assumes, then is it those big experiences of intense happiness that we really want? Are those peak moments what really make us happy?

Buddhist teachers, from Gautama himself on down, have always talked about balance, about following the Middle Way between extremes of any kind, including extremes of happiness and sadness. Most of your life is just like *this*, meaning it's neither very happy nor very sad. But we're forever running away from that middle ground and trying to liven things up by finding stuff that will excite us, stir us up. And then when we do try to meditate a little bit, we have a really tough time settling our minds. Now, why is that...?

Moving right along, researcher Tim Wilson says, "We don't

realize how quickly we will adapt to a pleasurable event and make it the backdrop of our lives. When any event occurs to us, we make it ordinary. And through becoming ordinary, we lose our pleasure." Now we're talking! No matter what happens to us, the very fact that it has happened to us transforms whatever it is into part of what we consider "mundane" or "ordinary." No matter if it's bungee jumping into the Grand Canyon or getting it on with Miss November, Miss August, and Miss January all at the same time, once you've done it, it gets filed in your brain under "been there, done that."

This is very important to notice. When you were a child, every single thing that happened in your life was supercool. Kids get all excited by things like rubbing their toes in dirt or filling up an old McDonald's® cup with water from a mud puddle. I have a very old memory of being a tiny little kid and pouring a glass of Kool-Aid® on my corduroy pants. I was absolutely riveted by watching the colored liquid soak into the fabric, reveling in the incredible sensation of the cold cloth beginning to adhere to my skin. I'm sure that later on I was also absolutely enthralled by the sensation of having my mom scream her head off at me, although for some reason I don't recall that. When we become grown-ups we lose this attitude. It's very sad. And it's one of the things that Buddhist practice aims to cure. Sit in zazen enough, and you begin to relearn how to notice the fascinating sensations that make up your ordinary life.

Okay, then, you're probably thinking, maybe our ordinary lives might be cooler than we imagine. But what about the things that we know for certain will make us super-duper happy — like suddenly getting a bazillion dollars in the mail from Ed McMahon? "A large body of research on well-being seems to suggest that wealth above middle-class comfort makes little difference to our happiness," the article states. It's not hard to believe when you take a look at some of our big celebrities. Britney and Brad and Lindsay and Tom have amassed more money, fame, and power than anyone could possibly expend in a dozen lifetimes, yet are they really any happier for it? It doesn't seem like it, if even a tenth of the stories in the gossip rags are even partially true. In my own case, the slight jump in income and fame I've experienced as a result of having a book published has been a pain in the ass as much as it's been a source of happiness. Just as our theoreticians might have predicted, I've found myself in pretty much the same condition as before.*

Okay, then, what about horrible, awful, life-altering tragedies? If we can't predict what's going to make us happy, we must at least be able to predict the things that are going to make us sad. But Gilbert found that most folks can adapt even to circumstances they've predicted would surely ruin their lives forever, the loss of a job or a close loved one, even the horrors of a terminal disease. This, he believes, is the result of what he calls our "emotional defense mechanisms" coming into play. But I don't think so.

I think it has more to do with our natural tendency to seek the balanced state. Our body/minds don't like to be thrown into states of high distress, whether we characterize that distress as "tragedy" or as "happiness." This is also, by the way, why so-called mystics who enter into what they like to call states of "bliss" or "transcendence" or what-have-you never stay there for very long and why so-called enlightenment experiences are always over almost as soon as they begin. Whether it's the extremes of happiness or sadness or the extremes of spiritual bliss, we don't like to dwell in extreme conditions. We always want to come back to less extreme, more balanced, and ordinary states.

Dogen addresses this throughout *Shobogenzo*, particularly in chapter 64, 家常, pronounced *kajo* and meaning "Everyday Life." The two Chinese characters in the title mean "home" and "usual." So what he's talking about here is the ordinariest of the ordinary.

---

* Although, just for the record, I still haven't experienced wealth above the middle class. You don't get rich writing Zen books or working for a company that makes cheeseball sci-fi movies.

In this chapter he quotes Great Master Musai, who expressed his enlightened state saying, "Having finished a meal, I calmly look forward to a nap." And then he quotes Zen Master Enchi Dai-an, who summed up the accomplishments of his life as a Buddhist master saying: "I lived on Isan mountain for thirty years, eating Isan meals, shitting Isan shit."

Dogen gives several similar examples and then ends the chapter with a joke.* A Zen master asks a newly arrived monk, "Have you ever been here before?"

The monk says, "Yep, I have."

The master says, "Have some tea."

Later he asks another monk, "Have you ever been here before?"

The monk says, "Nope, never before."

The master says, "Have some tea."

The chief of the temple office asks the master, "Why'd you say, 'Have some tea' to the monk who has been here before and also say, 'Have some tea' to the monk who has never been here before?"

The master says, "Hey, chief."

The chief answers, "What?"

The master says, "Have some tea."

Dogen explains this joke — the surest way to kill any joke — in a typically idiosyncratic way. He says, "*Here* is beyond the brain, is beyond the nostrils. Because it springs free from 'here,' it has already arrived here and it has never been here before."

Remember the master asked the monks if they'd ever been here before. Here, this place where we really exist right now, is eternally free from the concepts we carry around in our heads about "here." What we're really living through and what we think we're living through are two completely different things. Dogen goes on: "This place is the place where the ineffable exists, but they discuss it only

---

* Not a joke that's gonna get him called back for a return engagement on Letterman anytime soon, but a joke nonetheless.

as having already arrived and never having been before." We miss out on the amazingness of where we are right now by comparing it with the past and trying to determine whether we've done this thing before or not. But even if we've done whatever it is we happen to be doing wherever it is we happen to be doing it a hundred thousand times before, something is always different.

Have *you* ever been here before? Maybe you've ridden this bus a hundred times. Maybe, if you're really starved for entertainment, you've read this book three times already. But does that mean you've been *here* before?

Our researchers seem right on the verge of getting this point. But somehow they let it slip completely through their fingers like a handful of warm Cheez Whiz®. They then proceed to draw some conclusions about their research, which Buddhism would not support. "The benefits of not making this error [in judging how happy we would be if we get what we want or how unhappy we'll be if we don't]," Gilbert says, "would seem to be that you get a little more happiness." Okay, says I, go on.

"When choosing between two jobs, you wouldn't sweat as much because you'd say: 'You know, I'll be happy in both. I'll adapt to either circumstance pretty well, so there's no use in killing myself for the next week.'" So far so good. But then Gilbert concludes, "But maybe our caricatures of the future — these overinflated assessments of how good or bad things will be — maybe it's these illusory assessments that keep us moving in one direction over the other. Maybe we don't want a society of people who shrug and say, 'It won't really make a difference.'"

But is that what we'd have if we gave up our overinflated assessments of the future? I doubt it. It seems to me it's only when you give up wrong notions of what will or won't make you happy that you can really experience each moment as it is. And, contrary to what you might think, this does not lead to a lack of motivation, to a state of just passively hanging out like a tree sloth and letting whatever happens happen. It certainly hasn't been that way for my Zen teacher. Now in his mid-eighties he's still writing books, still working a regular day job, still jetting off to Chile and Israel to talk about Buddhism, and still leading the ragtag group of students — including imbeciles like me — who stop by at his dojo. He has no plans to retire either. He'll just keep on doing until he can't do no more. I'm certain one day, probably many more years from now than anyone expects, he'll just keel right over on his cushion while leading some Zen retreat somewhere. For me, I certainly don't feel like I need the lure of future happiness to do any of the things I do — or you wouldn't be reading this book right now.

It's actually quite the opposite of what Gilbert expects. On the one hand, Gilbert's right in that after studying and practicing Zen for a few years and discovering that your future's not going to be either very much more brilliant and wonderful than it is right now or very much more horrible either, you don't sweat it. But you don't give up either. Gilbert seems to assume that the only reason you make any effort is that you anticipate the rewards that effort will bring later on. But ask any artist or athlete, and they'll tell you that it isn't the results of their efforts they crave so much as the enjoyment of actually doing whatever it is they do best. What if we could apply that attitude to the whole of our lives?

Activities like sports or art or even s-e-x can lead to something like the Buddhist state of balance. But what makes zazen even better than those things is that the practice forces you to zoom right in on the dullest, most tedious situation you could possibly face. It teaches you how to find the beauty in a state you normally regard as not even worth noticing. Once you've managed this, the ability to enjoy everything else in your life follows naturally.*

---

* This is why I'm dead set against nominally "Buddhist" practices that take away from noticing what's here and now in favor of trying to induce some kind of special, "enlightened" state. That's a buncha BS, if you ask me.

If you can adapt this philosophy to everything you do, you don't end up giving up on life and doing nothing. Far from it. Rather, you end up free from the pervasive worry and fear that have always kept you from doing the things you really want to do.* In fact, it's only that part of you that is already free from fear, worry, and anticipation about the future — which is already in the Buddhist state — that can truly act and accomplish anything at all worthwhile.

Real happiness comes when you are truly living this moment, no matter what it is. It's not the least bit futile to pursue this kind of happiness. In fact it's your sacred duty as a human being.

---

* Ah, but be careful, 'cuz what you *think* you want to do and what you really want to do most often turn out to be quite different.

Chapter 16

The Day They Shot a Hole in the Jesus Egg

I'm on an airplane on my way back to Los Angeles after five days in Ohio with Zero Defects. In a very real way the experience resembled a Zen retreat. Those five days were very much an intensive and concentrated experience. I worked, ate, slept, and breathed the Zero Defects life for five straight days. It only occurred to me yesterday that I had not seen a TV set the entire time I was there, save for the one used at the place where I did my book signing to show videos of some of Ohio's legendary punk bands. I've never even been to a Zen retreat where there were no TVs — granted, those who were participating in the retreats themselves weren't watching, just the cooks and the monks who lived at the temples.

All of us involved knew that the only way to make this thing work was to really concentrate on what we were doing. We had to have tremendous faith and belief in Zero Defects, or nothing was gonna get done. And, as I said, just to make it more of a matter of faith for me, I had set myself the task of thoroughly documenting the event on video. So every moment that I didn't spend playing I spent either interviewing people, arranging to interview people, or

— unfortunately — dealing with video equipment disasters of my own making.

One of the things a lot of the interviewees talked about was the faith we all had in the community that existed in the hardcore scene back then. It was very clear that the only way to make the scene work was through real cooperation.

A lot of other hardcore scenes were characterized by violence. But not ours. For example, there was a rule at the shows we set up that people who wore spikes were not allowed to slam dance. Spiked wristbands and collars were, of course, a major part of punk fashion, as was full-contact slam dancing in which people careened about the dance floor like whirling dervishes and smashed into each other like dodgem cars. Jimi Imij and Vince Rancid, who more or less ran the shows in those days, would police the audience for people wearing spikes and make these folks take them off before allowing them on the dance floor. Some people protested; apparently one guy had to be held down on the ground and forced to remove his wristband. But most of us were glad to comply.

Although the scene ended, its ideals have been retained by most of those who participated. That's not to say there haven't been some bad moments in the lives of those people. I've heard stories of alcoholism and even one of death as a result of a severe heroin addiction. Bad things did happen. I think most of us realized that the bad things that went on occurred mainly when we gave up our faith.

But faith is just one side of the coin. The other is doubt. Tim liked to say that to practice Zen, you need equal amounts of doubt and faith. It took me a long time to understand what he meant by that. But nowadays I've adopted the slogan. Faith keeps you going, but doubt keeps you from going off the deep end.

Faith and belief are tricky subjects, though. So let's talk about the problem of faith and belief and how it ties in with Dogen's philosophy.

In the liner notes to the CD *The Day They Shot a Hole in the Jesus Egg*, by the Flaming Lips, the Lips's leader, Wayne Coyne, says, "The desire to believe is so instinctual and so pleasurable that for most people it is never challenged. But [when I was younger] I had challenged it and decided to side with science." This is a problem just about any philosophically minded person faces in the twenty-first century. As much as we might want to believe in our religions and faiths, we find it impossible to accept them, knowing as we do that science works and makes sense.

But, Wayne says, as he got older, his desire for religion grew. "The temptation to retreat into a world of angels and demons intensifies as one experiences the meaninglessness and evil of reality. The more one understands reality, the more one is comforted by this ingenious fabrication [of religion].

"I was resigned to believe only in 'the real,' but I longed to be immersed in the 'Guiding Light.'"

Wayne makes perfect sense here. This is the reason that you'll often find extremely smart people joining some of the flakiest cults around. Even though we know there are rational explanations for pretty much every phenomenon in the universe, rational explanations alone make us feel cold and alienated. The trouble for us in the twenty-first century is that we have all these high-definition liquid-crystal plasma TV sets, satellite radios, laptops, and other technology surrounding us all the time, proclaiming loudly and unmistakably that science works, that materialistic philosophy makes sense. It takes a hell of a lot of effort to try and pretend you don't believe in science.

I say "try and pretend" because I do not believe it is possible anymore not to believe in science. TVs work, radios work, computers work, all the things surrounding us that have been created by applying scientific principles to the real world work. To say that science is somehow wrong in the face of all that is absurd. We've seen already how crazy this makes certain people, what with death-and-doom apocalyptic cults all over the world trying to use the very things that science has provided them with — like jet airplanes, for example — to somehow demonstrate that so-called spiritual philosophies denying the validity of science really do have all the answers. Fortunately, not too many people find such demonstrations convincing.

What makes us crazy is that we tend to see it as an either-or situation. Either science is correct, or spirituality is correct. We cannot find any middle ground.

But Buddhist philosophy rejects both pure science and pure spirituality. One contemporary Zen master, Joshu Sasaki, likes to tell his students,* "There is no God, and he is your creator." This isn't just an absurd Dada-esque statement or some bit of funny-sounding nonsense either. It's the real truth of the situation as far as Buddhism is concerned. Reality includes both the spiritual and the material, yet it transcends both.

Coyne defines the word *reality* the same way most citizens of twenty-first-century Earth tend to. Because we believe so strongly in materialistic philosophy, the word *reality*, for most of us, means the material world as explained to us by science. But to Buddhists the material world is a kind of illusion.

Now, be very careful here. There are any number of religious philosophies out there based on the notion that the material world is an illusion and that therefore the real world is somewhere else. We may experience this other truer reality, they say, after we die, or maybe we can touch it when we're deep in some meditative trance. Or else they tell us we'll get to glimpse it during so-called enlightenment experiences, which momentarily rip us out of the mundane material world and send us zipping off to some fantastic, way-out other world far more real than this one. Then when we come back from that psychedelic Wonderland, we can tell everybody how we've visited "reality" and come back here to tell the tale. If you're really convincing, you might even be able to attract busloads of followers who'll accept your story and give you lots of money to pursue your fantasy. Nice work if you can get it, I suppose. But I've never been

---

* Who include Leonard Cohen, of all people.

all that interested in "realities" that didn't include the world I have to deal with every day.*

The difference between those philosophies and Buddhism is that while Buddhism says the material world is an illusion, it does not then go on to postulate that there is some other world somewhere else that is somehow more real than this one. This is an extremely important point.

But how can this view possibly make sense? If this material world we live in is an illusion, then reality *must* be somewhere else, right?

At the risk of refuting both Madonna and George Harrison, the Buddhist view is that we are not living in the material world. When we say the "material world" we are referring not to reality itself but to a set of assumptions we have about reality. What we call the "material world" is actually just a particular representation of reality that we carry around in our heads. A great many of our assumptions have been proven true by science. The assumption that water freezes at 32 degrees Fahrenheit,** for example, is absolutely undeniable. The assumption that if you stick your hand in a blender while it's set on puree, you're probably going to regret it does not require further testing.

We carry bucket loads of these assumptions around in our minds at all times. We've learned them in school, through observation, through admonitions by our parents not to play hopscotch on the highway. The sum total of all these assumptions is a thing we like to call the "material world." And for most of us, just like for Wayne Coyne, this material world is synonymous with reality. No need to

---

* The other day I watched some guy from an Indian religious sect lecture about the "spiritual world." According to him it's a place where grass and trees and flowers can talk, among other things. Sounds like something from a cartoon. I like cartoons fine. When they're cartoons. I'm not interested in pretending they're real.

** Or 0 degrees Celsius, if you want. I know it's a more sensible system. But in eleven years of living in Japan I still couldn't get my head around the idea that when someone said it was 30 degrees outside, that meant it was a hot day.

even ask why this is so. It's reality because it's obviously real. We divide reality into two parts we can call body and mind, or material and spiritual, or reality and fantasy. The fantasy of a sledgehammer can't squash your fingers, but a real sledgehammer can. Real sledgehammers are made of matter; imaginary sledgehammers are not. Matter is real. So reality must be matter. It's a total no-brainer. And if matter is real, then anything not made of matter must be unreal. Argument settled.

But can we really say that only matter is real, and mind is not? Have you ever experienced one and not the other? To a Buddhist the material world, true as it may be, is, at best, just one quarter of the true picture.

One of the big reasons some people find Buddhism depressing or even nihilistic is that they equate the Buddhist use of the word *reality* with the scientific understanding of that word. Science tells us, for example, that consciousness is nothing more than electrical impulses bouncing around in that three-pound (1,400-gram) lump of meat you carry around in your skull.

According to Buddhism the scientists who say this are perfectly correct. What we call "consciousness" is just electrical impulses bouncing around in that lump of meat in our skulls. Nothing more. But Buddhism takes things several steps further. See, when you say "electrical impulses in the brain," you believe that because you've managed to encapsulate that little sliver of reality in five easy-to-pronounce words, you have, therefore, understood it. You're ready to move on to bigger and better things.

That sort of understanding can be useful when you want to put A together with B and get to C. But it's not true understanding in the Buddhist sense of what understanding means. In chapter 33 of *Shobogenzo*, "Kannon," which we talked about earlier, a monk answers a certain question by saying, "I understand." Dogen says, "The understanding described by 'I understand' is the 'I' itself; at the same time we should consider its existence as 'you.'" So the Buddhist view of understanding is far more universal than our usual way of using the word. "Understanding" in the Buddhist sense isn't just intellectual. It is not limited to your own idiosyncratic understanding. It's not that "I" stand over here and "understand" some stuff over there. "Understanding" in the Buddhist sense is "I" itself and also includes "you." It's an understanding that includes and is included by the whole universe.

Wayne Coyne talks about the meaninglessness and evil of reality. We've already looked at the Problem of Evil. So what about Wayne's other point, that reality is meaningless? To a Buddhist the whole universe is meaning itself. We wring our hands over the meaninglessness of it all only when we experience things we can't assign to easy categories of preconceived "meaning." Things mean what we decide they mean. And if we can't decide what they mean, we call them "meaningless."

Whether or not we can slot the true meaning of all that we experience into the neat little culturally accepted categorical boxes stored in our brain labeled "meaning" is of no real importance. Meaning in Buddhism isn't merely meaning in terms that thought can grasp. It is more of a particular facet of the universe itself. It's not that our experiences have meaning, it's that all experience *is* meaning. To paraphrase Dogen, you understand this meaning by using your whole body and mind and by using the entire universe.

Real understanding comes when you penetrate deeply into reality itself, when you actually see things for what they are without the intercession of your ideas about what they are. You cannot do that with your brain alone. It is not intellectual understanding. It is not meaning in a sense that your brain can ever even hope to grasp.

Buddhism can say that consciousness is nothing more than electricity in the brain while at the same time avoiding materialism or nihilism because it also questions our ideas about what electricity in the brain actually is. Electricity in the brain is an amazing thing. It's a mystical thing. No doubt about it. Just look at what that electricity is doing right now. It's creating whole worlds out of nothing more than some squiggly black shapes on a piece of paper. You are reading my mind just by looking at those shapes. What's more, we can communicate with Dogen, a guy who died eight hundred years before our grandparents were even born, just by looking at tiny little marks on pieces of paper. And that's just the tip of the iceberg of what electrical impulses in the brain are capable of.

Some people wonder if consciousness survives the death of the brain. But this very wondering is simply more of the brain's activity. It's the activity of the personal ego trying to suss out what its own future might have in store. But the very concept of the personal ego having anything at all in store in its future may be nothing more than another creation of that personal ego. As such it has hardly any significance at all in terms of what reality actually is.

Dogen gives his take on the notion that the whole material world is an illusion in a chapter called 夢中説夢, which is pronounced *Muchu-setsu-mu* and means "Preaching a Dream within a Dream." This was already a clichéd phrase within Buddhism even by the year 1242, when Dogen wrote the piece. A great many Buddhists tended to understand the phrase to mean that the universe was unreal like a dream and that Buddhist teachers just talked about unreality in the midst of unreality. That wasn't how Dogen understood it at all.

"The pervasive disclosure of the entire Universe is the dream-state," he wrote. "This dream-state is just the clear-clear hundred things — and it is the very moment in which we doubt that it is so; it is the very moment of confusion." The "clear-clear hundred things" refers to an old Buddhist phrase spelled out in Chinese characters as 明明たる百草, which in the Japanese of Dogen's time was pronounced *meimei taru hyakuso* and means literally "clear, clear hundred weeds."* Weeds was just poetic shorthand for miscellaneous

---

* And if you want to get real picky about it, the final character I've written here is wrong. Dogen actually used a character that means the same thing but can't be found on modern Japanese computers.

and sundry things, a bit like the way we use the word *stuff* in English. So we might rephrase Dogen by saying "ridiculously obvious bunches of stuff."

So to Dogen the material world was unreal like a dream, and yet the dream state itself was our reality. We may not know just what reality is. But this is the way we're experiencing it right now, so this is what we have to deal with. So deal with it, already. On the one hand it is right and proper to understand that what we're perceiving as the material universe is not the sum total of reality. On the other, we don't need to screw around trying to imagine just what reality is or to picture reality as existing way off in some other realm we cannot experience right now. Nor do we have to have some kind of specially sanctioned enlightenment experience in order to truly live our lives.

Dogen goes on to say, "People who prefer not to learn the Buddha's truth, when they encounter this preaching a dream in a dream, idly suppose that it might mean creating insubstantial dreamy things which do not exist at all; they suppose it might be like adding to delusion in delusion. [But] it is not so. Even when we are adding to delusion in delusion, we should endeavor just then to learn in practice the path of clarity of expression on which the words 'delusion upon delusion' are naturally spoken." Even when we are confused about reality, our own confusion is reality itself. Understand that, and you understand everything.

All this isn't to simply dismiss Coyne's points or to say he's wrong. The entire essay is highly recommended, as is the CD.* In fact, the conclusions Wayne draws are exactly the Buddhist point of view, so I'll let him finish this chapter. He says,

> If religious folks could submit to "GOD" because he's great and powerful perhaps we could submit to "the Universe" because it's great and powerful.

---

* Especially the song "Unconsciously Screaming."

We had lost the lord but gained the world.

Instead of looking up and seeing Heaven and its endless possibilities and saying "that must be God" we looked up and saw the Universe and its endless possibilities and thought the Universe has made us. Yep. But the rest is up to us.

Chapter 17

Death

The only really bad thing about interviewing all those folks from the old Ohio hardcore scene for my documentary was the fact that several people I would have liked to talk to are dead. It's always sad when someone dies too soon. In our scene there weren't that many. But there were a few, and I admired them all.

Keith Busch was never part of the hardcore scene as such. But he was a tremendous source of inspiration. He was a bit older than we were, maybe by just five or six years, but that seems like a lot when you're eighteen or nineteen. Keith understood us and helped out whenever he could. And that was important. But Keith had a hard life and ended up dying of hepatitis while still in his thirties.

Everybody called Robert Morningstar "Iggy." Like Keith, he was older than the hardcores and was never really part of the scene. But his band, the f-Models, was one of the few in the area that played their own songs and had a loud, aggressive style. It's a fair guess to say that about half the members of the bands on the hardcore scene probably first met each other at f-Models gigs. But Iggy liked to drink and was prone to severe depression. He took his own life when he was just twenty-seven, the standard age for rock-and-roll deaths.

Dave Araca drew the cover for the New Hope compilation LP, one of the few documents of our hardcore scene. Dave was a member of both the Dark and the Guns, two of the scene's best-loved bands. The Guns were one of the few groups that survived the end of hardcore and went on to be embraced by the area's heavy metal fans, who liked their metal a bit brainier than was standard for Cleveland. I've got some photos of our gigs in which Dave is prominent in a bright-yellow shirt that says oDFx (Zero Defects) on the back. He was a great guy, a true original. He passed away suddenly of an aneurysm. No one's really sure what caused it.

Duke Snyder was the bass player for the Plague. I never knew Duke all that well. But my friend Fraser Suicyde shared a house with him for a while. Duke was one of those guys everybody liked. But Duke got into heroin, and it killed him.

Religions are in the death business: preparing people for death, pretending to send them off after they've died, making believe they know what happens afterward, and explaining to the dead person's relatives where they think their loved one might be now. Without death most religions don't have a whole lot to live for.

Unfortunately, Buddhism in Japan these days is hardly an exception. Generally speaking, Japanese people go to Shinto shrines for ceremonies related to birth and coming of age; they go to Christian churches — or reasonable facsimiles — for weddings; and to Buddhist temples for funerals. It's safe to say that if it wasn't for death, Buddhism in Japan would be pretty much a goner.

I don't know when I first became aware that people and things died — if it was when my pet chameleon got crisper than a potato chip after I'd left his cage out in the sun all day or when I first discovered that hamburgers were made from dead moo-cows or when my great-grandpa Cor-cor* bit the big one, but sometime during my kidhood I started thinking a lot about death. I think most people go through a phase like this. Buddha himself did. When he was a little twerp, he was watching some farmers plow a field and saw a worm get cut in half. He realized then that the only way people lived was through the deaths of other creatures, and he began wondering about his own mortality.

I had learned from the *Davey and Goliath* episodes I'd watched that if you were good during your lifetime, God would send you to heaven after you die, and if you were bad, he would send you to hell. But I never really liked those two options. My family moved to Nairobi, Kenya, when I was eight after my dad got transferred to the Firestone plant they'd just opened there, and I suddenly became aware that not everyone in the whole wide world believed you go to heaven or hell after you die. I discovered that people who did believe that were something called "Christians." And, much to my astonishment, I learned that most of the people in the world were not Christians. I remember thinking it was really unfair that God had doomed all these poor Hindus, Muslims, Buddhists, and assorted other peoples — who my Sunday-school teachers hadn't bothered to tell me even existed — to eternal damnation just for believing in the wrong things. I mean, some of them had never even been exposed to Christianity. What chance did they have? It was totally unfair. Then I started thinking maybe I didn't believe that was what happened when you died either.

My best friend in Kenya, Tommy Kashangaki,** was Catholic. Catholicism, I discovered, was a different species of Christianity from the one I knew about, which was something called "Protestantism." Sha-zayam, what else didn't I know? I learned from Tommy that the

---

* His last name was Corbin, and that's what I called him. Sue me. I was a little kid, okay?
** Where are you these days, Tommy?

Catholics allowed people a couple of other choices of places to go after shuffling off this mortal coil. Those who'd never had the chance to become Catholics were allowed to hang out in a place called purgatory and could get into heaven after a while if . . . well, I never quite figured out the criteria. They also had a place called "limbo," which I never did quite get, but then again, a lot of Catholics I know today don't really get that one either.

But that was just the Christian view. My dad had an Indian friend named Ramesh, who was a Hindu. And from talking to his kids, I learned that the Hindus had an altogether different idea about what happens after you die. According to them you didn't go to heaven or hell or even to purgatory or limbo. Instead you got reborn as a different person or maybe even an animal. That sounded kinda cool to me. Maybe I could get reborn as a Komodo dragon or something. Plus, it was a lot fairer of God to give folks a second chance than that whole heaven and hell deal.

But still, there were lots of holes in that argument too. Like, for example, the steadily increasing human population. Where were all these new souls coming from? And in most of the books I read describing the process, it seemed like all these reincarnations were basically steps leading toward a slightly different kind of heaven at the end of it all. If you finally managed to get everything right in one of these lifetimes, you got to go to somewhere cool and you never had to come back again. Plus, the evidence for reincarnation all seemed pretty flimsy, depending as much on faith as the evidence for heaven and hell did. Both arguments rested on the idea of people still being alive in some weird, inexplicable way after they were quite clearly and unambiguously deader than a doornail. So even though reincarnation made a bit more sense than heaven and hell, I wasn't ready to settle on that explanation either.

Throughout my teenage years I continued jumping from religion to religion, trying to see if the things any of them said about death made sense. But none of the explanations I heard satisfied me.

And like Wayne Coyne of the Flaming Lips, when I tried to side with science, I found the drily scientific explanations of death, though intellectually appealing, didn't work for me on a deeper level. It wasn't just that I didn't want to believe there was nothing after you died. There were a lot of areas science didn't seem to be able to reach. Yet religions that tried to deny science by requiring me to believe in a lot of supposed miracles for which there was no reliable evidence seemed totally stupid and lame.

Now, there's Buddhism and there's Buddhism. It's a shame, but there are plenty of people running around today proclaiming to be Buddhists who have some plenty wacky ideas about heaven and hell and life after death. But the Buddhism that Dogen taught was different. Dogen insisted that what he taught was the true essence of Buddhism. I don't see any reason to doubt this.

In Dogen's Buddhism I found a view of death that was so completely removed from any other I'd come across before that at first I couldn't even make heads or tails of it at all.

Dogen gives his views on death in a teeny little sliver of a chapter right near the end of *Shobogenzo*, chapter 92, which he called 生死, pronounced *shoji* and meaning "Life and Death."

He starts off by saying, "Because in life-and-death there is buddha, there is no life and death. Again, we can say: Because in life-and-death there is no 'buddha,' we are not deluded in life-and-death."* The word *buddha* here refers not to the historical person but to the state of understanding he attained, which is why I've left it lowercased, much to the consternation of my computer's spell check function. This state, Dogen maintains, is available to all of us any time we choose to recognize it.

But, he cautions us, "If a person looks for buddha outside of

---

* It's actually a neat piece of first-semester-level Japanese, so for foreign-language fans here it is in Dogen's words: 生死のなかに仏あれば、生死なし。またいはく、生死のなかに仏なければ、生死にまどはず.

life-and-death, that is like pointing a cart north and making for [the south country of] Etsu, or like facing south and hoping to see the North Star. It is to be amassing more and more causes of life and death, and to have utterly lost the way of liberation." So we have to use life and death themselves to understand life and death. Meaning that only if we live through life and then die can we be said to have truly grasped either one. Otherwise, we're just "amassing more and more causes of life and death." In other words, when we get more and more into our own ideas about life and death, we start believing that the concepts we've created in our heads are more real than the actual things themselves. We may not fear real death so much as we fear our ideas about death.

But most of our religions teach us to do just the opposite of what Dogen recommends. We're told to envision something, God or heaven or what have you, that exists somehow outside the realm of life and death. Then we're supposed to pretend that this idea we've formed, which we desperately cling to in the face of continuously mounting evidence that it's completely wrong, will somehow save us from the one thing we know for damn sure is gonna happen to us one of these days.*

To try and understand this a little better, let's look for a minute at how we define death. For most of us, death means the end of consciousness. But what's consciousness? There's an idea that consciousness is a constant factor throughout your life. Here's consciousness, and when you put a box of Apple Jacks® cereal in front of consciousness, it's conscious of Apple Jacks® cereal, and when you put a *Penthouse* centerfold in front of consciousness, it's conscious of April's Pet of the Month. Consciousness may at this point wonder how much that piercing hurt and where it can get a job doing piercings like that. But I digress. The point is, is that really how it works?

As far as Buddhism is concerned there is no continuous something

---

* That we're gonna die. Duh!

called consciousness that sits back and experiences stuff. Your consciousness of eating breakfast ceases when you put the last tasty spoonful of Apple Jacks® in your mouth. Your consciousness of the lovely Pet of the Month ends when you've finished, um, reading about her turnons and turnoffs. Your consciousness of taking a dump ends when you pinch off that last satisfying loaf. So if death is defined as the end of consciousness, then you are dying constantly.

You take the existence of consciousness for granted because you're used to making arbitrary categories out of your real experience. There's you. There's a bowl of Apple Jacks®. And between the two is consciousness, which informs you that there's a bowl of Apple Jacks® in front of you. But Buddhism accepts no such separation. There is one thing, the universe, and it includes you and Apple Jacks® and "your" consciousness thereof, all of which are ultimately the same thing.

No one of these things can ever be taken out of the picture and considered by itself in any meaningful way. Yet our brains are always attempting to do just that. That's the brain's function. And a useful function it is. But it is not the truth of the matter. Understand that one point, and you've understood all of Buddhism — not a single one of your thoughts or perceptions is true.*

If your consciousness does not exist now, why waste your energy worrying about it disappearing someday?

You cannot die because you were never born to begin with. Yet Shunryu Suzuki — who's deader than a doornail now but who was one of the few people I know of who really understood Buddhist philosophy very thoroughly — said, "You will always exist in this universe." But how can that be? If there's no reincarnation and if consciousness simply ends when you die, how can any Buddhist say you will always exist? Could it be that we're totally mistaken about what we really are?

---

* And that goes for my thoughts and perceptions as well. So there.

Look at this moment right now. Where did it come from? When it's gone, where will it go? You don't know. Neither do I. Neither did Dogen or Gautama Buddha. The difference is that Buddha and Dogen were able to understand the real fact of not knowing very clearly and precisely.

People are usually inclined to think that birth, or life, is great and that death sucks. Birth is the beginning. Death is the end. But Dogen thought differently. In chapter 23 of *Shobogenzo*, titled 行仏威儀, pronounced *gyobutsu yuigi* and meaning "Dignified Behavior of Acting Buddha," he talks about four kinds of birth, "birth from the womb, egg, moisture, and metamorphosis" (胎卵湿化生). The first three refer to the scientific understanding that existed in his day. The belief that things could be born from moisture was widely accepted in the West as well until advances in microscopic technology showed that insects and microbes once thought to generate spontaneously in water were actually born from tiny eggs or from cellular division. Birth from metamorphosis concerns those nonphysical things that are born from change, like a new idea, a new way of thinking, a new constitution, a new marketing division in the company you work for, a new religion, and so on.

Even so-called inanimate objects are born and die. A rock is born as a rock when it splits off from the earth and begins its separate existence as a rock. It dies when weather and time wear it away into sand, at which point grains of sand are born, though these too will one day end their existence as grains of sand. A rock ends its life as a rock by beginning its life as a bunch of grains of sand. Our own birth and death may be exactly the same thing. It may be that what we call "birth" and "death" are nothing other than our own perception of things moving from one conceptual category into another, while in reality nothing actually appears or disappears.

We complicate things by imagining that there's something called "sentience" or "consciousness," which exists somehow apart from matter. Religions love to extrapolate endlessly on just how the sentient soul enters and leaves the material body. But Buddhism does not accept this distinction between matter and consciousness. As the *Heart Sutra* says, "Form is Emptiness, Emptiness is Form." In other words, matter is consciousness, and vice versa. There is no sentience that sits back and observes matter. Sentience is matter itself.

A little further along in chapter 23 Dogen says, "Let us consider for a while among the miscellaneous beings born from these four kinds of birth, could there be any which have birth but no death? Are there any which receive a single line transmission of only death without receiving a single line transmission of birth? We must unfailingly study in practice the existence or nonexistence of kinds which solely are born or which solely die." Birth and death always come as a pair. Whatever is born will die. Birth is special precisely because death exists. A world in which everything that ever existed just continued in a single form forever and ever would be a very boring place indeed.

The reason we fear death may come down to a deep confusion in how we view our lives. If we could look at it a different way, there might be nothing to fear. Dogen says it this way (I am quoting from "Shoji" again):

> To understand that we move from birth to death is a mistake. Birth is a state at one moment; it already has a past and will have a future. For this reason, it is said in the Buddha-Dharma that appearance is just non-appearance. Extinction also is a state at one moment; it too has a past and a future. This is why it is said that disappearance is just non-disappearance. In the time called life, there is nothing besides life. In the time called death, there is nothing besides death. Thus, when life comes it is just life, and when death comes it is just death.

So in Dogen's view life and death are just momentary states. Each exists in its own unique place. When he says that appearance is nonappearance and disappearance is just nondisappearance, he's not trying to sound all groovy and "Zen." What we call "appearance" or "life" isn't confined to the mental categories and limitations of the word *appearance* or the word *life*. Our misunderstanding and confusion stem from the way we try to force the real world into neat little mental categories. Life and death are not "life" and "death," to put it the way Dogen might have. To understand real things in terms of mere words is an exercise doomed to failure because words are by nature limited, while the real world is infinite.*

People have asked me from time to time to teach them meditation techniques to help them deal with the persistent fear of death. Forget about it! There aren't any. For one thing, to some extent the fear of death is a perfectly natural thing. It's your self-preservation instinct. You don't want to get rid of that! Of course, thinking about death over and over and over doesn't do you any good. But if that's what's happening, try looking at those thoughts and seeing what they are. Every thought, no matter how profound, how beautiful, how scary, how true — is nothing more than electricity bouncing around in your brain. Thinking the same thoughts over and over and over tends to create neural pathways of least resistance in your brain. The electrical energy always present in your brain then tends to travel through these familiar pathways. It's hard for me to see any persistent fear as anything more than that.

But if you feel like you just gotta, gotta, gotta fear death, then fear death all the way. Experience total, absolute fear. Go all the way down to the bottom of fear. Don't fear your fear. Stare it down with absolute confidence. Your fear of death is nothing more than your ego trying to establish and maintain itself. The logic it's using goes like this: if you fear death, you must therefore exist. Unfortunately for Mr. Ego, this is not true. Fear of death proves nothing but the fact that electricity is running around in your brain. It does not prove

---

* Even the word *infinite* isn't infinite because it's used as a contrast to things we suppose are not infinite.

that you exist as a discrete entity forever separate from the universe "you" encounter.

While you're alive just enjoy being alive. When death comes, it will come. Trying to speculate about what might happen after you die is completely useless. Death isn't somewhere you can go the way you can go to Cincinnati. Death is your state at the moment of death. Life is what's happening right now. If you can't grasp what's going on right now, how are you going to understand something that's going to happen in your future? Leave death to death. Look at your life right now, and try to understand it for what it really is.

Chapter 18

God

Since we've talked about death, let's get into that other subject religions like to deal with, the big man himself, the man upstairs, the bearded guy on the throne in the painting on the Sistine Chapel ceiling, the guy who zaps you with a lightning bolt if you take his name in vain. Of course I'm talking about none other than our old friend Mr. God.

Zero Defects has a strange relationship to God as hardcore bands go. Our singer Jimi Imij is the only Quaker I know of in the world of punk rock. Jimi's real last name is Friend. His family members were never staunch Quakers. But, even so, Jimi's relationship to his religion was extremely important to him even back in the day. I was really intrigued by this when I joined the band, and I always tried to engage him in religious conversations.

When I first came across Buddhism, I was fascinated by the fact that it was supposed to be a religion without God; at least, that's what certain books I read about it implied. How could you have a religion with no God to worship? This was a real big problem to the first

Western scholars who studied Buddhism. In some of the really crusty old books you'll even find Buddhism described as a kind of atheism.

The idea that Buddhism is atheism with a happy face is very attractive to certain types of people. These are usually people who have been raised in very religious families or who for whatever reasons have come to reject religion and the idea of God. On the one hand, if God is defined as a big, huge white man with a long beard and magical powers who sits on a throne somewhere way up in the sky and sends people to hell for not kissing his ass well enough or in just the right way, then Buddhism does not accept the belief in that kind of God. Yet every decent Zen teacher I have ever encountered does believe in God. I believe in God too.

The problem with the usual religious view of God is that it is far too limiting. The God they believe in is much too small, a pitiful caricature of a jealous and mean-spirited dictator. The way most religions define God is an insult to God.

When I encountered my first atheists, I found their ideas intriguing. Now, these atheists were just guys on my high school debate team. They were as deeply nerdy as anyone could possibly be. They rejected everything the popular crowd in my school believed in, which is what we had in common. Now, I was a nerd too, mind you. But I was never as nerdy as these guys. I mean, these were pasty-faced bony guys who spent their Saturdays locked in a basement together playing Dungeons & Dragons. Some of them probably still haven't gone on their first dates. I was a pasty-faced bony guy who spent my Saturdays locked in a basement trying to learn the bass line to Devo's version of "(I Can't Get No) Satisfaction." You see the difference, I hope.

These debate-team atheists were also extremely intellectual. They thought everything through very, very thoroughly. They were well read and knew all kinds of things about the cutting edge of science and philosophy. They were very proud of the fact that they did not believe in God. But they were also very convinced of their nonbelief, to the extent that their nonbelief became a kind of belief. They even tried to convert nonbelievers in atheism to atheism. Most atheists I encountered were like this to some extent. So I had to reject atheism for the same reason I had rejected all other forms of belief I encountered: there was too much a sense of it being some kind of ultimate truth.

Buddhism isn't about belief, though. So it is no more of a problem for someone who believes in atheism to practice Buddhism than it is for someone who believes in fundamentalist Christianity to practice Buddhism. That is to say, no decent Buddhist teacher is going to reject you as a student just because you have those kinds of beliefs. But I would say to any passionate atheist the same thing I'd say to any passionate Christian, Muslim, Jew, Wiccan, or member of the Church of the SubGenius. If you come into Buddhism with strong beliefs, you should know from the outset that your beliefs will be severely tested. Buddhism is perfectly realistic. If your beliefs are not realistic, you must be able to throw them away, no matter how precious they are. This includes the belief in atheism.

You might be inclined, then, to try and classify Buddhism as a kind of agnosticism. But agnosticism implies that we don't address the problem of the existence or nonexistence of God because we just don't know. Maybe God exists. Maybe he doesn't. That's not the position of Buddhism either.

To understand how God works into the Buddhist picture, you need a bit of historical background. The prevailing religion in India in Buddha's day accepted the existence of a whole pantheon of powerful supernatural beings. But these gods weren't generally considered omnipotent or even immortal. They went through the same cycle of birth and death as every other thing in the universe. They just happened to take quite a bit longer to finally kick the bucket.

The closest the ancient Indians ever got to anything like the concept of the God of the Israelites was a guy they called Maha-Brahma, the chief of all the Indian gods. Buddha studied up on this idea, but it left him unimpressed. He commented on an old Indian text in which Maha-Brahma says, "I am the Supreme One, the mighty, the all-seeing, Lord of All, the Maker, the Creator, Father of all that is and will be," saying that poor Maha-Brahma was obviously suffering from delusions of grandeur brought on by a runaway ego. The statement didn't cause the kind of furor you might have expected if, say, some ancient Hebrew soothsayer had said the same thing about Jehovah, since the Indians were used to thinking of their gods as being prone to such foibles.

I discovered the concept of God long before I encountered atheism when I started getting into *Jesus Christ Superstar* at the age of ten or so.* Since I had no idea what God was supposed to be, I asked around. I soon discovered that most of the people I asked about God didn't have any better idea what He, She, It was than I did. The few people I encountered who did have a fixed idea of what the heck God was supposed to be always came off as a little weird to me. They seemed to just blindly accept the existence of this, I dunno, this *something or other* they couldn't really describe but that they believed was very big and very, very scary.

But the evidence they had to support such an all-consuming belief looked pretty flimsy to me. They had this book — some had different books than others, but they all had a book — which had been around for an awful long time, and they had a community of other people who professed the same belief in this invisible whatever it was that was out there *somewhere* and which they were certain could really hurt them if they got on its bad side. The old book(s) said that God used to pull off a lot of miracles and stuff. But God didn't seem to do any of those things anymore. So if you wanted to believe in him, you needed to have what they called "faith." Faith, as far as I could understand it, mainly involved believing that the people who

---

* Hey! I grew up in the seventies; that stupid movie was everywhere. And, by the way, I still dig it.

wrote the book — whichever book it was — were not crazy since no one could possibly ever prove what did or did not actually happen all those centuries ago. Suffice it to say, I never really got the whole idea.

God, as far as I could see, was supposed to be the ultimate thing in the whole universe. In fact, he was so ultimate he didn't even exist within the universe as we knew it. He somehow stood *outside* all creation, watching over it and only getting involved when he wanted to. That is to say, he was removed from the laws of cause and effect — which he had supposedly created to fool us into believing he didn't exist, thereby cleverly testing our faith when the things in his book didn't match up with the stuff we actually encountered every day. Though he was supposedly removed from our universe, it seemed he could be emotionally affected by the things his creations did down here since he was always getting his knickers in a twist about their doings.

The whole notion of God has always been very weird to me in many, many ways. But it's this idea of a supreme being that somehow exists in a state beyond the laws of cause and effect that Buddhism takes particular issue with. As we know, according to Buddha everything in the universe is subject to the laws of cause and effect.

For some believers God is perfection. This world is not perfect, but God is. Therefore God must be somewhere other than this world. But isn't perfection just a concept we invent for ourselves? No two people ever have the same idea of what exactly perfection means. How could even God ever satisfy everyone's requirements for what he ought to be?

But, even though I am a Buddhist, an adherent to a religion that they say has no God, I do believe in God. I feel I have no choice but to believe in God, since God's existence is too obvious to be denied. In fact, I'm far more inclined to doubt the existence of Brad Warner than I am to doubt the existence of God. So I should probably explain just what I mean by the word *God* and how I can believe in God even while rejecting the ideas most religious folks I've encountered have about God.

Gudo Nishijima is fond of saying, "God is the Universe. The Universe is God." This eliminates the logical absurdity of a God who exists somehow apart from his own creations. I like this idea a lot. For Nishijima this world is a very mystical place. "When we think about the Solar System," he says, "I usually wonder why those big heavenly bodies can be maintained in space. Our scientific knowledge has developed so much, and we know that everything in the universe has gravity. But when we think about why there is such a miraculous thing as gravity, it is not so easy to find the answer. Therefore it is necessary for us to think that the world, where we are just living now, is very mystical and miraculous in spite of our expectation."

To me God is what you get when you take everything in the universe as a whole and call it by one name. And God is also you and me in the sense that we are the means by which God observes his creation. If God is omniscient, he must also therefore be nonomniscient. I mean, if he knows all and sees all — and I mean *all*, as in every last thing — he must also know the state of not knowing all and not seeing much of anything. I don't want to get too psychedelic on you here. But if God is everything, as most true believers say, then God must also be you, reading this book. And if God knows everything, he must also know the state in which he cannot possibly know if he exists.

Some people might assume that by saying God is the universe, I'm positing a very cold, uncaring outlook. But it's not that at all. The universe cares more about you than you do about yourself. It loves you and tries at all times to prevent you from doing harm to yourself and others by providing consequences for such actions. In this way anyone who pays attention can see clearly for him- or herself exactly what is right and what is wrong without ever having to look to any book — holy or otherwise — for a list of dos and don'ts.

To me God is the same as what Buddhists call the Rule of the Universe. Or to put it another way, the law of cause and effect isn't just something *made* by God that he stands apart from. The law of cause and effect *is* God. Though we use the words *rule* and *law*, it's not like a law written in a book. It's a living, ever-changing thing. The Rule of the Universe is intensely moral in that it includes all those things that ensure that you suffer the proper consequences should you attempt to do things you ought not to do. Someone asked me once what "Higher Power" a Buddhist could choose to believe in if he or she became a member of a twelve-step program that required such a belief. I think that the fact that you can't drink too much alcohol without becoming very ill — addiction being an illness, after all — is evidence enough that the Rule of the Universe is a benevolent Higher Power that wishes us not to become alcoholics. I would trust in the law of cause and effect as my Higher Power.

When God is the universe and the universe is God, we've removed ourselves completely from both the simpleminded view of God as a big white dude on a throne somewhere and the mystical view of God as a nebulous spirit or force within the universe. God is as concrete as the concrete under your feet and as insubstantial as the memory of your first kiss.

Chapter 19

It! The Thing from Beyond the Realm of Mind

Though Dogen doesn't really address the subject of God in the sense that Westerners usually conceive of him, he does talk about something else very much related to Buddhist ideas about God.

In chapter 29 of *Shobogenzo* Dogen quotes a Zen master named Ungo Doyo,* who said, "If you want to attain to the matter which is it, you must be a person who is it. Already being a person who is it, why worry about the matter which is it?"

Did you get all that? It's really not as goofy as it sounds.

The word translated as "it" here is the Chinese word *inmo* (恁麼), which is the title of Dogen's chapter. In ancient China the word *inmo* was used to indicate something the speaker didn't really need or want to explain directly, much in the manner that the word *it* is used in this famous exchange between Jerry and Elaine on *Seinfeld*:

---

* The words *ungo doyo*, by the way, are used in the film *Tarzan's Desert Mystery* (1940), where they are translated as, "Let's go to the river where the water makes smoke."

ELAINE: You know that friend of yours you set me up on a date with last night? When we were in the car just about to say goodnight, he took it out.

JERRY: It?

ELAINE: It.

JERRY: Out?

ELAINE: Out.

Also like our word *it*, *inmo* can be used to indicate something you cannot possibly explain, as in *It Came from Beneath the Sea* or *It: The Terror from Beyond Space* or even the Stephen King novel *It*. The Zen master Dogen uses the word *it* to talk about the ultimate truth.

So why is the ultimate truth "it"? It's a truth, right? And like any other truth it should be easily expressible in simple words like, "Two plus two equals four" or "Corporate rock still sucks" or "You've got a big green thing hanging out of your nose."

Most of the "truths" out there in the spiritual marketplace claiming to be ultimate are like that. They're supposed to be easily contained within certain special books — subject, of course, to the special interpretations of special people specially qualified to explain them to us. Personally, I've never found such truths very interesting.

The supreme truth in Buddhism isn't like that. The Buddhist supreme truth doesn't describe everything in some really cool way. It *is* everything. This is why it's impossible to talk about. For Buddhists the truth of the universe isn't just some handy way of explaining the universe. The truth of the universe *is* the universe itself. So *it* — the supreme truth — is you, and it is the universe as well.

The reason it's hard to get our heads around concepts like that is that most of our philosophies come from a completely different place. As I write this chapter, I'm sitting on a plane bound for Tokyo to attend a meeting with some famous American guys who might want to use our company's services to make a movie that parodies the Japanese giant monster movie genre — a pretty cool idea, if you ask me. Anyhow, the guy in front of me is reading some book whose dust jacket claims it's the only book he'll ever need to read in order to find the true meaning of life. The chapter he's on is titled "Why Am I Here?" It's a very common spiritual question, one you'll find addressed in a buttload of those kinds of books. From the Buddhist point of view this question is absurd. It assumes the existence of two distinct entities, "I" and "here," which one can consider separately.

But that's not how a Buddhist looks at the question at all. *I* and *here* are not two things but, in fact, are one and the same. What the Zen master in Dogen's story says is that the truth of the universe — *it* — is known by a person who is already *it*, who is already the truth of the universe.

In the chapter about it, Dogen takes the idea of the "universe" several steps further than most of us do, saying, "The whole Universe in ten directions is just a small part of the supreme truth of bodhi." Ten directions means north, south, east, west, northeast, northwest, and so on, plus up and down.*

So, as far as Dogen is concerned, even the whole universe as far as we can perceive or conceive of it — perception being the material side and conception being the spiritual or intellectual — is just one small part of the supreme truth. The truth, he says, abounds way beyond even the entire universe. Now, there's a mindblower. Even the entire universe is not big enough to contain the supreme truth that Buddhism talks about. So obviously we're not talking here about the kind of "truth" that can fit on a bumper sticker.

But how do we know that this *it* exists? How do we know there even is a supreme truth? How do we know we aren't just random animals existing in a universe devoid of meaning? "We know it is

* Add 'em up yourself, okay?

so," says Dogen, "because the body and the mind both appear in the Universe, yet neither is our self."

Stop and look at that statement for a second or two.

Notice again that we're on totally different ground here from that covered in most of the philosophies that get filed in the "Eastern Wisdom" section of your local book supermarket, which assert that "we are not the body, we are the spirit-soul that flies within." As far as Dogen is concerned, not only are we not this body but we are not a soul within this body.

"The body," says Dogen, "lives on through years and months, but it's not the self." Where is that snotty-faced kid who you called "me" when you first learned to say "spaghetti" instead of "pasketti"? That kid is gone without a trace. Yet something you still insist on calling "you" is here reading this silly book.

Dogen follows up, saying, "The sincere mind, too, does not stop, but goes and comes moment by moment." The word translated here as "sincere mind" is 赤心, pronounced *sekishin*. The two characters mean "red" and "mind," and the word refers to the raw, red mind as it is. This unadorned mind changes from moment to moment. It can't possibly be that "self" we view as permanent and unchanging.

If you study a lot of Zen books, though, you'll often come across references to the philosophy of "mind only." This is sometimes described by Western — and not a few Eastern — commentators on Buddhism as Buddhism's philosophy of "radical idealism." Idealism, in philosophical terms, is the concept that ideas alone are real. Radical idealism is idealism taken to its ultimate extreme. The words *mind only*, they assert, surely mean that these Buddhist dudes must have believed only in the existence of consciousness and not in anything else. Dogen's own students must certainly have interpreted it the same way, because the very next thing Dogen does is explain why this "mind only" idea has been wildly misinterpreted. To illustrate, he tells an old Zen story that goes like this:

A Zen master and his student are listening to some bells ringing in the wind. The Zen master, being a smart-ass, asks his student, "Is it the sound of the wind or is it the sound of the bells?"

The student, being plenty clever with this Zen stuff himself, says, "It's beyond the ringing of the wind and beyond the ringing of the bells; it's the ringing of my mind."

The Zen master pushes further saying, "Okay, wise guy, then what is the mind?"

The student says, "The reason it's ringing is because all is still."

The Zen master likes this answer a lot and eventually gives the student his permission to teach. I know, I know. As far as any sane person is concerned, it's just a couple of loonies talking about bells. But let's see what Dogen has to say.

Dogen says that "many people have misunderstood [the story as follows]: The student's words 'It is neither the ringing of the wind nor the ringing of the bells, it is the ringing of the mind' mean that there is in the listener, at just the moment of the present, the occurrence of mindfulness, and this occurrence of mindfulness is called 'the mind.'"

So Dogen wasn't satisfied with the common idea that we have a mind and that our mind responds to things like the sounds of ringing bells or the sounds of the latest Metallica CD or whatever. Nor was he real hot on that favorite of all Buddhist buzzwords — even eight hundred years ago — *mindfulness*. Then, as now, *mindfulness* too often implied the idea he rejects here, the idea that being consciously aware of stuff all the time — as if that were even possible — is the same as enlightenment.

Instead, Dogen picks up on the student's later reference to stillness. He says, "The blowing of the wind being still, the ringing of the bells is still, and for this reason he [the student in the story] says all is still."

Dogen pushes on: "He is saying that the mind ringing is beyond the ringing of the wind, the mind ringing is beyond the ringing of the bells, and the mind ringing is beyond the ringing of the mind. Having pursued to the ultimate the close and direct state like this, we may then go on to say that it is the wind ringing, it is the bells ringing, it is the blowing ringing, and it is the ringing ringing."*

I know that's another one of those weird-ass quotes. But, trust me, Dogen wasn't just a crazy man explaining the craziness of other crazy people in some crazy-ass way. The word *stillness* is often used in Buddhism to refer to the present moment. According to Buddhist philosophy, each moment is cut off from the ones that came before and the ones that will come after. As with frames of film, there is no movement in each individual moment, but when taken together they appear to be in motion. So when the student here says, "All is stillness," he's referring to the state of being fully present in just this moment. Dogen refers to this as the "close and direct state." It's our real state at every moment, something we couldn't possibly lose, no matter how hard we tried.

Dogen then gives another example of the same thing. He tells a story of a Zen master walking by two monks who are looking at a flag and arguing. One says the flag is flapping. The other says the wind is flapping. The Zen master says, "You're both idiots! It's your minds flapping!"**

Dogen comments on this, saying, "The words 'You are the mind moving' are fine as they are, but we could also express it as 'You are moving.' Why do we say so? Because what is moving is moving, and because you are you. We say so because [you] already are people who are it."†

Here Dogen is attempting to express his understanding of what we human beings truly are. We can perceive flags and wind and bells and sounds and the rest of the universe because we are the universe itself. In another part of the chapter Dogen expresses this in a way I

---

* Would somebody *please* go and deal with all that ringing? It's driving me nuts!
** Though it would've been cooler if he'd said, "It's your lips flapping, chuckleheads!" then clonked their bald heads together like Moe from the Three Stooges.
† The word translated as "it" here is *inmo*.

happen to like a whole lot: "We ourselves are tools which it [*inmo*] possesses within this Universe in ten directions."*

He goes into this particular idea again in an even cooler way in chapter 53 of *Shobogenzo*, titled "Mujo Seppo" (無情説法), which means "The Nonemotional Preaches the Dharma" or "The Insentient Preaches the Dharma." That chapter has this kind of neato sci-fi–sounding paragraph:

> There are thousands of eyes on the tips of the fingers, there are thousands of eyes of right Dharma, there are thousands of eyes in the ears, there are thousands of eyes on the tip of the tongue, there are thousands of eyes on the tip of the mind, there are thousands of eyes of the thoroughly realized mind, there are thousands of eyes of the thoroughly realized body, there are thousands of eyes on top of a stick, there are thousands of eyes in the moment before the body, there are thousands of eyes in the moment before the mind, there are thousands of eyes of death in death, there are thousands of eyes of liveliness in liveliness, there are thousands of eyes of the self, there are thousands of eyes of the external world, there are thousands of eyes in the concrete place of eyes, there are thousands of eyes of learning in practice, there are thousands of eyes aligned vertically, and there are thousands of eyes aligned horizontally.

This passage always reminds me of the old Roger Corman B-grade sci-fi classic *Beast with a Million Eyes*.**

Now, as cool as it might be to envision thousands of googly stalks with bloodshot eyeballs on the ends of them suddenly sprouting out

---

* Which is われらも尽十方界のなかにあらゆる調度なり in Japanese, if you're just dying to know.

** Except that when you finally get to see the beast itself in that film, it's a fairly lame rubber puppet with only two eyes. The premise is that some kind of alien force is attempting to rule the world by taking over individual people and animals, thus giving it millions of eyes to see through. It turns out the puppet — I mean the *alien* — is a creature from a different planet that this thing has taken over. We never actually get to see what the million-eyed beast looks like.

of someone's tongue, this isn't really what Dogen had in mind. Dogen conceives of the universe itself as one gigantic entity whose eyes and ears are what we identify as ourselves and other people, as well as animals, inanimate objects, and pretty much anything else you can think of. In chapter 63, "Ganzei" (眼睛) or "Eyes," Dogen talks about what he means by the word *eye*. He says, "This Eye [there are no plurals in Japanese so "this eye" can also be read as "these eyes"] is, from the beginning, neither subjective nor objective. Because there are no hindrances of any kind, a great matter like this also is without hindrances." So Dogen uses the word *eye* to discuss the universe's ability to perceive and experience itself. The concrete manifestation of that ability is you and me and your sister's boyfriend with the stupid tattoo and those guys who try to sell you flowers by the freeway exit ramps — and the flowers, and the exit ramps, and ... well, you get the picture, I think.

Though he says that neither body nor mind can be called "self," Dogen claims that "the state of sincerity does exist but it is not something which lingers in the vicinity of the personal self." In other words, the state of sincerity is way too cool to hang out with the likes of you.

But what's the "state of sincerity"? Do you ever get so into doing something that you lose all sense of time and place, forget your own name, and feel there's no "you" separate from the thing you're doing? That's the state Dogen's talking about. It's the state we're all in all the time when we're children. We lose it as we grow up. That's our tremendous mistake. As a culture we think we have to lose our childlike innocence, our sense of fun, our sense that every moment is a great adventure. We think we have to throw that away in order to be mature. But we don't.

Dogen says that the *it* the ancient Zen masters talk about isn't the personal self, but, "even so," he says, "there is something which, in the limitlessness, establishes the [Bodhi] Mind." Establishing the Bodhi Mind just means having the will to try and find out what is actually true about you and the universe you live in.

In Dogen's view this establishment of the will to discover the truth is a very significant matter. "We know that we are people who are it just from the fact that we want to attain the matter which is it." The phrase "people who are it" was used by ancient Zen teachers to refer to people who possess the necessary state of sincerity to discover the truth of the universe for themselves. Whether or not you feel "enlightened" is beside the point. "Already we possess the real features of a person who is it: we should not worry about the already-present matter which is it. Even worry itself is just the matter which is it, and so it is beyond worry. Again, we should not be surprised that the matter which is it is present in such a state. Even if it is the object of surprise and wonderment, it is still just it." Whether or not you notice *it*, it's always there.

Establishing Bodhi Mind, says Dogen, is not our own doing, and yet it is. In a sense we establish the will to know the Truth while the Truth simultaneously establishes the will to know us. If you sincerely want to know who and what you truly are — if you're not just doing it for show, to look like a "really spiritual person" to all your friends — then you're going to find it sooner or later. More likely later. But don't let that get you down. It is far better to take your time. Rushing things will just screw up your head.

This *it*, this something that is the source of the universe and the source of you — that is, in a sense, God — is not something you can ever hope to understand. Not even Buddha himself could understand it. Even if every living thing in the whole universe somehow connected themselves together like one gigundous mainframe computer, this *it* still could not be defined because by its very nature it is beyond definition. The best way to express it, says Dogen, is just to say, "Already you are a person who is it: Why worry about attaining to the matter which is it?"

The sounds you hear and the forms you see are it. They — and you — are the body and mind of the universe itself.

Or, as you say when playing tag: You're it!

Chapter 20

Buddha Is Boring

Now God, he's an interesting guy to talk about. But Buddha? Looking for some airplane reading for the flight to and from Ohio, I stuffed this book called *Gotama Buddha: A Biography Based on the Most Reliable Texts*, by Hajime Nakamura* in my bag before I sprinted off to catch the bus for the airport. Let me tell you, friends, this is an amazing book. Just reading it put me into an altered state of consciousness. I entered a realm where perceptions of form and matter vanished, to be replaced by an amorphous void beyond all thought and senses, a world of peace and quiet undisturbed by the anxieties and uncertainties of the material universe. In other words, I fell right to sleep.

I swear, every time I read a page or two of that book I'd nod right off. In fact, I started doing it deliberately after a while. Whenever I'd wake up midflight, I'd pull out the book, and within minutes I'd be out like a light.

---

* He spells it *Gotama*; some people spell it *Gautama*. Since the name wasn't originally even written in roman letters, it's hard to say which is correct.

This is not to say that it's a bad book. In fact, I think it's very good. It's just that the subject matter — the life and times of Gautama Buddha — is so hopelessly dull.

Mel Gibson managed to generate a lot of controversy — not to mention a lot of moola — with his movie about the life of Jesus. It's a good thing he didn't make a film about Buddha. He'd have lost his shorts on that. I mean, the life of Jesus is very cinematic. You've got betrayal, death, miracles. Just think how much money the apostles could have made if they'd been able to option the film rights to the Gospels.

But it would be nearly impossible to make a movie about Buddha that was anything other than boooooring. It'd end up being like one of those horrible Euro-trash art films in which the characters just walk around and talk to each other for three and a half hours. Worse yet, you'd have long stretches where the hero of the film did nothing except sit still with his legs crossed. Even I wouldn't go see a movie like that.

But at the risk of putting you to sleep, I thought I'd have a whack at telling you the basic story of Buddha's life in case you don't know it. Because boring as it is, it's an important story nonetheless. Now, Dogen doesn't say too much about the life of Gautama Buddha in *Shobogenzo*. He makes references to it here and there, of course, but he doesn't include anything like a narrative biography of the founder of the philosophy since he could reasonably assume all his intended readers were well acquainted with the tale. But since I'm writing for twenty-first-century Western readers, I don't want to make that assumption. So here we go.

The guy we now know as Buddha was born the prince of a northern Indian kingdom about twenty-five hundred years ago, give or take a century either way. On his birth his parents had a fortune-teller tell his future, as was the custom of the day. The fortune-teller said that young Siddhartha — that's what they named him, must've been fans of Herman Hesse — would either become a great king or a great religious leader. His father, the king, wanted the boy to follow in his footsteps, so they spoiled him rotten. But, much to his dad's displeasure, the little Buddha-to-be had a thoughtful, introspective nature. As I already mentioned, one day while he was out watching some farmers plow up dad's fields, he saw a worm get cut in two by a plow. He suddenly became aware of the tremendous price other forms of life paid just so he could remain alive and healthy.

As the years went by, the boy's introspective nature grew. Legend has it he was never allowed out of the palace, lest he see something that might upset him, though this is probably an exaggeration. But one day, so the story goes, young Siddhartha bribed his dad's charioteer to take him out on the town. Once outside the palace walls he saw four sights that changed the course of his life. First he saw an old man, all wrinkled up and bleary-eyed like Keith Richards on a day when his smack supply has run out, shuffling down the street supporting himself with a cane. He'd never seen anybody old before, the story says, and asked the driver what was wrong with the guy. The driver said, "That's just an old dude. Everybody gets old someday."* Next he saw a sick person, his nose running, his eyes watering, coughing up sputum all over the place, like Dave Navarro on a day when *his* smack supply has run out. Siddhartha, according to the story, had never seen anyone sick before, so he asked his driver what the deal was. The driver said, "He's a sick dude, your princeship. Everyone gets sick some time or another." Next up he saw a corpse lying in the street, all stinky and buggy-eyed, flies buzzing around, like Sid Vicious the day *his* smack supply ran out for good. The Buddha-to-be asked the driver what was up with that. The driver said, "That guy's croaked." Siddhartha gave him a puzzled look. "You know, gone to meet his maker." No response. "A stiff. Gorked. Soon to be pushing up the daisies." The prince still didn't get it. "He's a dead

---

* If you've seen Bernardo Bertolucci's film in which Keanu Reeves plays Buddha, you might envision the charioteer as the guy who played opposite Keanu as Bill in *Bill and Ted's Excellent Adventure*.

dude," the driver said; "all of us have to die someday." This really freaked out little Siddhartha. He had no idea such things happened.

Finally, as they were headed back home, Siddhartha saw a wandering monk with a shaven head dressed in the traditional mustard-colored robes. He looked so peaceful and so serene even in the midst of all the other gnarly stuff they'd seen that day, that little Sid asked the driver what the deal was with him. "That's one of those monk dudes," said the driver. "He has renounced the things of the world and seeks peace of mind." At that moment Siddhartha knew what he was going to do with his life.

Still, our hero hemmed and hawed about it for a while, even ended up getting married and knocking up his wife. But one day he decided he had to make his break. It was the very same night his son was born. He snuck out toward the palace gate, stopping briefly by his wife's room. He started to take a peek inside at his new kid but stopped short. He knew that if he took one look at his son, he'd never leave the palace. So he steeled himself and went out.

Once he was outside he shaved off his hair, threw away his fancy clothes, got himself some robes, and went looking for a teacher. First he came across a guy named Alara Kalama, who taught a method of reaching the abode of nothingness. In nothing flat Siddhartha had learned how to reach the abode of nothingness, and Alara Kalama wanted to make him his successor. But this wasn't what Siddhartha was looking for, so he passed. Next he met Uddaka Ramaputta, who taught folks how to get to the abode of neither perception nor non-perception. Once again, Siddhartha learned how to get to the abode of neither perception nor nonperception in short order. Uddaka Ramaputta offered to make Siddhartha his successor. But Siddhartha said "no dice" to that and moved on.

At this point he decided to try ascetic practices, the kinds of self-torture that are in vogue among many spiritual seekers in India even today. He spent six years wandering around the forests in the company of five similarly inclined companions wearing clothes made of straw or tree bark; sometimes they went around buck naked. He didn't take baths, and so much mud and dirt got caked up on him that moss began to grow on his body. Sid cut down his food intake to one meal a day, then one meal a week, then one grain of rice a week — so the stories go. They say he even gave up food completely and lived on cow poop. And when even *that* didn't seem severe enough, they say, he took to eating his own poop. He slept on beds of thorns or on the dirt in cemeteries or even on piles of human bones, a practice that's still performed by Indian ascetics today. After a while he ended up so emaciated that his skin was translucent, and if you pressed on his belly you could feel his spine.

Finally, Siddhartha figured out that this was stupid. If he kept it up, he wouldn't end up enlightened; he'd just end up dead. So he made up his mind to start eating and wearing clothes and taking baths again. Legend has it that at that very moment a young girl just happened to be passing by on her way to serve an offering of rice gruel to one of her village deities. She saw Siddhartha and decided to give the food to him instead. When Sid gobbled up the gruel, his five companions figured he was a sellout and wanted nothing more to do with him.

Though Siddhartha was still interested in finding the truth, none of the teachers he encountered seemed to have any clue about how to go about pursuing it. So he figured he had to do it on his own. He recalled how one day, when he was a little kid, he'd sat under a tree in the lotus posture. Remembering how calm and balanced that had made him feel, he decided to forget all the other hoo-hah his former teachers talked about and make that his practice — just sitting there. What a nut job! Everybody knows you can't learn anything by just sitting in one spot.

Nonetheless, Sid found himself a tree and sat down, vowing to continue his meditation until he'd grasped the truth. The stories say that he was set upon by Mara, the closest equivalent in Indian cosmology to the devil, who offered him great riches and bodacious babes and all kinds of cool stuff if he would stop. When he refused those temptations, Mara sent bands of demons and ghosties and spooky things of all kinds to scare him, but that didn't work either. Siddhartha touched the earth as a gesture of grounding himself in reality and went right on with his meditation. You'll often see statues of him in this pose.

On the morning of his forty-ninth day of sitting Buddha saw the morning star rising, and at that moment he finally got it. We'll get to what he "got" in a minute.

At first he figured there was no way anyone was going to understand what he'd figured out that morning. So he kept it to himself. But after a while he decided he ought to make a stab at teaching it to others. First he looked for his two previous teachers but found they had already died. Next he went to his former five companions, the ones who'd branded him a sellout. When they saw him, they decided they'd give him the cold shoulder. But when Buddha came closer they could see in his eyes and his face that something important had changed. So they figured they'd hear him out just this once. Buddha gave his first sermon to them. They liked what they heard and ended up becoming his students.

Buddha's time was a lot like ours in many ways. Though they may not have had the Internet and reality TV shows, India in his day was the most highly developed civilization in the world. Its people had enough material wealth that they could waste time on useless things like arguing about philosophical issues. The philosophical issues that got them most hot and bothered were very similar to the ones people debate today. There was a basic conflict between spiritual or idealistic philosophies and the emerging materialistic philosophies that would, in time, form the basis of the scientific view.

Today we're faced with the same dilemma. Our spiritual religions proved themselves deficient long ago. The Renaissance, the Protestant Reformation, the American and French Revolutions, and all the rest of the stuff you learned about in your high school history classes carved away at the foundation of the spiritual worldview in the West until, by the nineteenth century, it was pretty well finished off. After that it seemed like science was going to give us the answers to all the big questions. But the more we searched within the world of science, the clearer it became that the ultimate answers were not to be found there either. There are still many who search for the elusive Theory of Everything in the realm of purely materialistic thought. But science can only ever hope to represent reality. The real Theory of Everything, to be worthy of its name, can't just represent everything. It must *be* everything.

Though it's become commonplace these days to dwell on Buddha's so-called spiritual quest, Buddhism is not spirituality. If you absolutely have to place it into that category to differentiate it from secular theories, okay. But Buddha's solution wasn't to deny the materialistic view in favor of a spiritual one. Materialism did present part of the picture. And he found that the same was true for spirituality. In fact, we could say that the entire first half of Buddha's life was devoted to a deep examination of materialistic philosophy. Of course, there are various forms of materialism. Marxist materialism strives to find a way to make everyone comfortable and happy in a universe devoid of any value other than that which is physically tangible. But when you get right down to it, if the only things of value are material, then the best way to have a good life must be to get as much stuff as you possibly can. So the Buddha-to-be spent the early part of his life pursuing personal wealth and fame and living a hedonistic lifestyle. Having thoroughly exhausted this path and finding it lacking, he went the opposite direction and embarked on a spiritual quest. It was only when he found that the spiritual side had no more answers than the material side that he found his ultimate truth.

Buddhism is the Middle Way between the two extremes of materialism and spirituality. And, in navigating this middle ground, Buddhism rises above both materialism and spirituality. The practice of zazen brings together a person's spiritual and material sides in a way no other practice can. That is why Buddha chose it.

It's also boring as hell, just like Buddha himself. But it's a big mistake to think that boredom is a bad thing. A boring movie about a boring religious leader may be bad in terms of what a major film studio would want to invest in. But boredom is what life is all about, really. Because if you're a healthy person, most of your life is probably pretty damned boring.

But it's only within the boring parts of your life that you can begin to see what your life really is. Yet we constantly seek to be *amused*, the root of which means "diverted." We want to be diverted from what's really going on. Our spiritual quests, for the most part, are a search for a new kind of amusement, a spiritual diversion. The solution Buddha found, while sitting there under the Bodhi tree, was simply to stop looking for diversions of any kind and to stay with what was happening here and now.

Chapter 21

Bad Hair Day

Back in the day, when I originally joined Zero Defects, hair was a major issue. Hairstyles are an important way of defining oneself and one's cultural affiliations. This is especially true for people in their teens and twenties. In the sixties young people showed their dissatisfaction with society by growing their hair. But by the end of the next decade long hair had become a sign of conformity to a specific set of ideals. The punks showed their disgust with the failed ideals of hippiedom by cutting their hair short. When just having short hair didn't seem radical enough, the hardcore punks went one better and shaved it all off. But this caused confusion because certain racists had already adopted the skinhead look. So the skinhead punks had to take great pains to distance themselves from white supremacists.

I cut my hair short at the end of the seventies to be more punk. But by 1982, the year I joined Zero Defects, I'd been growing it back for a couple years, and it was pretty long. This didn't really sit well with the band, which included two skinheads. But they were still more committed to the idea of personal freedom than they were to enforcing the punk dress code, so I was never really pressured to get a haircut. I was teased a lot for looking like a hippie, though. Actually, I was trying to master the hairstyle of Ozzy's late guitarist, Randy Rhoads. I stuck to my guns and never did cut it short — though I dyed a white skunk stripe down the middle for a while. When the fanzines printed photos of the band, I noticed that I usually wasn't included in the shots they chose. Guess I was bad for the image. It was funny when Henry Rollins grew his hair long a couple of years later and suddenly my old friends were commenting about how progressive I'd been. Ha!

Of course, Buddhists discovered the psychosocial effects of the shaven head a few thousand and some years before the punks showed up. The chrome dome was intended to symbolize the monk's detachment from things of the world — like cool hair. These days, though, I'm not so sure how well that aspect of the deal works, since so many people shave their heads to look cool. Unfortunately, I do not look cool with a shaved head. I look like a Martian. I only shaved my head one time. That was when I officially joined the Soto sect.

Here's how joining the Buddhist order works. There are a number of ways one can officially become a member. In Gautama's day you shaved your head, got some robes, and went up to Gautama himself, who would ordain you with the words, "Welcome, monk." Very simple, very easy. These days things have gotten way more complicated.

See, Buddha died, but the organization just kept on growing, so things became more bureaucratic. Of course, there were reactions to the bureaucracy, various splinter groups were formed, and so on. Nowadays in Japan you have a few major organizations, one of which is the Soto sect, which traces its ancestry back to Dogen and beyond. The Soto sect is a big, monolithic beast of an organization with all kinds of bylaws and such. My teacher, Gudo Nishijima, is an ordained member of the Soto sect. As such, he can ordain whoever he wants as a monk. But those monks don't automatically become members of the sect unless they go through the proper procedures.

At first I had no intention of joining the Soto sect. Those of you who've read *Hardcore Zen* know I had strong misgivings about even being ordained by Nishijima, let alone joining some kind of a big-ass corporation. Besides that, I knew that Nishijima didn't require the head-shaving business but that the Soto sect did. So, no thanks.

But when I decided to move back to the United States, I thought that since I was in Japan already and the procedure would be relatively simple and painless, I might as well officially join the sect now rather than end up later on regretting not having done it.* I talked to Nishijima about it. At first he was real down on the idea. He doesn't have a whole lot of interest in the Soto sect, which he considers to be little more than a guild of funeral directors. Though he's been invited numerous times to speak at Eiheiji, the sect's head temple, he considers such talks a waste of time and prefers, instead, talking to ragtag groups of foreign idiots like me. But after a while he decided ordination might be worthwhile, so he agreed to make it happen. What I had to do — apart from shaving my head — was to fill out some forms, get myself a set of special joining-the-Soto-sect robes, then make a trip with him out to the temple where he'd been ordained and go through a brief ceremony.

A weird thing happened once word got out that I had decided to join the sect. All of a sudden several other guys who'd been ordained by Nishijima decided they wanted to join the sect as well. So there ended up being six of us on the trip. We all piled into a car on the bullet train headed down south from Tokyo to Shizuoka, where the temple was located, and off we went.

The ceremony itself was pretty dumb, if you ask me. Nishijima sat on a big, goofy-looking chair with this silly-looking hat on. We all stood in a line and one by one went up to him and let him mime

---

* Weirdly enough, nearly every time I tell this story to anyone they refuse to believe that my thoughts about it went no deeper than that. But what can I say? I'm a shallow guy. That is really as far as I thought it through.

the action of shaving our heads, which already looked like cue balls anyway. He recited some stuff, the other monks who lived at the temple recited some stuff, we all recited some stuff together. Incense was burned, commemorative photos were taken that would be sent to Soto HQ for their records, and that was it. Bob's yer uncle, we was monks. A couple of weeks later I got my certificate in the mail.

Later I had this bizarre conversation with a guy I knew who was way, way too impressed with the fact that I'd actually gone through this ceremony. He absolutely refused to believe that I did not find the whole thing immensely profound and deeply moving. But I assure you I did not. It was sort of fun, in a way, but not the least bit moving.

As much as I hated looking at myself in the mirror after that, I did discover that there are some real advantages to having no hair. It's really easy to manage, for one thing. Back when I had my Randy Rhoads do, it used to take me ages of messing around with styling gel and hairdryers and crap to get it looking just right. And even when I did achieve the desired effect, as soon as I walked out of the house some random gust of wind would come along and undo all my hard efforts. Being bald is really easy. You never have a bad hair day. At least not about your hair. But even bald-headed Buddhist monks can have bad hair days about all kinds of other stuff. So how does a Buddhist deal with a bad hair day? Dogen quotes a story in a book called *Shinji Shobogenzo* — which is like a shorter companion piece to the *Shobogenzo* — that addresses that.

A monk asks a Zen master, "When all houses close their doors, how do we behave ourselves?"

The Zen master says, "What about the situation in the zazen hall?"

Six months pass before the monk can come up with a snappy comeback. Finally he says, "There is no one who will accept him."

The Zen master says, "Okay. I'll give you a 'B plus' on that answer."

Hearing this, the monk — who figured that was an A-plus answer for sure — throws a big ol' conniption fit in front of the Zen master and begs him to tell him what he could've said to get a better grade. But the Zen master just clams up.

So the monk gets all heated up, grabs hold of the Zen master by the collar, and drags him right out of his room and into the hallway. He balls up his fists and shouts, "Look, you old windbag, if you don't give me the answer I'm gonna pound your stupid-looking bald head in!"

The Zen master says, "I have found the words." The monk starts bowing and bowing and bowing, right down to the floor like something out of a bad cartoon.

The Zen master says, "There is no one who is even aware of him." All at once the monk finally gets it.

Yeah. I know. Another couple of Zen goofballs. But wait.

"When all houses close their doors" refers to a situation in which the whole wide world seems to be against you, when you're having a bad hair day and nothing's going right. For lots of people — especially dumb asses like me — this is what Zen practice is like all the time. One bad hair day after another.

You sit there and sit there and sit there, and nothing is ever solved; there's no enlightenment at the end of the rainbow; it's just a lot of boredom and pain in your legs. Even when you do have cool mystical insights, your teachers tell you to forget about them. Zen is crap. This is the idealistic point of view. Nothing, no matter what it is, will ever be able to match your idealized vision. The good stuff is never as good as what you had imagined, and even the worst bad stuff is never quite as bad, just like those researchers quoted in Jon Gertner's *New York Times* article said in chapter 15.

Instead of answering the monk's question like a normal person, the smart-ass Zen master asks the poor monk about the state in the zazen hall — meaning, what's it like when he's doing zazen. See, if the goal of zazen were to achieve a heightened awareness, states of sacred bliss, or some such thing, then zazen on a bad hair day might be considered worse than zazen on a good hair day. But zazen isn't like that. Whatever it is is just what it is. If you can stay reasonably still and at least *try* to keep your mind focused on the task at hand for the time period you've allotted yourself, you get a gold star. Whether or not it works out the way you want it to is of no concern. Being just what you are right now is the very definition of success in zazen.

It takes the monk six long months, but he finally gets a sense of what the master's been telling him and expresses his understanding by saying that "no one will accept him." By "him" the monk is referring to himself in the third person, as Buddhist monks sometimes do. "Accept" means "accept as a student." In other words, no one can teach him. He alone possesses and manifests the truth of the universe — just like you. Yeah. You heard me. You *alone* possess the truth of the universe, just like *everyone* and *everything* else throughout all of creation.

The master says it's a good answer but that it doesn't go far enough. When the monk asks the master to explain what the monk's mistake was or to express his own enlightenment clearly, the master refuses. He wants the monk to find the answer for himself. That way it would be far more meaningful.

Just stop for a second here, and look how easily this poor monk gets distracted. First he says that he alone possesses the truth. But the minute his teacher withholds his approval, the monk suddenly forgets that he possesses the truth and starts thinking the master's got it and therefore can give it to him. This happens all the time with students of Buddhism. They'll get it and a half second later forget what they've just understood. I can't tell you how often this still happens to me.*

So after the monk gets all pissed off and threatens him, the master tells the monk that no one is even aware of him. This time "him" means both the master and the monk.

---

* It happens to everyone, by the way. The people you gotta watch out for are the ones who'll tell you they have the Final Answer.

It also means you and me.

The master's answer is even more severe than the monk's. Not only are we alone in the universe, but no one else even knows we're here.

Think about it. Other people may be able to get some rough idea of what we think and feel. But no one else can ever be "aware" of you in the truest sense. Only you can know what you really think, feel, and experience. Yet a lot — perhaps even all — our conflicts are based on the assumption that whoever we've disagreed with thoroughly understands what it is we're trying to tell her. Ten times out of ten, though, she does not. Half the arguments I've had in my life boil down to cases of two people who think exactly the same thing but express it differently.*

It's a pretty frightening thing to imagine being totally alone in the universe, which is why most of us don't even want to entertain the possibility. You can picture some very melodramatic person suddenly ripping his black Morrisey T-shirt and beating the ground with his fists while shouting in despair, "I'm totally alone in the universe!" I can recall a few times in my childhood when I suddenly noticed how alone I really was and literally started screaming and shouting about it. Alas, to no avail. Everyone just thought I was being a problematic child. What I didn't know then was that I was far from being alone in my aloneness.

Interestingly enough, though, Dogen places this story just a couple of pages after another story that seems to be saying precisely the opposite thing. That one ends with the words, "A lone naked body in the ten thousand phenomena is just the ten thousand phenomena."** "Ten thousand" is an old-fashioned Chinese way of saying "a whole

---

*   And far too often our solution to this dilemma is to try and make others understand us by hurting them the way we feel we have been hurt. As if no one but us has ever experienced pain before....But remember, kids, *everybody* has experienced just as much pain in their lives as you have in yours, and they don't need you proving to them what "real pain" is. Sorry for the digression. I just think it's a really, really important point.

** Especially if it's Lucy Liu's lone naked body! Angh! Angh! Angh! Sorry.

big bunch" or "everything." I hate it when Zen dudes from Western countries start rattling on about the "ten thousand things" as if they're characters out of the old *Kung Fu* TV series.

We are alone in the universe because the total universe is us.

I know that sounds bizarre. It goes against all common sense. But it happens to be true. You can never separate yourself from the rest of the universe. You're just one aspect of the totality and at the same time you are that totality itself, since there is nothing else you could possibly be.

So what's all this weird philosophy got to do with the poor monk who's having a bad hair day — or bad scalp day, since his head was probably shaven — or, for that matter, with you or me when things aren't going right? Everything. And it's got everything to do with us when things are going just perfectly, for that matter.

When things don't go the way we want them to, we start to feel at odds with everything. We start to invent impossible hypothetical situations. If only this or that condition were met, we think, every-thing would be fine. If only she loved me as much as I love her. If only I had enough money. If only my job didn't suck so bad. And on and on and on. People involved in Zen meditation tend to imagine "if only" scenarios concerning how much better off they'd be if only they could get enlightened.

On the other hand, during those rare times when things are go-ing perfectly, we develop this terrible anxiety about when it's going to end and things'll get sucky again. We can't enjoy life when things are going badly, and we can't even enjoy it when everything is hum-ming along just fine.

But to a Buddhist, the whole world is me. I *am* that sucky job. I *am* the girl who doesn't love me as much as I love her. I *am* the pair of "vegetarian" Doc Martens I special ordered by mail that pinch my feet so bad I can't wear them for more than ten minutes and yet cost over 150 nonreturnable bucks.

Now you're probably saying to yourself: How could that possibly be? I mean, it's perfectly obvious that there's a very clear division between you and other people and things. If you and I were the same, then my publishers would send you my royalty checks.* If you and Donald Trump were manifestations of the same ineffable unified reality, you could charge whatever you wanted on his credit cards. Right?

But it's just like how when you poke a safety pin through your nose you feel pain in your nostril and not in your left big toe, even though both your left big toe and your nostril are part of one single human body. The universe may feel pain, or joy, or existential longing for that which has past, or an ingrown toenail, or whatever, in that part of it called "Bob Canastaberry" and not in that part of it called "Amy Logenbottom." Yet in ways you can't possibly hope to notice, as well as in ways that are hopelessly obvious, whatever affects one part of the universe affects the whole thing. Because both Bob and Amy are the entire universe. And so are you.

I know it sounds goofy. But at the risk of sounding like a broken record I'll say it again. You've spent your whole life learning how to clearly differentiate between that which is you and that which is not you. You've honed it. You know every detail of this thing you've chosen to call "you" and all the ways in which it stands in clear contrast to things outside itself. And it's not that the conclusions you've come to are entirely wrong. It's just that they're far too one-sided. You believe that just because one thing is true, it's exact diametrical opposite can't possibly be true as well. Think again.

The oneness of you and the entire universe isn't just a way of thinking about things, a philosophical speculation. After a few years of practice this becomes the only possible way of looking at the world that makes any sense at all. You are forced to accept it whether you like it or not.

And I, for one, did not like it one teeny bit when I first began to

---

* And you'd probably complain about how small they were too.

notice it. I'd heard the old saw about how "all is one" more times than I could count. But when the reality of that finally began to sink in, I hated it.

Lots of people find the whole "all is one" thing really attractive. Not me, boy howdy. Are you kidding? I was voted "most individu-alistic" in my senior class in high school.* I'd invested lots of time and effort to standing out from any crowd. As a hardcore punk rocker I'd even refused to cut my hair short just to make certain I'd stand out even in a crowd full of stand-outs. The idea that I might be one and the same as all the idiots of the world who I despised so vehemently made me gag.

See, for one thing, when you see things this way, it's im-fogging-possible to blame anyone else for what's wrong in your life. And man, oh, man, is that ever a hard thing to face. Here I was, a punk rocker, completely unable to blame any of the standard things punk rockers blame for what was wrong with my life and the world in general. I could no longer point a finger at the Republicans or at the NRA or at that brainwashed herd of corporate rock–worshiping sheep they called my "peers" or at the System or at anyone else, for that matter. Try that one on for size sometime, substituting your own set of things you usually blame for what's wrong with your life. Don't make any excuses or exceptions for any reason whatsoever. Accept all responsibility yourself and see how easy or nice the whole "all is one" thing sounds to you.

Ouch.

For some of us the very idea of looking at stuff that way seems patently ridiculous. We cannot fathom that such a view could possi-bly be true. There *must* be things we can blame on others when those things are clearly *their* fault and not ours! But a Buddhist can never view anything in those terms. Unlike our usual way of looking at

---

*   I happened to be on the committee that came up with the categories, but — hey — it wasn't like I could've won in any other category.

things, the idea that we have only ourselves to blame for our circumstances — whatever they might be — removes any desire we might feel to cause pain to others or to fail to put our own lives in order.

You can't control your circumstances. Control is an illusion. But how you respond to them is totally up to you. And once you learn to respond better, an interesting thing happens. The world starts to behave exactly as you want it to. Or is it just that you no longer expect it to behave in any way other than it does? Maybe. And maybe not. Honestly, I'm not sure.

Yet, as Dogen's story says, the outside world — which is so intimately connected with you that there is no separation between the two — couldn't give a rat's ass about you. And yet the universe that doesn't even give a rat's ass about you *is* you. And because of this, it cares more about you than *you* could ever care about you.

There's the magic. That's where things become so beautiful that it hurts to even try and comprehend them. You are completely part of this nasty old, beautiful old world. Not just part, even; you are the whole shebang. Just like a bubble floating on a river, getting pulled this way and that by the currents, rising and falling, eventually to end with a pop, after which none of the other bubbles will know that the bubble you loved and cherished so much you called it your self was ever even there. Is that bubble separate from the river, or is it just one aspect of the river to which we arbitrarily give the name "bubble"?

Six of one, half a dozen of the other.

How do you live when you see things that way? Do you angrily rail that no one will ever know your true feelings? That nobody really cares?

Or do you see things as they are and float along enjoying doing what needs to be done until you can't do anything at all anymore?

Chapter 22

The Same Difference

I arrived back in Los Angeles to a cocktail of jet lag, smog, and warm December sunshine. Don't get me wrong. I would never knock the weather out here. But, dammit, it just ain't natural for it to be this warm a week before Christmas.

In Ohio I was a rock star. But out here in California, I was a Zen teacher. It's hard to say which I prefer. Being a rock star is fun. But being a Zen teacher has better hours. Rock stars get to do interviews. Zen teachers just get a lot of questions thrown at 'em. One of the most frequently asked is the one about the relationship between Buddhist teachings in the form of lectures and books and suchlike and Buddhist practice in the form of zazen.

In lamenting the futility of Buddhism, our old pal science writer John Horgan talks about a Zen teacher who said that "language prevents us from seeing the world as it truly is." He responds, "I thought how tired I was of this Zen cliché. How many millions of words have Zen masters spouted telling us to get beyond words?"

The answer is — a whole lot of 'em, including the ones in this little book. And the reason Buddhists spout so many words telling us to go beyond words is to get us to go beyond words.* Without hearing that words are unnecessary — spoken in unnecessary words — most of us would never make the effort to see why that might be so. Dogen talks about "seeing the moment of their [words'] complete nonnecessity." It's not enough just to hear the words that words are unnecessary. We have to make the real effort to go beyond them.

People make a big deal about going beyond words and concepts. But, really, it ain't no big thang. What is beyond all words and concepts is just this — just your life right now. Even if you can explain it with words, the words cannot capture what your life really is.

In chapter 24 of *Shobogenzo*, called 仏教, which is pronounced *Bukkyo* and means "Buddhist Teachings," Dogen talks about a dude who goes up to a Zen master and says, "The Patriarch's intention and the intention of the teachings; are they the same or different?"

The Zen master looks him up and down and says, "When chickens are cold they perch in trees. When ducks are cold they enter the water."

The "Patriarch" here refers to a guy named Bodhidharma. He was the Indian monk credited with bringing zazen practice to China. Now, guys before him went to China to teach Buddhism. But mainly they stuck to teaching the words of Buddhism and not its actual practice. Bodhidharma was different. He taught Buddhism by doing Buddhism, specifically by doing a whole lot of zazen.** So when Zen students ask about Bodhidharma's intention, it's a way of referring to the practice of seated meditation. The "Patriarch's intention," then, is zazen, and the "intention of the teachings" is written or spoken Buddhist philosophy.

Legend has it that Bodhidharma sat in a cave for nine years just staring at a wall until his arms and legs fell off. Sounds like a tall tale

---

* Duh!

** The practice was called *dhyana* in India, which was pronounced *chan* by the Chinese and *zen*, or *zazen*, meaning "sitting zen," by the Japanese. Once again, don't say you never learned nothin' from one of my books!

to me. Still, a lot of Japanese temples have little wooden statues of armless, legless egg-shaped Bodhidharmas with a cartoonish-looking bearded face set in a perpetual scowl. Miniature versions of these statues are still common playthings for children. Like the Weeble toys, Bodhidharma wobbles but he won't fall down.

The real Bodhidharma must have had arms and hands, though, because he wrote a famous poem about the place of written teachings in Buddhism.* It's this little poem that inspired the student to question whether Bodhidharma's intention in coming to China was the same or different from the intention of the written teachings of Buddhism. So let's take a look at the poem:

Separate transmission outside the teachings (教外別伝)
Nondependence on writing (不立文字)
Direct pointing to the human heart (直指人心)
Seeing one's nature and becoming Buddha (見性成仏)

Not much of a poem, eh? It doesn't even rhyme. If it had started off, "There once was a man from Nantucket, who got enlightened before he kicked the bucket," it might have hung together better as a poem in English. But Bodhidharma was writing in Chinese, and, from what I gather, it sounds a lot better in that language.

In the chickens and ducks story the guy is asking his Zen teacher about the first line of the poem, the one about "separate transmission outside the teachings." Our Zen student is asking about the relationship between the teachings of a guy like Bodhidharma, who was supposed to be a man of few words who taught his students face-to-face, and that mountain of books with all these millions of words in 'em — which Bodhidharma seems to be refuting in his poem but

---

* Or maybe he didn't; recent historians of Buddhism have questioned whether Bodhidharma is the true author of this piece. But it certainly shows his influence, and even if someone else actually wrote it, the writer based it on things Bodhidharma had said.

which people still call "Buddhism" anyhow. A lot of folks figure that Zen is all about tossing the spoken and written Buddhist teachings out the window and looking for something more profound and direct. And there *are* Zen stories about Buddhist scholars who suddenly burn all their books and get enlightened. But Dogen wasn't very fond of that attitude. So he uses this story to address the problem.

In his commentary Dogen says that what the Zen master really means here is, "It's the same difference, blockhead."* What Dogen actually said is that the answer "expresses sameness and difference, but not the sameness and difference which is at the mercy of people who hold views on sameness and difference."

The Zen master in the story was implying that chickens solve the problem of cold by going up in the trees and ducks solve the problem of cold by going in the water. In other words, written teachings address the problem of how to live a sane and peaceful life in one way, and the actual practice of zazen addresses it in another. Comparing them is like comparing apples to oranges or trying to judge Johnny Ramone's guitar style by the same criteria you'd use to judge Yngwie Malmsteen's. It makes no sense.

So why is this important? I'm glad you asked, Grasshopper.

See, a whole lot of the time when human beings disagree with each other, it's because they don't know the difference between real differences and pretend ones.

Dogen says the sameness and difference expressed in the story we just looked at "is not the sameness and difference which is at the mercy of people who hold views on sameness and difference." In other words, there is real sameness and real difference in this big wide universe of ours. But that real sameness and difference are not the "sameness and difference" you carry around in your head all the time.

So what's the difference between these different samenesses and

---

* Okay. I added *blockhead.*

differences? To take an easy example, if you were born in an English-speaking country like America, you learned that there was a color called blue and a color called green. The sky was blue, your parents taught you, and traffic lights that meant "go" were green. But if you were born in Japan, you learned that there was a single color called *aoi* and that the sky and traffic lights — which are the same color there as they are in America — were both shades of *aoi*. Now, any non-color-blind Japanese person will tell you that the color of the sky on a sunny day is not exactly identical to the color of a traffic light. There is *real difference* between the two colors. They just use the same word, *aoi*, to define various shades of similar color. There is *real sameness* in the word used to describe those two different colors.

It's not just people from different cultural backgrounds who have this problem with real differences and made-up ones. Think about all the words and concepts we take for granted. What is love? What is hate? What is freedom? What is God? What is defense of one's people? What is terrorism? It's all very complicated, when you get right down to it.

Buddhism proposes something very, very radical about the nature of all this sameness and difference. Buddhism says that no matter how we slice up reality to fit it into our brains — no matter what definitions we come up with of sameness and difference — reality itself remains forever unsliced, remains forever just as it is. And it further asserts that the sliced-up image of reality in our heads never, ever in a million billion, quadrillion years matches up with reality itself.

To Dogen, the written teachings of Buddhism were the same as and yet different from the one-on-one teaching between a Zen master and her or his student. To explain this further, he cites another old Zen story:

A monk goes up to a Zen master and asks, "The three vehicles and the twelve divisions of the teaching being unnecessary, just what is the ancestral Master's intention in coming from the west?"

The Zen master says, "The three vehicles and the twelve divisions of the teaching completely being unnecessary."

The ancestral Master is Bodhidharma once again, and his "coming from the west" refers to his concrete real action of traveling from India to China to teach zazen. Dogen goes into detail about the three vehicles and the twelve divisions of the teachings, but I'll let you look that up for yourself. Suffice it to say they basically serve in this story as shorthand for the kind of stuff students of Buddhism learn either from books or from memorizing stuff their teachers say even if the students don't really get it.

Dogen explains the story like this. "We do not deny the existence of the three vehicles and the twelve divisions of the teaching; we should glimpse the moment of their complete nonnecessity. Because they are complete nonnecessity, they are the three vehicles and twelve divisions of the teaching. Because they are the three vehicles and twelve divisions of the teaching, they are not 'three vehicles and the twelve divisions of the teaching.' For this reason, we express them as 'the three vehicles and twelve divisions of the teaching.'"

Just after saying this, Dogen was snagged in a giant butterfly net by two men dressed in white, then whisked away to a very special kind of hospital where they taught him to weave baskets, and he lived happily ever after.

No, no, no! What he said actually makes sense.* In fact, it's extraordinarily practical and vitally important. All humankind's problems today stem solely from our inability to see that words are just words. We have the ability to eradicate hunger, war, poverty, lack of proper sanitation, bad Eddie Murphy movies — the whole enchilada right now, today, this very second. The only thing stopping this from happening is our unwillingness to see ourselves and the world we

---

* At least finish the chapter before you call the nice young men in their clean white coats to come and take me away, okay?

live in for what it truly is beyond the mental concepts we use to organize it for ourselves.

When you can really understand that the concepts you carry around in your brain are no more than mere concepts, the entire universe changes completely.

The understanding I'm talking about here isn't just intellectual understanding. Actually *living this truth* is what's really important. When you only understand it intellectually, you still attach undue importance to your own conclusions about how things are.

Another thing that came out of Bodhidharma's little poem that's really messed up lotsa folks is the one little word the old man chose to lead off the very last line. In English it means "seeing one's nature." In Japanese the word is pronounced *kensho*.

Ah ha! I saw the eyes of all you Buddha nerds out there suddenly light up on that one. The normal people are just going, "Ken Sho? Didn't he fight Bruce Lee in one of them old karate movies?"* Ah, but the Buddha nerds are all going, "Great! He's finally gonna talk about *kensho*!"

For those of you who don't waste all your time hanging out in dodgy Buddhist chat rooms on the Internet or reading crappy books about Zen, *kensho* is another word for the Big E, Enlightenment. Lots of folks latched onto this little word like a crab onto a rock star's scrotum. So let's talk a little about *kensho*, shall we?

---

* That was Sho Kosugi, by the way, or maybe Ken Watanabe.

Chapter 23

Enlightenment Is for Sissies!

In my role as bass player for Zero Defects, questions about enlightenment never come up. Nobody expects a punk rock bass player to have had any kind of paranormal experiences or to possess any Mystical Knowledge of the Great Beyond. Unfortunately, the same is not true in my role as a Zen teacher. No matter how often I insist that there ain't no such thang as enlightenment, there's always someone who thinks I'm putting them on, that I'm being cagey about it or something. Or they decide there really is enlightenment out there somewhere, but Brad just hasn't achieved it. It's always kind of a relief when folks decide that, because then they'll go bug someone else and leave me alone. Still, I feel kind of bad when that happens, because I know there are plenty of con artists out there who'll tell you they do have it and are prepared to sell it to you.

A chapter of my last book ended up being used in a book called *The Best Buddhist Writing of 2004*. While I was honored to have been chosen for inclusion, the intro the editor wrote really rubbed me the wrong way. In the chapter he picked I talked about the day I was walking to work and things just kinda fell into place very nicely. No big deal, really. But the editor described the chapter as being about my experience of what he called *kensho*, "a sudden hit of the Enlightened Mind," is how I think he put it — he never sent me a copy of the book so I don't own it. The chapter was not about that at all. I've never experienced *kensho*, and I hope I never do. The people I've encountered who claim to have had such experiences have never said anything to convince me it was an experience worth having.

Just to get you up to speed if you're not a Buddha Nerd, enlightenment goes by a variety of names in Buddhist literature. The two most common Japanese words are *kensho* (見性), which Bodhidharma used in his poem, and *satori* (悟り). *Kensho* means "seeing into one's true nature," while *satori* is just a Japanese word meaning "understanding" — although these days it is used almost exclusively to refer to enlightenment.

A lotta times when people first hear the story of Buddha's life, they focus on what folks like to call his enlightenment experience. He's out there on his firm mound covered in dewy soft grass under that tall, strong, upright tree. Slowly, gently he slides into the meditative state. Once he's in, he meditates harder and harder, going faster and faster through the various spiritual stages, his understanding getting bigger and bigger as he keeps on meditating harder and harder and harder, pushing and thrusting deeper and deeper into his psyche for enlightenment. And then finally, all at once he has this massive spiritual climax to end all climaxes, spurting all over space and time and even going splat right in our twenty-first-century faces.

Plenty of people come away from that story thinking that after his enlightenment ol' Mr. Buddha no longer had to make any kind of effort to maintain the balanced state he'd acquired. Enlightenment, they think, turned him into something superhuman, a kind of god. Folks like that tend to project this view onto Buddhist teachers in general, thinking that their enlightened state allows them to glide effortlessly through their lives with nary a worry or care. It's this kind of enlightened state they seek. Unfortunately, there are people who take advantage of that mistaken understanding and make a lot of money doing so. They even put out magazines. But real Buddhism does not teach anything of the sort.

The earliest Buddhists, for example, didn't see it that way at all. You'll recall the story of how Mara, the evil demonic tempter, offered Buddha riches and power and babes by the score if he'd just give up this whole zazen deal, but, of course, Buddha refused. The way the story gets told most of the time these days, Buddha meets Mara once, defeats him, gets enlightened, and never deals with the guy again. But in the earlier texts Mara pops up again and again, even after Buddha has had his supposed enlightenment-to-end-all-enlightenments. We're not supposed to accept that Buddha was subject to weird visitations by supernatural beings all his life. The point being made is that even Buddha was not free from normal human temptations and folly even after his awakening, that he had to constantly guard and keep the state he'd achieved.

Dogen is famous for maintaining that there is no difference between practice and enlightenment, that the moment you sit on your cushion and do a bit of zazen you are enlightened already. It was and still remains a controversial idea. What's the point of sitting there with your legs all twisted up in knots for hours and days and months and years if you're not going to get enlightened by doing it?

But in Dogen's way of thinking, zazen itself is the practice of enlightenment — meaning enlightenment is not something you can achieve; it's something that you *do* every single moment of every single day until you can't do nuthin' more. Becoming calmer, more easygoing, less neurotic, even gaining a deep and profound understanding of what you and the universe actually are — these are nothing but side effects, little perks. They're the bonus tracks of Buddhism, the unreleased mixes and alternate takes. But they're not the album itself.

There's a real danger to this practice of pursuing so-called enlightenment experiences. Remember, according to Buddhism there is no self, and everything is one. This sounds like a philosophical position. But Buddhists through the ages have discovered that it is an absolute fact, as concrete and observable as any other phenomenon in the universe. Certain practices can give a person a very, very shallow and incomplete glimpse of this rather quickly. Some of these involve psychological games; others involve special ways of breathing and suchlike; sometimes sleep deprivation and isolation tanks are employed. And though the experience may be just the tip of the left big toe in the kiddy pool, a lot of people have a bad tendency to figure they've been plunged into the depths of the mid-Atlantic.

If the person who glimpses this is not very mature, this understanding can and does lead to all kinds of not-at-all-nice things. To take one sadly far-too-common example, you can begin to believe that since all is one, and I am the same as everyone else, then I am the same as my best friend, and it is therefore perfectly all right for me to schtup his wife because, she's, like, *my* wife too, right? And besides that even, she is ultimately the same as me 'cuz, like, everything is the same as me. Therefore on the basis of Ultimate Reality — which, of course, I am privy to, having been enlightened and all — I'm not really doing any harm to anyone but myself. And, hey, I can handle it, so everything is cool. There are all kinds of sleazy variations on this theme involving not just sex but money, power, fame, and all the rest. This is just pure speculation on my part, but I've often suspected that people like Charles Manson and Adolf Hitler may have had some kind of low-level "awakening experience" that led to their being able to do what they did.

This is one among many reasons why I am not the least bit interested in practices that encourage the quest for enlightenment experiences. I much prefer Dogen's way of not dividing practice from experience.

Although Dogen doesn't divide the practice of zazen from enlightenment, he does talk about something quite different that is often assumed by confused readers to be enlightenment of the Big Fat

Download from on High That Fixes Everything Forever Amen variety. Dogen uses two particular phrases to describe this something. One is 発無上心, which is pronounced *hotsu-mujoshin*, and the other is 発菩提心, which is pronounced *hotsu-bodaishin*. The first character in both phrases, *hotsu* (発), means something like "aspiration," while the last character in both phrases, *shin* (心), means "mind" or "heart." *Mujo* (無上) means "supreme" (literally the two characters are "nothing" and "above") and *bodai* (菩提) stands in for the Sanskrit word *bodhi*, meaning "awakening."

These two phrases are rendered a number of different ways in English by different translators. The most common way is the "aspiration for enlightenment." Occasionally you'll see it translated as "seeking the absolute" or "desire for the supreme." But I much prefer Gudo Nishijima's way of putting it: "will to the truth."

Dogen emphasizes over and over again the paramount importance of Buddhists having the will to the truth. He believed that this was one of the most important aspects of Buddhist pursuit.

Yet, though he believed we needed to have the will to the truth, in the chapter "Kuge" (空華), or "Flowers in Space,"* Dogen quotes a Chinese poem by a guy named Chosetsu that says, "To approach the Truth intentionally is wrong." Dogen explains this, saying, "To turn one's back on the Truth is wrong. The Truth is the approaching and the turning away, which, in each instance of approaching or turning away, are the Truth itself."

Do you see what he's saying here? It's pretty neat. Even the very action of your approaching or turning away from the truth is nothing other than the truth itself. The truth is inescapable. Turn away from it, and it's right there in front of you. Approach it, and you're already there. The trick is to learn *this* moment, no matter what it is.

---

* A bit like *Pigs in Space* but with flowers, though it's not clear if Dogen meant "outer space" in the way we conceive of it since the idea of outer space hadn't been invented yet.

To envision something you call the "truth" and then make efforts to arrive at it makes no sense.

In other words, that big ol' hard-on you have for getting enlightened is the very thing that will prevent it from ever actually happening. Tough break, I know. But that's the way it is.

The will to the truth means seeking that which is 100 percent free of any kind of bullshit. It means a will — as in "willingness" — to see and to conform with what is true, whether or not that truth is comfortable, whether or not it's what you want to be true, whether or not it matches your fantasies about what is true, whether or not it's what everyone always told you was true. That one supreme, absolute, awakened truth is what is *just* here, *just* now. If you cannot find the truth here and now, then even if you somehow made it to whatever sort of "enlightenment" you envision for yourself, you couldn't possibly recognize the truth of that state either.

Some folks get really disappointed with the idea that here and now is enlightenment itself. We know all about here and now. Boooooring! We want to go somewhere else. We're sure that all the cool stuff has got to be out there somewhere because it sure as hell ain't here.

So for those of you who might think of it that way, let me offer you my take on why even perfect unsurpassed enlightenment isn't any better than the state of washing some unexplainable brownish-green gunk off your favorite pair of Converse high-tops.

I'm sure that every person reading this book has some possession somewhere in their house or their garage that, at one time, they wanted soooooo bad they could hardly think of anything else. Maybe you gave up a hell of a lot just to get that pearl-white, three-pickup Gibson Les Paul Custom guitar, or whatever it happens to be. Maybe you worked late, didn't go out with friends, sacrificed eating lunch four days a week just to be able to afford it. Or maybe the thing you wanted was very rare. You searched and searched and searched. You spent hours every day trolling eBay for possible names your item might be listed under. You lost out on three or four auctions before you finally snagged a genuine glow-in-the-dark plastic model of the giant spider creature from *The Angry Red Planet.*

Whatever it was and however you managed to get it, now it's yours. So how do you feel about it now? Stop and think for a sec.

It seems to me there are a few basic ways of dealing with this kind of thing. Sometimes people become obsessive about their acquisition. They polish it and enclose it in a glass showcase. They insure it. They do anything and everything in their power to keep that item from ever, ever becoming any different from the way it was when they first took possession of it. And they go absolutely ballistic if the thing gets a scratch or scuff on it. They seem to believe that by preserving the thing in its pristine form, they can preserve that thrill they got when they first made it their very own. We do this with the people we feel we possess too, and that's a big problem. But we'll leave that aside for now.

Others like to create a category for the item to be an example of. They strive to collect every single item that falls into that category, searching the world over for the one they might have missed — all in an effort to reexperience the thrill they got from making that very first something — whatever it was — their own. Pretty soon they amass a huge collection of their chosen fetish objects. This is the one I personally have to work hard at avoiding. And still, my collection of old sci-fi memorabilia is pretty impressive....

These are pretty much the ways folks deal with so-called enlightenment experiences. Some people obsess over them, trying with all their might to hold onto that one shining moment of clarity just as it was the moment they were struck by it. They want to freeze that little moment forever and ever. Those who are successful at convincing others they have done this impossible thing can make a very good living as gurus and dispensers of eternal cosmic wisdom that's about as substantial and nutritious as cotton candy.

Other folks become collectors of enlightenment experiences.

They categorize them into levels of awakening. They compare their enlightenment experiences with each other the same way a group of seven-year-olds might compare Yu-Gi-Oh! cards. They envy those with the cooler experiences and lord it over those who've attained lower levels of enlightenment, condescendingly offering their benevolent help and support.

Enlightenment experiences do happen. And, on some rare occasions, they can even be valuable. But not usually in the way you'd imagine. Their value lies mainly in your ability to forget about them. The best way to deal with such experiences is to just let them settle where they are. Let them become a part of your life but not an obsession. Maybe it'll happen again. Maybe it won't. Either way, you'll continue to lead your life as it is, moment by moment. But, most important, be strong enough to give up the illusion that whatever you experienced has anything to do with the idea of a once-and-forever-type enlightenment. As Dogen puts it, "There is a state in which the traces of realization are forgotten; and it manifests the traces of forgotten realization for a long, long time." Real enlightenment is not an experience. Real enlightenment is the ongoing work you do to keep from getting caught up in your experiences.

Your ordinary life, whatever it might be, is the absolute truth of your ordinary life. The universe that enters your eyes shines from your eyes as well. If it's dull and mundane, you have no one else to blame. Or as Dogen says in "Four Elements of a Bodhisattva's Social Relations" (chapter 45 of *Shobogenzo*), "When we leave the truth to the truth, we attain the truth. When we attain the truth, the truth inevitably continues to be left to the truth."

Chapter 24

The Eight Truths
of Great Human Beings

Zero Defects never "made it" in the world of rock and roll, and we never will. We'll never even get to be as cool as the Sex Pistols and turn down an invitation to be in the Rock and Roll Hall of Fame in Cleveland, because no one will ever ask us to join. Such is life, I suppose. It wasn't about getting rich and famous anyway. But we were good at what we did, and what we did was important, even if very few people noticed it. And big deal if they didn't.

When I wrote *Hardcore Zen*, I made a few ripples in the world of Zen. But I sometimes feel like I just ended up creating more confusion. Like the whole deal with *The Best Buddhist Writing* book. In the end, though, you just say what you say, and people get it or they don't. And if they don't get it, that's fine too.

I often wonder how Dogen must have felt about his life's work. Sure, he had a few students, and a couple of them must have gotten just a little of what he was going on about. But the world at large certainly did not. It's interesting to me that he chose to leave a record of his thoughts, and a very extensive one at that. While he was not the first Buddhist teacher to do so, he was one of very few who did.

And I can't think of anyone who left quite as much writing behind as he did. It's as if he must have had some intuition that one day, in a future he could scarcely even imagine, people might yet understand what he wanted to convey.

I feel a tremendous debt of gratitude to Dogen for that and also a sense of deep responsibility to try my best to put his words into practice. As far as I am concerned, Dogen might as well have been writing a love letter directly to me, and to all of us way out here in what, to him, would have been a far-distant future filled with miracles and tragedies beyond anything he could have dreamed possible.

Since we started out by looking at "Genjo Koan," the first chapter in the ninety-five-chapter edition of *Shobogenzo*, it makes sense to end by looking at the very last chapter. This chapter was the final thing Dogen ever wrote, just a few months before he bit the big one. Legend has it that the last thing Buddha talked about was a list of desirable personal qualities that came to be called the Eight Truths of Great Human Beings.* When Dogen believed his time was almost up, he decided to write about these.

The first thing great human beings need, according to Dogen, is "small desire." After this is a little note that says, "Not widely to chase after those among objects of the five desires that are as yet ungained, is called small desire." It's not clear if the little notes like this one, which appear throughout the text, were added by Dogen himself or by his student Ejo, who copied it after his death. But even if the additions are Ejo's, they're most certainly based on things Dogen said — possibly even stuff Dogen said directly to Ejo as he copied the thing.

At any rate, the five desires are the desires of the eyes, ears, nose, tongue, and skin, which are also explained as desires for wealth, sensual contact, food, fame, and comfort.

---

* 八大人覚, pronounced *hachi-dai-nin-gaku*.

After this, Dogen quotes Buddha, who said, "People of abundant desire abundantly seek gain, and so their suffering also is abundant. People of small desire never curry favor and bend in order to gain the minds of others. Further, they are not led by the sense organs. Those who practice small desire are level in mind; they are without worries and fears; when they come into contact with things, they have latitude; and they are constantly free from dissatisfaction."

Notice that we're talking about small desire here and not about some imaginary state of desirelessness. We can never be completely free from desire, anyhow, as I said earlier. But the less desire you have, the less of a pain in the ass your life will be. It's only when you desire things that you can't be yourself and that you end up worrying way too much about what everyone thinks of you.

Or think of Fritos®. Small desire for a handful of Fritos® won't do you a lot of harm. But abundant desire for a giant bag full of 'em every single day will make you very fat.

It's not that Buddhists recommend giving up desire because they want us to all be stoic and not have any fun. It's actually the total opposite. Every object you acquire comes with a certain degree of responsibility for that object. Most of us don't realize this, which is why we treat most of the stuff we own so incredibly badly. But whenever you bring something into your realm, you are committed to that thing just as if it were a pet or even a child. This includes cars or bicycles or bags or Fritos® or vinyl reissues of the first Negative Approach album or whatever you get. You need to take care of these things. When you don't, you cause yourself and others a heap of trouble. Just look at what overconsumption has done to our environment. No, Buddhists don't recommend small desire to make us all unhappy. The only way to really be happy is when you desire as little as possible.

The next point kind of expands on that idea. Dogen says that great human beings should "know satisfaction." The little note then says, "To take within limits from among things already gained is called to know satisfaction."

He quotes Buddha as saying, "Those who do not know satisfaction, even when living in a heavenly palace, are still not satisfied. Those who do not know satisfaction, even if rich, are poor. People who know satisfaction, even if poor, are rich."

There are plenty of examples of folks who have everything and still seem to need more and more and more. Right after I moved to Los Angeles I took one of those Hollywood homes of the stars tours and got to see some amazing examples of excess and waste. I mean, the late TV producer Aaron Spelling's house has something like eighty bedrooms. He had his own bowling alley, for cryin' out loud. What does anybody need with their own goddamned bowling alley? There are shops in Beverly Hills where the fabulously wealthy pay five hundred dollars for bath towels. It's all completely ridiculous, yet incredibly stupid behavior like this is held up to the public as the most desirable way for a person to live. And most of us swallow it and feel bad because our lives aren't like that.

But Hollywood stars aren't really all that different from most of us. They just have the wealth to take things to ridiculous extremes. Yet knowing satisfaction is the simplest way to get rich quick because everything you have becomes everything you want.

Truth number three says that great human beings "enjoy tranquility." This is followed by a little note that says, "Departing from all kinds of noise and living alone in an empty space is called to enjoy tranquility."

Now, remember that Dogen spent most of his life living with a group of monks. So when he talks about living alone he isn't saying we should all go find caves in the mountains to squat in and survive on nuts and berries till we croak. It's more a matter of your approach to groups and crowds. In his commentary on this Dogen quotes Buddha as saying, "Those who take pleasure in groups suffer many troubles — like a flock of birds gathering on a great tree and then worrying that it will wither and break." And ain't that the truth? Let me give you my personal take on this one.

As I've mentioned, in high school and college I wasn't part of the popular crowd. Didn't go to shows much, didn't really hang out. I enjoyed being alone. And yet I felt like shit about it a lot of the time. The idea that hanging out with a crowd of people was the "thing to do" was so strong within the culture in general that I felt like I must be missing out on something. But whenever I did go out, all I ever found was a bunch of people getting drunk or stoned and talking about idiotic garbage I had no interest in.

Whenever I found myself part of such a crowd, I always ended up stressing out, trying hard to be liked by the group, to say just the right things, to hold the right views and opinions, to fit in. I guarantee you that every other person in the group felt exactly the same way. We all do that all the time. And what's the point of lots of useless socializing? Again, Dogen isn't trying to get us all to be nerds and not have any fun. He's trying to point us toward a better, happier way to live with the proper balance of solitude and social interaction.

Next, Dogen says, great human beings like "to practice diligence." The comment off to the side says, "It is ceaselessly to endeavor to perform good works and so it is called devoted effort — devotion without adulteration, and effort without regression."

By way of explanation Dogen quotes the Buddha as saying, "A trickle of water that constantly flows is able to drill through a rock." Buddha also said, "If the mind of a practitioner often tires and quits, that is like twirling a stick to start a fire and resting before it gets hot." This is an especially important message for people engaged in zazen practice. It's easy to get frustrated at your lack of progress.

Dogen's Buddhism is all about understanding what you really are right here and right now. And reality often includes the fact that you cannot see reality as it is. The ability to understand that you do not understand is what real enlightenment is all about.

Eventually little bits of understanding — most of which you don't even notice when you gain them — will start to accrue, and one day you'll reach a point where the general principles will become abundantly clear. But the idea of wanting to get "full enlightenment" — whatever the hell that is — all at once without any effort is like a ten-year-old kid wishing with all her might she could be a grown-up right this very second. I know I threw away plenty of my own kidhood on that useless fantasy. How many once-in-a-lifetime experiences have we missed completely because they were just *ordinary* once-in-a-lifetime experiences and not *supercool kick-ass* once-in-a-lifetime experiences? Everything you ever do, no matter what it is or how "enlightened" you are when it happens, is always, always, always a once-in-a-lifetime experience. Don't miss your life.

Number five says great human beings do not lose mindfulness. Off to the side it says, "It is also called to keep right mindfulness. To keep the Dharma and not to lose it is called right mindfulness and is also called not to lose mindfulness."

In another chapter of *Shobogenzo* Dogen describes what he means by mindfulness, saying it's "the donkey looking at the well, the well looking at the donkey, the donkey looking at the donkey and the well looking at the well." So what the heck is that supposed to mean?

Normal folks would say that mindfulness in this situation would be a donkey staring at that well and thinking, "Yup. Here I am. Looking at the well." But in Dogen's view the well looking at the donkey was equally significant. But that makes no sense at all. How can the well look at a donkey?

To a Buddhist everything is alive, including wells. The only things that aren't alive are those fantasies we create in our heads. In *Shobogenzo Zuimonki* Dogen says, "Without knowing who taught you, you think mind is the function of the brain — thought and discrimination. When I tell you that mind is grass and trees you do not believe it" (*Shobogenzo Zuimonki*, trans. Shohaku Okumura). Grass, trees, donkeys, wells, triple-fudge banana splits covered in whipped cream with a cherry on top — they're all alive and conscious as far as Buddhism is concerned. This is not a form of animism, by the way.

It's not that these things have souls or consciousness or whatever. Life is the universe, and the mind manifests itself as the things and phenomena of this world.

When you encounter the universe, both of you are alive. If that were not the case, the encounter could never happen. True mindfulness is the awareness that everything you encounter is a vigorous expression of the same living universe as you. This, by the way, is one of the aspects of understanding I'm referring to when I say that Buddhism is definitely not a form of atheism, which, as far as I can tell, posits that the whole universe, including ourselves, is basically dead.

And Dogen takes even this two steps further, saying that mindfulness also includes the donkey looking at the donkey and ol' Mr. Well looking at ol' Mr. Well. So our own awareness of ourselves also comes into the picture.

Dogen quotes Buddha again here, saying, "If your power of mindfulness is solid and strong, even if you go among the bandits of the five desires you will not be harmed by them." Real freedom from desire comes when you can desire as much as you please and still not feel bound to satisfy all those desires. It goes back to the whole "knowing satisfaction" thing Dogen told us about earlier.

It's a hard trick to learn, to be able to desire stuff without feeling you need to satisfy those desires. I'll give you an example that, I'm afraid, is a bit uncouth. I'm not sure if Dogen would approve of this example. But he's dead anyway, so he'll never know about it. So here goes. Once a few years back when some guys from my company and I were out somewhere in Tokyo, this really delicious-looking girl in a tiny miniskirt and knee-high black leather high-heeled boots walked by. I kinda ribbed one of my co-workers and said, "Hey, check out that action." I know this is awful, and I tend to try and refrain from this sort of behavior now. But, let me clue you in to something: ain't no man or woman so enlightened that he or she doesn't notice that kind of thing — though the genders may be reversed — and don't let nobody tell you otherwise. The myth that "enlightened beings" take no notice of such things has caused a whole mess of trouble in a whole heap of spiritual communities.

Anyhow, my co-worker's response was, "Man, I don't even want to see that, 'cuz I know I can never have it." I found that a little surprising. It's not that I don't understand his feelings. But my take on it is completely different. For one thing, I don't feel like there's anything there I can't have. She was freely giving her beauty to anyone who had eyes to see it. The fact that I'd never end up getting under that little skirt was inconsequential. If all I get is a peek, that's all I get, and that's fine by me.

Of course, that example may be a bit too easy. It's harder when we're confronted with things we feel like we really could have. That's when the bandits of the five desires can do their dirty work a lot more efficiently. This is especially true for us today since even the poorest among us have way more material wealth and way more things to spend it on than Dogen could have imagined. Still, the virtue of being able to be happy with what you already have is important to cultivate.

Next up, number six says, "To practice the balanced state of dhyana." The note next to this one says, "To abide in the Dharma undisturbed is called the balanced state of dhyana." *Dhyana* is the Sanskrit word that was eventually transformed into the Japanese word *Zen*, as in *zazen*. So "practicing the balanced state of dhyana" means doing zazen. Easy peasy lemon squeezy.

Dogen quotes Buddha, who said, "It is like a household that values water attentively repairing a dike. For the sake of the water of wisdom, we attentively practice the balanced state of dhyana and prevent the water of wisdom from leaking away." Practicing zazen regularly, every single day, gives your balanced state of mind a little charge that keeps everything running the way it should, just like plugging in your iPod at night makes sure it'll work the next day. If you can just manage a half hour in the morning and a half hour before bed, you can maintain a nice balanced state of mind throughout the day. Of course, a few days of intensive practice every so often doesn't hurt either.

Number seven on the list is, "To practice wisdom." The note says, "To engender hearing, thinking, practice, and experience is called wisdom." Dogen then quotes Buddha, who said, "By constantly reflecting on and observing yourself, you will prevent wisdom from being lost."

Real wisdom is the ability to understand the incredible extent to which you bullshit yourself every single moment of every day. We're all so used to swallowing our own lies that we can hardly even recognize them for the load of horse hooey they really are anymore. We've built up a vast array of mental gimmicks to excuse ourselves for not facing up to what we know perfectly well is true. See, that's the real shocker. At some point, if your practice deepens enough, you'll not only discover what's really true. You'll discover that you were never, ever, not for even a fraction of a nanosecond in your whole entire life the least bit unaware of the truth. And you'll see that you couldn't possibly be unaware of the truth because the truth is what sustains you, that you are nothing more than a manifestation of the truth of the universe. But just because you get this doesn't mean you're enlightened. You have to live it every moment of every day. And if you think that's effortless, think again.

Even once you've caught on to that, it's still extremely easy to slide back into your old patterns, which is what Dogen's addressing here by saying wisdom needs to be practiced. Every single so-called enlightened being throughout human history has faced this fact. Practicing wisdom is hard work. Real Buddhism is hard work.

Finally, number eight on Dogen's list is, "Not to engage in idle discussion." The thingy off to the side says, "To experience, to go beyond discrimination, is called not to engage in idle discussion. To perfectly realize real form is just not to engage in idle discussion."

This is a funny one. After seven deep and profound proclamations he ends the list with the equivalent of "and quit all this chattering among yourselves." But remember that Dogen, and Buddha himself, who made up the list in the first place, were addressing their fellow monks, people who had left home and family to dedicate their lives to the pursuit of the truth. Now, if you've ever spent time among any group of monks, you'll know how easily they slip right back into the habits they've supposedly left behind in the secular world.

All the pettiness and stupidity that exist in the regular world don't just magically disappear when a few folks decide to form an "alternative" community. The punk community is a good example. We started off with great intentions of creating a completely alternative way of living, only to end up being little more than a microcosm of everything that was wrong with the way of life we had supposedly rejected. Same thing happened to the hippies and to the Beats and to pretty much every alternative community that ever existed all through history. As Pete Townshend said, "Meet the new boss, same as the old boss."

Buddha and Dogen didn't want the communities they founded to go the same way as other similar communities they'd seen. So their final admonishment to their followers was to avoid engaging in the kind of idle chatter that reinforces all the old habits they needed to leave behind in order to really pursue what was — and is — ultimately true.

Chapter 25

The Ultimate Truth

I don't write too much about the Ultimate Truth because as soon as you start saying anything about that kind of stuff, certain people take it as a challenge. They want to argue about it. I'm not interested in arguing. Truth is not something that will ever be proven by debate anyway. Other people take whatever certain teachers — sometimes even me — say about the Ultimate Truth at face value and start up with the "Tell me more, O Master" routine. But truth can never be explained in that way either. I suppose I could make a good living just doling out more and more talk in exchange for cash. But people who pay money for that kind of talk really bug me.

But here I am at the end of my book, and my editor wants me to write something that sounds more like an ending. That last chapter, he said, just left the reader hanging. Okay, then, what could be more like an ending than the Ultimate Truth? So here I go.

I think the reason some people get mad and others get all bleary-eyed when I say anything about the Ultimate Truth is that they think I must be saying that I know the Ultimate Truth and that I want to tell them about it. But that's not the case at all. In fact, what I am saying is that you — yeah, you out there with your hand in your underwear — you know the Ultimate Truth perfectly well right now. And what's more, you don't need me or anybody else to tell you about it.

Look. I'm glad you bought my book, or ripped it off, or whatever you did.* I'm happy to spend some time sharing my dumb-ass stories with you. If you come to one of my Zen classes, we can sit together for a while and watch the Ultimate Truth unfold. Maybe afterward we'll go bowling. But I'm not interested in selling anyone the Ultimate Truth. It's not something that can be sold, transferred, or transmitted.

We try all kinds of different ways to find the Ultimate Truth. Some of us build giant telescopes and send them up into orbit to try to find it in the far reaches of space and time. Don't get me wrong — I love those cool pictures of nebulae and planets. But the Ultimate Truth isn't out there either. Other people try to grasp it by thinking deeply about it or trying to calculate it somehow. But if the Ultimate Truth could be thought through or calculated, wouldn't someone have done it by now? None of our great enlightened masters, not even Dogen or Buddha, could put it into a set of words or a formula everyone could understand and agree on. Some of us think the Ultimate Truth might be found in an ancient book said to be the words of the Creator himself. I've never seen anything come out of that approach other than blind conformity, deep confusion, and acts of international terrorism.

Here is my conviction. I say this without qualifiers, without adding "maybe" or "I think" to it because it's not a "maybe" or "I think" matter. The Ultimate Truth is not hidden from view. It's not far off in the outer reaches of intergalactic space. It's not contained within the profound words of some ancient book. It can't be taught to you by someone who possesses secret knowledge. It's not

---

* Though I'd be happier if you actually bought it, and so would the folks at New World Library.

in a formula or on a graph. It can't be reasoned out and set in type. It's not a principle, divine or otherwise. It's not buried in the past or concealed in the future.

The Ultimate Truth is not a secret. Don't ever let anybody tell you that it is, 'cuz they will try to. But that's all marketing. It's nonsense. It's a lie. The Ultimate Truth is right there in front of your eyes at all times. There is nowhere you can run to to get away from it. Nowhere you can hide from it. It never leaves you. It couldn't. You are an expression of the Ultimate Truth.

In the *Shobogenzo* chapter "The Triple World Is Just the Mind" Dogen says, "The reality of the past, present, and future [i.e., the Triple World] does not obstruct the here and now. The reality of the here and now blocks off the past, present, and future. The whole Universe in ten directions is a real human body." This moment includes the limitless past and limitless future. The entire universe in all directions is nothing but you. But be careful about this point. It's also nothing but me. And nothing but your landlady and Adolf Hitler and Paris Hilton and her Chihuahua. The problem with folks like Adolf and Paris is that they don't know that everything already belongs to them, so they try to buy or steal it from others. It's as if your left pinkie toe decided it was the most important part of your body and tried to suck everything out of the rest of your body to prove it. That's how cancer works. Don't be like that.

If you tell people that the Ultimate Truth is right here and now, lots of folks will be terribly disappointed. There's gotta be something better than this! But there isn't. And that's not a bad thing. Pay attention to what this really is, and you'll see there could never be anything better. No matter what it is. I say this because I've observed my own life, and even during my worst times I've been exactly where I wanted and needed to be. I don't think I'm unique in this, either. No matter what I'm going through, *this experience here and now* is always real. Whatever I think might be better than this is always a fantasy. Reality beats fantasy every time.

But you want to live forever, you say? Or at least you want someone to promise you you'll live forever. In the *Heart Sutra* is a line that goes, "Fu-sho, fu-metsu," which means "no birth, no extinction." You were not born, so you can never die. Brad Warner was born March 5, 1964, in Hamilton, Ohio. One of these days he'll die, and after that you'll never see him again. At the same time, though, what the *Heart Sutra* says is absolute fact. But Buddhists never talk about eternal life. Don't be concerned about life eternal. This is eternity. The present moment is eternal. It's always here, and it always will be. You are not just a thing that inhabits this moment. You *are* this moment.

I've said it a lot already, and I'll say it again: the Ultimate Truth is this moment you are experiencing right now. Yep. You right there, on the very toilet you're sitting on. This is the Ultimate Truth. It can't be anything else. It can't be anywhere else. It can't be anyone else. This body. This mind.

In his book *Zen Mind, Beginner's Mind* Shunryu Suzuki says, "Usually we think of our mind as receiving impressions and experiences from outside, but that is not the true understanding of our mind. The true understanding is that the mind includes everything." This is not some kind of radical idealism that denies the existence of the outside world. The outside world is real. At the same time, everything you have ever encountered and everything you will ever encounter is nothing but you. There is no one else it could ever be. Yet I can't date your girlfriend, and you can't use my credit card. Don't be unclear on this point, or someone will punch you in the face.

I don't need to tell you that the Ultimate Truth isn't contained in this book. If you haven't figured that out by now, there's no hope for you. Still, maybe you think that it's in some other book, if only you knew which one.* Or you may think that if you read a whole bunch of

---

* It'll be in my next book, which will be printed in a limited leather-bound edition and will cost $3,845.

books, you can mush all of them into your head and somehow get it. I've gone through all that myself. It's a dead end. But you don't need to take my word for it. Heck. Maybe it's in that one book I haven't read yet. I don't think so. But go right on ahead and check it out for yourself. There are good books out there, to be sure. And they're worth reading. But the Ultimate Truth is not to be found in any of them.

In the end all I can give you is my take on the matter.

We've been socialized for a very, very long time to look at the world and to conceive of the world in a specific way. This understanding of reality is almost entirely wrong. That's why it never really works very well, and we end up sad, disgusted, and miserable.

When you do the practice of zazen for a long time, the noise in your head gradually quiets down. Once it begins to get quiet in there, a different kind of understanding becomes available. This understanding is not new. It's always been there. You've just been shouting it down for so long, you forgot it even existed. The truth is very quiet. It doesn't need to scream and shout to make its presence known and felt. Your thinking mind, on the other hand, is constantly bellowing and screeching. And you listen to all that nattering like a fool. I do, too, far more often than I should, even now. We all do.

It takes effort to get to the point where you can see what an idiot you've been for listening to your own drivel because society is continuously telling you that the best way to deal with any problem is to think about it. To go against this tendency is to take up arms against all human society — your mom, your dad, your teachers, your friends, and even yourself.

Nearly all of us believe unquestioningly in the reality of our self, our ego. We have absolute, unshakable faith in its existence. But when you look for it carefully, you can never find it. Do it sometime. I mean, really do it. Don't just accept the way things have been explained to you. Try to find the real substance of this self you assume exists. It's really absurd. You think you have this self. But who is the one who possesses this self? When you talk to yourself in your mind, who is speaking, and who is that someone speaking to? Why are there two entities? Why do we say "my self" as if some "me," other than the self, owns this thing called "self"?

To quote Shunryu Suzuki again: "Your eyes are always on your side for you cannot see your eyes and your eyes can't see themselves." Everything you encounter is part of this body/mind, as is that which encounters these things and phenomena. But you can't hold this truth in your brain for even a second. It's not an object you can be aware of or experience. That which longs to experience reality is just reality itself.

If you're truly interested in Ultimate Reality, you will not fail to find it. But if you're not truly interested, there is nothing anyone can do to help you. No matter what books you read, no matter what teachers you visit, no matter how many hours of meditation you practice in whatever school you choose, if you're not serious about Reality, everything you read or hear and every hour you spend in practice will be put into the service of increasing and enhancing your own ego. It happens all the time. Even practitioners of zazen are not immune. There is nothing that cannot be corrupted and bent into the service of a powerful ego. Yet reality will always remain just as it is, no matter how hard you try to escape it.

As I write this, I have just returned to Los Angeles from San Francisco, where I met with Tommy Strange, the guitarist and founder of Zero Defects. Tom didn't make it to our reunion show. But he did approve of Jeff Hardy, longtime fan of the band, as his replacement for the gig. He even said later that Jeff played a lot better than he could have. But Tom's a nice guy, and he would have been tremendous. I've seen Tom just one other time since the band broke up in 1983, a brief breakfast together when I was in San Francisco promoting one of my company's movies. While I was up there this time, I stayed with Frank Mauceri, founder of Smog Veil Records, a label dedicated to reissuing the best of the Ohio punk scene.

The interviews I did with Tom and Frank will be the last pieces of the puzzle in terms of *Cleveland's Screaming*, my documentary about the northeast Ohio hardcore scene of the early eighties.* Finally I feel like I'm just about ready to call the thing finished. Now I've gotta go look for distributors. Sheesh! The work just never gets done!

But that's the way life is, isn't it? There's always something. Just when you knock one mole on the head, up pop three more. Same thing happens in zazen practice. It's useless to long for the Enlightenment to End All Enlightenments. The Ultimate Truth never rests. But that's just the way we like it.

So sit down and shut up, already!

---

* Most likely in stores by the time this book hits the shelves. Ask for it by name!

Acknowledgments

I'd like to be real Buddhist about this and just thank all sentient beings. That way I wouldn't have to try and remember a lot of names and no one would get upset if they weren't listed or if someone else got listed before they did. But I guess I gotta do it the old-fashioned way.

First and foremost I need to acknowledge my teachers Gudo Wafu Nishijima and Tim McCarthy. Without their efforts I would never have even considered studying Buddhism at all. Then, of course, there is my editor, Jason Gardner, and all the staff at New World Library who made this book possible. Thanks also to my parents, Dan and Sandy Warner, for making me possible. I have to thank my wife, Yuka, for all her support. Also thanks to all the people who show up for my weekly zazen classes and talks, particularly Bret Johnson, who has made it to nearly every class. Don't you have anything better to do on Saturdays? Also Christine Buckley, who set me up at the Hill Street Center in Santa Monica to begin with, and Chris Chapple for making the Hill Street Center happen.

Thanks as well to all the people who came to the Cleveland's Screaming show in December 2005. Especially thanks to everyone who participated in the making of the Cleveland's Screaming movie, particularly Jimi Imij, Mickey X-Nelson Hurray, Tommy Strange and Jeffro Smull of Zero Defects, as well as Mike Mohawk, Tom Miller, and Sean Saley of Agitated. I mustn't forget the Munchkins, Tom Dark and the rest of the Dark, the Offbeats, the Guns, the Plague, Vicki Sprague, and everyone else who contributed. You'll all get thanked again on the DVD box.

I'm not gonna make a three-page list of everyone I know like I did for the last book. But all of you who were thanked there are thanked again here. Go read the other book for the list of names.

About the Author

Brad Warner was born in 1964 in Hamilton, Ohio, and lived in a suburb of Akron until he was eight years old, when his father took a job at the Firestone Tire Company's new plant in Nairobi, Kenya. Brad returned from Africa to the Akron area three years later with a different perspective on the world. In 1982 he joined the hardcore punk band Zero Defects (oDFx), whose song "Drop the A-Bomb On Me!" can be found on the P.E.A.C.E./War compilation. At around this time he began studying Zen with Tim McCarthy of the Kent Zendo. In the eighties he released five albums of neo-psychedelic rock on the Midnight Records label under the name Dimentia 13. In 1993 he moved to Japan and the following year fulfilled a childhood dream by getting a job working for the company founded by the man who invented Godzilla. That same year he met Gudo Wafu Nishijima, an iconoclastic Zen teacher who published the only complete English translation of Dogen's masterwork *Shobogenzo*. Brad was ordained a Buddhist monk by Nishijima in the late nineties. In 2004 he returned to America and now lives in Los Angeles with his wife and a lot of plastic monster toys.

His websites are:
http://homepage.mac.com/doubtboy
and
http://hardcorezen.blogspot.com

He also writes a weekly column for the Suicide Girls website:
http://suicidegirls.com/news/contributors/brad_warner

cleveland's screaming!

Brad Warner's documentary about the Cleveland/Akron, Ohio hardcore scene of the early 1980s, featuring never-before-seen performances by Zero Defects, Pagans, Rubber City Rebels, Starvation Army, Offbeats, Agitated, Defnics, Hammer-Damage and many more Ohio punk legends!

**AVAILABLE ON DELUXE 2-DISC EDITION DVD
SUMMER 2007**

ZERO DEFECTS (AKA ZERO DEFEX, ODFX) AVAILABLE NOW ON CD AND 7 INCH VINYL!

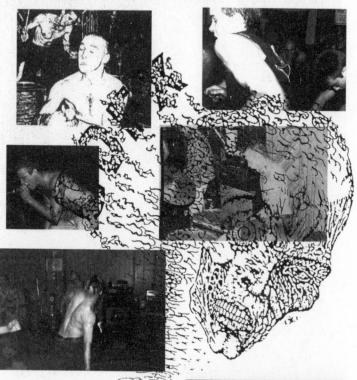

All of Zero Defex's studio recordings plus amazing vintage live performances remixed and remastered available for the first time in 25 years!